☆ ALWAYS SUPPORT HEAD, SHOULDERS, HIPS

✳ MOI → Px → comp. mech. → S/sx → Tx

☆ Universal Assessment Tool → Awake Verbal Pain Unresponsive (A.V.P.U)

The Art & Technique
of
Wilderness Medicine

✳ Bloody Nose → pinch & lean forward

A Field Manual

By Paul Nicolazzo

Spiral Binding
ISBN 0-9670228-1-9

Dedication

This field manual is dedicated to my parents, Peter Nicolazzo, DO, and Elizabeth Nicolazzo, RN, who sparked my first interest in medicine, to Peter Goth, MD,who led me to the teaching path; to Jim Morrissy, EMT-P, and Steve Lyons, EMT-P, who helped educate me; to Melissa Shaw, DVM, who freely shared enormous amounts of her love, time, and knowledge; and to all my students who continue to ask questions I cannot answer....

Acknowledgments

The manual could not have been written without the help of many people. Special thanks to Melissa Shaw, Rob Bates, David Johnson, and Kent Tableman, who helped educate me medically. To Laura Ordway, Mike Spilitros, and Glenn Rink who gave practical editing advice from a user's' perspective. To Sussi Rowntree who helped with the "final" editing. To Brad Dimock who made valuable graphic suggestions. To all my friends who reviewed the draft copy. And finally to Mark Twain whose advice I read once but forgot: "If I'd known how much trouble it was to write a book I should never have started it in the first place." He was right...but now that I'm done I'm glad I did. I hope you are too.

Disclaimer

This is a field manual for wilderness medicine. It is intended to help you make decisions in a remote pre-hospital setting. It does not replace training and practice. Medicine is a changing art form utilizing many techniques that also change with time. You are encouraged to confirm the information in this manual with other reliable sources and to keep abreast of changes. The author, publisher, and editors are not responsible or liable for the ongoing accuracy or use of the material in this manual.

Illustrations

Amanda Joubert

Layout

Paul Nicolazzo

Published by

the Wilderness Medicine Training Center
Post Office Box 11
Winthrop, Washington 98862
(509) 996-2502
office@WildMedCenter.com
http://www.WildMedCenter.com

Copyright ©1997

by Paul Nicolazzo

Contents

Contents

Contents iii

Introduction

General Information

Medicine is a blend of art and technique. Skills in both areas are acquired through rigorous training, practice, and insight. Your ability to use the information within these pages is directly related to your skill level. The techniques described and illustrated in the text require both training and practice in order to be effective. Some of the recommended treatments should only be undertaken under the supervision of a licensed physician. If you have not already done so, you are encouraged to take an in-depth course in wilderness medicine, to solicit the advice of a licensed physician where necessary, and to remain current with developing information. For state-of-the-art courses in wilderness medicine contact *the* **Wilderness Medicine Training Center** at www.WildMedCenter.com or (509) 996-2502.

As previously mentioned, medicine is both art and technique. **Changes** in technique occur as research reveals new information. Significant changes in the material covered by this field manual *after* publication are noted on *the* **Wilderness Medicine Training Center's** website. Go to www.WildMedCenter.com/changes.html

Medical Legal Issues

Wilderness medicine is a relatively new form of medicine that has emerged with the recent increase in wilderness travel (and subsequent injuries). It is defined as the skills necessary to assess and treat injuries or illness in a prolonged pre-hospital setting. Since assessment and treatment often occur in severe environments with minimal facilities available, practitioners require a broader range of knowledge and skills than standard urban medical courses offer. Unfortunately the United States legal system has yet to recognize the differences between urban and wilderness care. Do not rely on the good samaritan law to protect you when using techniques not presently sanctioned by the Emergency Services (EMS) system (wound cleaning, ruling out spinal injuries, reducing dislocations, dispensing medications, stopping CPR etc.). Your best legal protection is to become trained and certified though a well known training organization, maintain that certification, and practice your expanded skills only under the authorization of a licensed physician (medical control).

How to Use This Book

This is a field manual. To assist you in locating information it is indexed in three ways with: a table of contents, color-coding by mechanism of injury (MOI), and through a problem and topic index. The table of contents is located at the front of the manual while the problem and topic index is located towards the back. **All the indexes have a black bar with reverse printing across the bottom of the page.** To use either the contents or the index locate the topic and turn to the section and page. If you have purchased a field manual with a screw pin binding, pages may be removed or added by unscrewing the binding, removing (or adding) the desired pages, and then re-threading the screws.

The manual is visually divided into four sections by color. The first section (white pages) reviews general anatomy, physiology and patient assessment, and basic life support (BLS). If you are already familiar with these topics you may wish to save weight and space by removing them (field manuals with screw pin bindings only).

An algorithm is a decision making process. The colored sections of the field manual (red, green, & blue) utilize a mechanism-based algorithm designed to assist you in the field assessment and treatment of common wilderness injuries and illnesses. Correct and fast identification of the mechanism of injury (MOI) is the first part of any clinical pattern. Injuries with an unknown MOI are difficult, if not impossible, to assess and therefore treat. For the purposes of this field manual there are three basic categories of MOI: trauma, environmental, and medical. For fast and easy reference, each section is a different color (red, green, or blue respectively) and all the indexes have a black bar across the bottom of the page. To use the decision making indexes, first identify the MOI then turn to the page marked INDEX for that section and continue to follow the page directions. Familiarize yourself with the INDEX for each section *before* an injury occurs if you want to use the guide efficiently. Again, if you have a screw pin binding, you can remove any unwanted pages to save weight or space.

A problem & topic index (also black), appendices, and SOAP notes may be found at the end of the manual. Replacement SOAP notes for field manuals with screw pin bindings are available from *the* **Wilderness Medicine Training Center.** A separate SOAP booklet containing ten SOAP Notes also available.

Examples

Problem 1

A friend has fallen 15 feet and landed on their head, chest, and arm.

- The MOI is Trauma.
- Immediately immobilize their spine until you can rule out a spinal injury. Finish your initial assessment and BLS treatment. Complete your focused history and exam as necessary.
- Turn to the Trauma Index and follow the Trauma Algorithm
- Turn to the pages that discuss the possible problems indicated by the Trauma Algorithm.
- Rule out/in each possible traumatic problem based on the presence of signs and symptoms.
- Prioritize and treat your friend's problems.

Problem 2

A friend is exercising in a hot humid environment, becomes dizzy and falls 10 feet onto their right leg and hip.

- The MOI is Trauma and Environmental
- Immediately immobilize their spine until you can rule out a spinal injury. Finish your initial assessment and BLS treatment. Complete your focused history and exam as necessary.
- Turn to the Trauma Index and follow the Trauma Algorithm.
- Turn to the pages that discuss the possible problems indicated by the Trauma Algorithm.
- Rule out/in each possible traumatic problem based on the presence of signs and symptoms.
- Turn to the Environmental Index and identify the environmental conditions (or specific MOI).
- Turn to the pages that discuss the possible problems indicated by the Environmental Algorithm.
- Rule out/in each possible environmental problem based on the presence of signs and symptoms.
- Prioritize and treat your friend's problems.

Problem 3

A friend comes to you and says that s/he has been feeling poorly for the past few days.

- The MOI is Medical.
- Complete your focused history and exam.
- Turn to the Medical Index and match your friend's signs and symptoms with the possible problems.
- Turn to the pages that discuss the possible problems indicated by the Medical Algorithm.
- Consider treatment based on your friend's signs, symptoms, and relevant medical history.

Introduction

Anatomy & Physiology

White Pages: This section reviews normal human anatomy and physiology from a medical perspective. The three critical systems (respiratory, circulatory, and nervous) are discussed in great detail. The digestive, urinary, reproductive, integumentary (skin), endocrine, and musculoskeletal systems are also discussed but to a lesser degree. The text and drawings examine the normal structure and function of each system. General problems relating to the structure and function are briefly identified. A more complete discussion of specific problems and their pathophysiology occurs in the remainder of the manual.

Patient Assessment System

White Pages: The Patient Assessment System (PAS) is an organized method for gathering, evaluating, and documenting patient information. It is universal to the medical field and necessary for efficient and successful patient care in a wilderness setting. Each component in the PAS is examined and directly related it to patient care. Patient surveys, the evaluation process, and the use of patient SOAP notes are also covered in detail.

Basic Life Support

White Pages: Basic Life Support (BLS) assesses and treats life-threatening injuries as soon as they are found. Assessment and treatment for patients with an obstructed airway, absent or inadequate breathing, no pulse, severe bleeding, and suspected spine injury are briefly discussed. In order to remain proficient, you should regularly train and practice your BLS assessment and treatment techniques prior to using them in a wilderness environment.

Trauma

Red Pages: Trauma is, perhaps, the most common mechanism of injury in the wilderness. Most traumatic injuries in the outdoors are minor musculoskeletal injures that rarely require an evacuation. When life-threatening injuries do occur, they demand immediate assessment and often evacuation. The severity of most critical injuries may be predicted based on specific clinical patterns. These clinical patterns are covered in detail in the trauma text.

Environmental

Green Pages: Water, heat, cold, snow, rain, sun, altitude, SCUBA and free diving, toxins, allergies, lightning, burns, bites, stings, etc. are all potential environmental MOI. They often affect multiple body systems at the same time. Most environmental problems are easier to prevent than treat. For that reason, the environmental text focuses on the pathophysiology and prevention of common environmental problems in addition to their assessment and treatment.

Medical

Blue Pages: Medical MOI impact body systems by directly affecting specific cells and tissues. Because some infectious diseases are fatal, prevention is often the best option. The text discusses the pathophysiology and prevention of many serious diseases encountered by outdoor and world travelers. Specific assessment criteria and treatment plans are given to support your understanding and risk assessment. Common noninfectious diseases and expedition medicine are also covered. Because medical problems (illness and disease) are extremely complicated and early assessment and treatment are often critical, you may need the assistance of a physician. Field treatment for many medical problems require appropriate nutrition, rest, and drug therapy.

Appendices

White Pages: The white pages at the end of the book address topics not covered in detail in the previous sections. They include *Drug Theory and Tables, Medicinal Herb Theory and Tables, First Aid Kits, References, Medical Abbreviations, and Symbols.*

Problem & Topic Index

White Pages *with a Black Bar across the bottom*: An alphabetical problem and topic *Index* that is independent of the MOI. Problems are listed according to their headings and page numbers.

Patient SOAP Notes

White Pages: You will find two sets of patient *SOAP Notes* at the end of the manual. They are designed to be quickly accessible. Turn the manual backwards and flip up the back cover to expose the first SOAP page. Review and practice with the SOAP notes before use to become familiar with their format. Additional SOAP notes may be purchased from *the* Wilderness Medicine Training Center.

About the Author

Paul Nicolazzo is the owner, director, and head instructor of *the* Wilderness Medicine Training Center. He has taught courses in wilderness medicine throughout the United States and abroad for the past fourteen years. He has been active in Search & Rescue since 1977; teaching both technical rock and whitewater rescue skills since 1979. Also an EMT since 1979 he currently responds with the Methow Valley SAR and Nordic ski patrol when home in Mazama, Washington. He is a professional member of the Wilderness Medical Society and the National Association of EMS Physicians. Paul has extensive guiding and teaching experience in whitewater paddling, rafting, climbing, mountaineering, and Nordic & telemark backcountry skiing. He continues to balance personal expeditions, guiding, and skills instruction with teaching wilderness medicine and rescue. Paul is an exceptional writer and educator who believes in teaching thought processes and concepts in addition to facts. His courses are dynamic, practical, and fun. Paul developed the Pacific Crest Outward Bound School's "site management" theory and continues to act as an educational consultant and staff trainer for the school.

Introduction 4

General Concepts

Balance

The collective goal for each of the body's systems is to maintain a balance between the body and its environment. Biologically this balancing act is known as *homeostasis*. Built into each complex body system are numerous compensating mechanisms that work to correct problems before they become critical. If any problem overwhelms the body's *compensatory mechanisms*, outside intervention is necessary to tilt the balance in favor of healing. Knowledge of both the structure and function of the human body is required for effective intervention.

Basic Structure & Function

In general, basic functions are carried out by individual organs and organ systems. Structurally, fluids and gases are transported between organs and systems via tubes (Blood travels throughout the body in the tubes of the circulatory system. Oxygen enters and carbon dioxide leaves the body through air tubes. Digestive, excretory, and reproductive systems all rely on tubes for transporting both fluids and solids). Control and integration are provided by the brain. And messages are conducted via nerves. *In its simplest form the major components of the human body are organs, tubes, and nerves.*

Cellular Physiology

Cells provide the basic building blocks for the human body. Cells in turn create tissue, organs, and organ systems. In order to perform efficiently all cells require a constant supply of nutrients and the steady elimination of waste products. Both nutrients and waste are transported to and from the cells via the circulatory system. They are either suspended within the blood (or lymph) as solutes or bound to carrier cells. They must be able to pass freely through the semipermeable membranes of the capillaries and into or out of the extracellular space. It is through the extracellular fluid that the cells either absorb nutrients or dispose of waste. Movement of both nutrients and waste across the cellular membranes takes place by diffusion or active transport. *Diffusion* occurs when solutes move across a membrane from an area of higher concentration to an area of lower concentration. Carbon dioxide, oxygen, and water are transported across cell walls by diffusion. Glucose is also transported across the cell wall by diffusion; however, its entry is facilitated by the presence of the hormone insulin. *Osmosis* is a form of diffusion where water, not a solute, diffuses through a semipermeable membrane to equalize the concentrations. Osmosis is an important element in understanding heat related illnesses. *Active transport* occurs when a cell uses energy to move a specific substance across its membrane. Sodium, potassium, other ions, and proteins are often carried into and out of cells by active transport.

All cells require *oxygen* and *glucose* in order to survive. Cells break down oxygen and glucose to produce heat and chemical energy. The energy is used by the cell to carry out its functions. A cell deprived of oxygen and glucose will eventually die. *Carbon dioxide* is a waste product produced during cellular metabolism. It is picked up by the blood and eliminated through the lungs. Other cellular waste must be transported to the kidneys for removal. If waste products build to toxic levels, cellular function will decrease and the cell will die. *In order for the transportation of both nutrients and waste to be effective, fluid levels within the human body must remain within tight parameters. Cellular function will significantly decrease or stop if fluids fall below acceptable*

levels. Water accounts for 70% of the weight of the human body and is responsible for transporting both nutrients and waste to and from cells. Without enough water the body will die.

In addition to water, cells need a balanced intake of **carbohydrates** (for energy production), **proteins** (for use as building blocks), and **fats** (also for energy). Vitamins and minerals work together and with **enzymes** to facilitate chemical reactions and maintain homeostasis. Numerous diseases may be traced to a lack of specific vitamins and minerals. Often the disease process may be reversed with early assessment and the appropriate nutritional supplements. **Vitamins** may be broken down into two major categories: water soluble and fat soluble. While fat soluble vitamins may be stored for long periods of time within muscle tissue and specialized liver cells, water soluble vitamins must be replaced frequently. Most water soluble vitamins (B, B complex, and C) are excreted by the body within four days. **Minerals** are naturally occurring elements. During digestion they are coated with a protein molecule (chelated) to aid in their absorption. Large amounts of fiber taken at the same time inhibits the chelating process and restricts mineral absorption. Similar to vitamins, some minerals (**electrolytes**) are water soluble and need frequent replacement while others, the majority, are stored in both bones and muscle tissue and require less maintenance.

Stuffsacks

Each of the body's components (cells, tissue, organs, body cavities, the body), both collectively and individually, are surrounded by a membrane or "stuffsack" and attached to one another with connective tissue. Membranes serve to separate, contain, and protect. Increases in membrane permeability tend to increase fluid or gas movement across the membrane in accordance with the pressure gradient. If the structures of the body are viewed as cells, tissue, organs, and organ systems where fluids and gases are transported through tubes, the concept of "stuffsacks" has clinical significance. *If a rupture or leak occurs in any tube or stuffsack the leak is contained within the next largest stuffsack.* This concept is perhaps the single most important concept in understanding the pathophysiology of most traumatic injuries.

Swelling

Swelling indicates structural damage and is caused by one of two mechanisms: bleeding or edema. **Bleeding** occurs when blood vessels are broken. Blood leaks from the damaged vessel into the local tissue spaces until it is contained within the tissue's membrane or "stuffsack." **Edema** occurs when plasma (not blood cells) leaks into the extracellular tissue spaces due to an increase in vascular permeability. Numerous mechanisms may lead to increased vascular permeability and subsequent edema: altitude, a weak heart, poor muscle tone, inflammatory response etc.

The Inflammatory Response

When cells are damaged or destroyed (by any MOI), cellular debris is released into the extracellular fluid. The "floating" debris activates a complex healing process known as the inflammatory response. Numerous chemicals, produced by mast cells, nerve endings, platelets, and white blood cells (WBC), are released locally. Together they increase the permeability of the local capillary network and encourage white blood cells to move across the capillary walls into the damaged tissue. Once there, the WBCs begin cleaning up, a prerequisite to healing. The area remains "inflamed" until most of the damage is repaired.

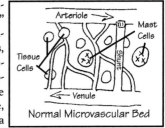

Normal Microvascular Bed

Anatomy and Physiology   6

A side effect of the increased permeability is localized swelling. The greater the tissue damage, the greater the swelling. Vasodilation (a component of the inflammatory response) increases the local capillary pressure forcing plasma (fluid) to move across the vessel walls into the extracellular space. Fluid continues to accumulate in the extracellular space (edema) until the pressure is equalized. The increased fluid causes the local tissue to swell. Both the edema and swelling are confined to the stuffsack that surrounds the leaky tissue (e.g.: muscle facia, organ membrane, skin, etc.) **In the majority of cases clinically significant swelling due to the inflammatory response has reached its peak within 24 hours of the initial MOI. Swelling primarily due to bleeding is much more rapid and usually occurs within six hours of a traumatic event.**

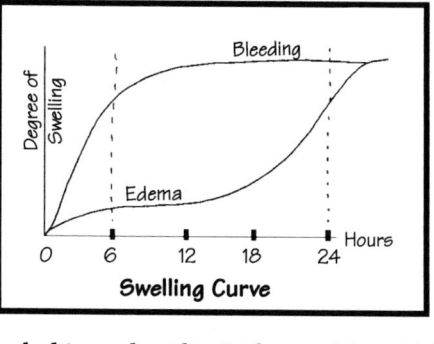

Swelling Curve

Cellular Debris 2° Cell Death

MAST Cell Response

Local Vasodilation &
Increased Vascular Permeability

Phagocytes Enter Tissue

Inflammatory Response

Body Systems

carries groceries
takes out garbage

The Circulatory System

The function of the circulatory system is twofold: it picks up nutrients from the proper organs and delivers them to all the body's cells. And, of equal importance, it picks up cellular waste and delivers it to the proper organs for removal. Medically this transportation process is know as *perfusion*. Without perfusion, cellular function would decrease or cease all together as the affected cells are denied access to the nutrients they need to support life or as toxic waste buildup begins to poison them. Both nutrients and waste are carried by the blood (a combination of blood cells and plasma) through an interconnected series of tubes to all the cells of the body. The blood is forced through the tubes by a powerful muscular pump. The circulatory system may be structurally divided into three major components: the heart or pump; the vessels or tubes; and the entire fluid volume of the body inclusive of both blood and plasma. Any problem that disrupts the function of any of the components will effect the function of the entire system and subsequently the entire body. Severe problems with the circulatory system usually lead to a systemic decrease in cellular perfusion (shock) and death.

The Heart

The heart is really two separate pumps and two receiving chambers within a single organ. The larger of the two pumps, the *left ventricle*, pumps blood to the body while the smaller pump, the *right ventricle* pumps blood to both lungs. Oxygen poor blood returning from the body is collected in the larger of the two receiving chambers, the *right atrium*, and oxygen rich blood returning from the lungs is collected in the smaller *left atrium*. Independent valves separate each chamber. The timing of the valves and the contraction of each ventricle is critical to functional circulation. The heart contains *specialized cardiac nerves* that are responsible for generating and coordinating the electrical impulses necessary for efficient pumping. The rate and strength of cardiac contractions is dependent upon both the specialized cardiac nerves and signals from the autonomic nervous system. Cardiac perfusion is accomplished via the *coronary arteries and veins.*

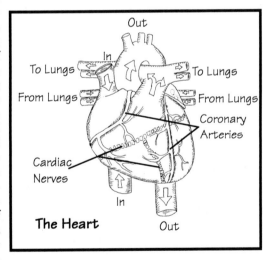

Out

To Lungs — In
From Lungs

To Lungs
From Lungs

Coronary
Arteries

Cardiac
Nerves

In

The Heart   Out

The Vessels

The blood and lymphatic vessels create a system of tubes that carry fluids to and from all the cells of the body. *Arteries* are muscular blood vessels that carry blood away from the heart and are responsible for the pickup and delivery of nutrients (vitamins, minerals, amino acids, glucose, etc.) from the liver and oxygen from the lungs. They also deliver cellular waste to the kidneys for elimi-

Anatomy and Physiology   8

nation. Because they are under increased pressure from their proximity to the heart, arteries have thicker and more muscular walls than either veins or lymph vessels. Veins and lymphatic vessels return blood and lymph (similar to plasma) back to the heart. They are also responsible for delivering carbon dioxide to the lungs for oxygen exchange. All vascular muscles are under the control of the autonomic nervous system and capable of vasoconstriction or vasodilation when properly stimulated.

Upon leaving the heart, arteries continually divide and subdivide until they form an interwoven web of microscopic tubes called capillaries. *Capillaries* are the circulatory system's link to cells and are found within all the body's tissues. Nutrients suspended in the blood's plasma move through the thin permeable walls of the capillaries to bathe and nourish individual cells. Waste products are released into the extracellular fluid, picked up by the capillaries and lymph vessels, and eventually removed from the blood by the kidneys.

Blood leaving the capillaries returns to the heart via *veins*. Movement of venous blood towards the heart is driven by the muscular contraction of the surrounding striated muscle groups (especially those in the legs) by "squeezing" the blood back to the heart.

Lymph vessels also pick up extracellular fluid and waste, passing it thorough filters (lymph glands) before returning it to general circulation via the central veins. Fluid moves through the lymphatic vessels in the same manner as venous blood returns to the heart: through contractions of the surrounding muscle groups.

Blood, Plasma, and Fluids

The blood is made up of approximately equal proportions of blood cells (including platelets) and plasma. Under normal circumstances the overwhelming majority of blood cells are **red blood cells (RBCs)** responsible for binding with and carrying oxygen to all the tissues of the body. The spleen is responsible for recycling old RBCs while new red blood cells are formed within bone marrow. Unless an infection is present, relatively few **white blood cells (WBCs)** are present in general circulation. *Platelets* are also present in small numbers and are responsible for clotting. *Plasma* is a water based, nutrient rich solution containing the salts, sugars, proteins, vitamins, minerals, etc. required by the body's cells for normal functioning. Because of their large size, blood cells remain within the capillary network while the vital nutrients held within the plasma are able to pass through the semipermeable walls of the capillaries to nourish individual cells. Once fluid and nutrients have passed through the restraining walls of the capillaries the mix is known as *extra or intracellular fluid* depending on where it is found. *Lymph* is similar to plasma in that it does not contain blood cells. Each type of fluid contains a slightly different mix of nutrients, waste products, and electrical charge depending upon the needs of the local tissue.

Shock

Shock is the major life-threatening problem of the circulatory system. It is medically defined as a systemic loss of perfusion. There are three basic types of shock: heart shock (cardiogenic shock), volume shock (hypovolemic shock), and vascular shock (septic shock, anaphylactic shock, spinal shock). Each are directly related to a failure in one of the circulatory system's major components. All forms of shock, regardless of the mechanism, may lead to death.

Failure of the pump (**heart shock**) may occur from a variety of mechanisms all resulting in a drop in perfusion pressure (cardiogenic shock) and arrest. Medical mechanisms involving the heart usually disrupt the heart's intrinsic electrical system by blocking one of the coronary arteries and depriving cardiac cells of oxygen and nutrients (heart attack). Infection may damage the heart muscle or any of its various components. Trauma can directly damage the heart's electrical system or the organ itself. Environmental mechanisms such as lightning may disrupt the electrical system directly while drowning affects the heart indirectly by damaging the respiratory system thereby depriving the heart of oxygen.

A break in any vessel causes an immediate fluid loss at the site of the break. If the vessel is an artery the amount of fluid loss is increased because of the increased arterial pressure. Fluid loss may also be caused by an increase in the permeability of the walls in the capillary beds (inflammatory response). Any loss of red blood cells causes an immediate decrease in the blood's oxygen carrying capacity. A loss of water (dehydration) causes an immediate decrease in the efficiency of the circulatory system's delivery system. Both cause a decrease in cellular function. Large amounts of fluid loss (blood, plasma, water), regardless of the cause, will cause a systemic loss of perfusion (**volume shock**).

Problems with the vessels that effect the entire circulatory system tend to be those that cause systemic vasodilation (anaphylaxis, spinal shock, septic shock). All may lead to a loss of perfusion pressure (**vascular shock**).

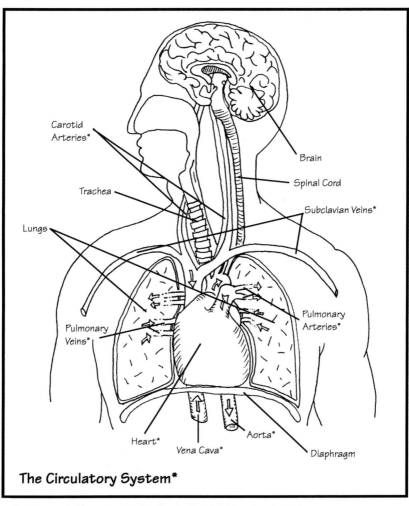

The Circulatory System*

Anatomy and Physiology 10

Supplies O_2 pH balance

Removes CO_2 -

The Respiratory System

The function of the respiratory system is to supply the blood with oxygen and remove carbon dioxide. The removal of carbon dioxide and water assists with the acid-base (pH) balancing of the blood. When the amount of carbon dioxide in the blood becomes too high, or the oxygen level too low, chemical receptors in the brain stem signal the diaphragm and intercostal muscles to contract. This begins *inspiration*. The muscular contractions enlarge the intrathoracic space, expand the lungs, and cause a negative pressure to develop internally. In a process similar to that of an expanding bellows, air is pulled into the body through the mouth or nose by the negative pressure. It passes through a series of smaller and smaller tubes (trachea, bronchi, bronchioles) until it fills microscopic air sacs (alveoli) and the pressure is equalized. The alveoli are enveloped by capillary beds and it is through the thin walls of the alveoli and the adjacent capillaries that the gas exchange takes place. While inspiration is an active process, expiration is passive. During *expiration* the muscles relax, intrathoracic pressure increases, and air is expelled. Normal respirations are smooth, easy, and quiet.

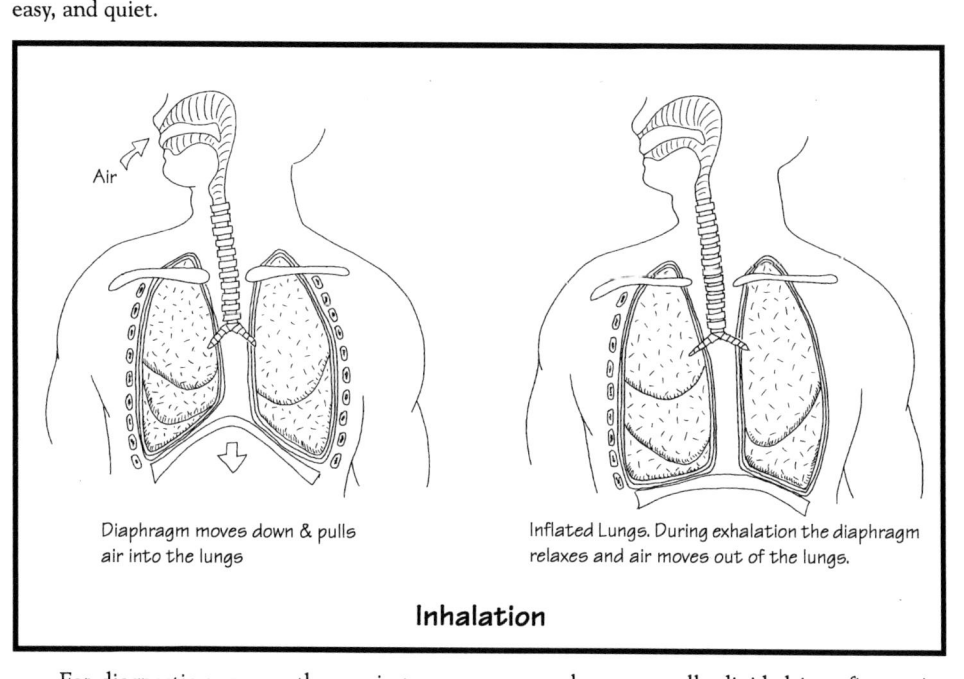

Diaphragm moves down & pulls
air into the lungs

Inflated Lungs. During exhalation the diaphragm
relaxes and air moves out of the lungs.

Inhalation

For diagnostic purposes the respiratory system may be structurally divided into five major components: the respiratory drive located in the brain stem; the upper airway; the lower airway; the air sacs or alveoli; and the musculoskeletal structure consisting of the chest wall, diaphragm, and pleura (the stuffsacks surrounding each lung). Any problem that disrupts the function of any of the components will affect the function of the entire system and subsequently the entire body. Problems with the respiratory system decrease or stop the gas exchange causing systemic cellular *hypoxia* (lack of oxygen) and often death.

The Respiratory Drive

All cells require oxygen to produce energy and do work; carbon dioxide and water are waste products of this process. An increased demand for work from individual organs increases the oxygen requirement of their cells. Chemical receptors located in the brain stem monitor **blood pH, carbon dioxide, and oxygen levels**. When the blood pH falls too low (becomes more acidic), the amount of carbon dioxide in the blood rises too high, or the oxygen level falls too low, the chemical receptors stimulate the diaphragm and intercostal muscles to contract; thus, beginning a breathing cycle. The respiratory drive regulates the rate and depth of the body's respirations to facilitate oxygenation and assist the kidneys with balancing blood pH. It is the interface between the nervous system and the respiratory system.

The Upper Airway

The upper airway consists of the **nasal and oral pharynges**. Both are hollow tubes surrounded by soft tissue that intersect at the back of the throat; both are capable of carrying air. Air entering the nose is filtered before entering the lungs while air entering the mouth may contain particulate matter. Food is prevented from entering the main air tube (**trachea**) by the contraction of a muscular flap (**epiglottis**). During swallowing the epiglottis lowers directing food or liquids into the esophagus. Large contaminants or foreign bodies are removed from the upper airway by sneezing and coughing. Directly below the epiglottis is the **larynx** or voice box. The upper airway ends at the larynx.

The Lower Airway

The lower airway is a series of air tubes that, beginning with the trachea just below the larynx, divide into bronchi, subdivide into secondary bronchi, then tertiary bronchi, and finally into bronchioles before terminating in the alveoli. The walls of the larger tubes, the **trachea** and **bronchi**, are supported by cartilage and lined with smooth muscle and ciliated (hairlike fibers) mucosa. The smaller **bronchioles** consist almost entirely of smooth muscle and are covered by a mucus membrane. Within the lower airway large particulate matter is removed by coughing while smaller particles are trapped by the mucus layer and expelled by ciliary action. An extensive lymphatic network within the lining of all the tubes is responsible for the removal of microscopic particles and organisms. The lower airway ends at the alveoli.

The Alveoli

The **alveoli** are microscopic air sacs or chambers completely enveloped by a capillary network. In structure each air sac resembles a grape clustered with other grapes. It is through the alveolar walls that oxygen is exchanged for carbon dioxide. The alveoli are the interface between the respiratory system and the circulatory system. Both systems must be functioning to ensure the oxygenation of cells.

The circulatory system is responsible for transporting oxygen and carbon dioxide between the alveoli and cells. Once oxygen has diffused through the thin alveolar and capillary walls, it is quickly dissolved in the plasma. Because plasma can only hold a small amount of gas in solution, most of the oxygen binds with **hemoglobin** molecules in the red blood cells for transportation. Upon reaching its destination the oxygen is released into the plasma, passes through the capillary walls into the extracellular space, and then diffuses into the cells where it is used to produce energy. Simultaneously, carbon dioxide and acids, both by products of cellular metabolism, diffuse from the cells into the adjacent capillaries. **Carbon dioxide** is carried by the blood in three ways: a small amount remains dissolved in the plasma as a solute; approximately one third combines with hydro-

Anatomy and Physiology   12

gen ions and is carried in the red blood cells as carbonic acid; and the remainder, over half, is carried in the plasma as a bicarbonate ion. Once in the lungs, the carbonic acid breaks down into water and carbon dioxide, diffuses into alveoli, and is expired. The breakdown of carbonic acid and the elimination of the resulting water and carbon dioxide decreases the acidity of the blood (increases blood pH). Prolonged rapid respirations (*hyperventilation*) may lead to *respiratory alkalosis* as too much carbon dioxide is lost.

The Musculoskeletal Structure

The musculoskeletal structure of the respiratory system includes the sternum, ribs, and thoracic vertebrae; the diaphragm and intercostal muscles; and the lungs and their pleura. The bone and cartilage of the sternum, ribs, and thoracic vertebrae give support while the *intercostal muscles* provide the basis for movement. Together they form the chest wall. As the intercostal muscles contract the ribs pivot along the spine and lift anteriorly, causing the chest to expand externally. The *diaphragm* is a large muscle that separates the chest cavity from the abdominal cavity. When stimulated it contracts downward, pushing the abdominal organs out of the way, to internally expand the chest cavity. The interior of the chest wall (*thoracic cavity*) and diaphragm are lined with a smooth resilient membrane (*parietal pleura*). The lungs are enclosed by a second membrane (*visceral pleura*) that lies against the partial pleura separated only by a lubricating fluid. The parietal and visceral pleuras separate the lungs from the middle section of the thoracic cavity (*mediastinum*) that contains the heart. The lungs contain the lower airway, the alveoli, and the blood vessels that are responsible for the delivery of oxygen and the removal of carbon dioxide. *In their most basic form the lungs are a series of air tubes and sacs tied to a second series of tubes containing blood and surrounded by a stuffsack.* It is the integrity of the individual pleura and the surface tension of the fluid between them that permits the lungs to expand with the contraction of the chest and diaphragm.

Respiratory Distress & Arrest

The major problems of the respiratory system are a complete or partial failure of the system's ability to supply the blood with oxygen and remove carbon dioxide. Partial failure of any of the system's components may cause *respiratory distress* while complete failure will cause *respiratory arrest* and potentially death.

The *respiratory drive* may be damaged and depressed through head trauma, toxins, lack of oxygen (hypoxia), electricity, stroke, altitude, etc. Serious damage leads to a decrease in the patient's level of consciousness, a decreased respiratory rate, and is rapidly followed by respiratory arrest. Problems in the *upper airway* are usually related to a complete or partial blockage. Blockage may occur from foreign objects (food, gum), localized swelling, fluids (blood, vomitus), or simply poor positioning of the unresponsive patient. *Lower airway* problems are usually related to the constriction of the smooth muscular lining of the respiratory tree due to a bronchial spasm and/or swelling. Common causes range from asthma to anaphylaxis to smoke inhalation. If the *alveoli* fill with fluid the gas exchange cannot take place. Fluid often develops during drowning, congestive heart failure, pneumonia, high altitude, etc. If the integrity of *chest wall or diaphragm* are broken during trauma, air or blood can leak into the pleural space and prevent one or both lungs from inflating. An abrupt pressure change through trauma or an improper ascent with SCUBA may rupture multiple alveoli and cause a similar phenomenon.

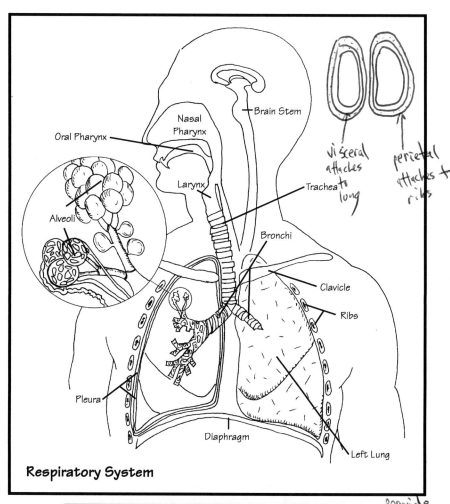

Respiratory System

Labels on figure:
- Brain Stem
- Nasal Pharynx
- Oral Pharynx
- Larynx
- Trachea
- Alveoli
- Bronchi
- Clavicle
- Ribs
- Pleura
- Diaphragm
- Left Lung

(handwritten) visceral attaches to lung

(handwritten) perietal attaches to ribs

The Nervous System

(handwritten) provide command & control

The nervous system works with the endocrine system to maintain homeostasis by generating and sending the electrochemical signals that provide control and integration for most body functions. Structurally the nervous system is divided into the ***central nervous system (CNS)*** and the ***peripheral nervous system (PNS)***. The CNS is further subdivided into the brain and spinal cord. The cells of the CNS are delicate and well protected by tough stuffsacks, circulating ***cerebrospinal fluid (CSF)***, and bone; damage to these cells is permanent. The nerves of the peripheral nervous system are far stronger and require less protection; they tend to follow the medial aspect of the long bones as they travel through the extremities. ***Peripheral nerves*** are capable of regeneration.

On a functional level the nervous system is divided into two divisions, the ***voluntary (somatic) nervous system*** and the ***involuntary (autonomic) nervous system***. The voluntary division

Anatomy and Physiology   14

of the nervous system contains both sensory and motor nerves. **Sensory nerves** carry input to the spinal cord and brain while **motor nerves** carry messages from them. Through its nerves, the somatic nervous system controls conscious functions, primarily striated muscle contractions. The autonomic division of the nervous system maintains or restores homeostasis by regulating smooth muscle contractions and the glandular secretion of hormones. Most autonomic functions are beyond conscious control.

The autonomic division of the nervous system is subdivided into the sympathetic and the parasympathetic systems. The **sympathetic system** stimulates effectors (cells or organs) while the **parasympathetic system** inhibits them. Both systems continually transmit impulses to the same effector and act in an antagonistic manner with the stronger impulse assuming control.

The Central Nervous System

The **brain** is the primary source of the signals necessary to control bodily functions. Its multi-layered structure is similar to an onion while its texture closely resembles spongy cottage cheese. Higher functions, such as sensory awareness, thought, and personality, reside in the brain's outer layers (**cerebrum**) while the more basic autonomic functions, like the cardiac, vasomotor, and respiratory centers, lie within its center (**brain stem**). The brain stem also contains numerous other reflex centers such as hearing, smell, pupil responses, coughing, sneezing, swallowing, and vomiting. The **cerebellum** lies adjacent to but outside the cerebrum and controls muscular coordination. Both the brain and spinal cord are bathed in circulating cerebrospinal fluid which provides both nourishment and protection. Both the brain and spinal cord are surrounded by three stuff-sacks (**meninges**) and bone. The skull protects the main onion and the spine protects the cord. The **cord** is simply an extension of the brain stem. Although its primary function is communication, reflex centers within the cord respond directly to pain by stimulating local muscular contractions (reflex arc). In both appearance and texture the spinal cord resembles twisted strands of "al dente" spaghetti.

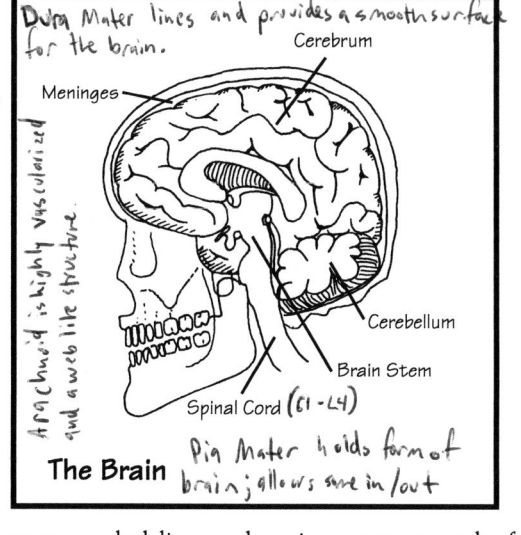

Dura Mater lines and provides a smooth surface for the brain.

Cerebrum

Meninges

Arachnoid is highly vascularized and a web like structure.

Cerebellum

Brain Stem

Spinal Cord (C1-L4)

The Brain — Pia Mater holds form of brain; allows save in /out

The cells of the central nervous system are extremely delicate and require a constant supply of nutrients and a stable internal environment to function normally. Changes in oxygen, sugar, temperature, electrical impulses, chemicals, and pressure adversely affect the brain and the patient's level of consciousness. Significant changes may result in death.

The Peripheral Nervous System

Spinal nerves branch from the cord at each vertebrae and form the central nervous system's interface with the PNS. Spinal nerves are mixed nerves capable of transmitting both sensory and motor messages. It is important to understand that each spinal nerve root enervates a specific region of the body (skin, hands, feet, organs, etc.). Knowledge of a few nerves, their pathways, and functions can assist in the field assessment of trauma patients with a suspected cord injury. Clinically useful motor functions and their nerve roots are: wrist and finger extension C-7, finger abduction/adduction T-1, big toe/foot dorsiflexion L-5, and foot plantar flexion S-1,2. Clinically useful sensory functions and their nerve roots are: top of the foot L-4, S-1, and hands (front and back) C-5,6,7,8. Refer to the Trauma section for the ruling out process.

The nerves of the PNS resemble strong elastic cords and are primarily responsible for both sensory and motor communication. In general, *peripheral nerves* follow the same routes through the body as do the major arteries and veins forming a neurovascular bundle. In the extremities the neurovascular bundle follows the medial aspect of each limb, through the joints, to its terminus in the hands or feet. Skeletal bones offer some protection from minor trauma.

Increased Intracranial Pressure (ICP)

An immediate life-threatening problem involving the *brain* is increased intracranial pressure. When brain cells become injured or die, the subsequent cellular debris initiates the inflammatory process. If the damage is severe, localized swelling occurs within 24 hours of the insult. The swelling may occur quickly if due to an arterial rupture, or more slowly if due to edema. In the closed compartment of the skull swelling means increased pressure. If the pressure builds to a point where it reduces perfusion to adjacent tissue, a negative spiral develops as the newly affected tissue dies. This results in additional swelling, a greater loss of perfusion, increased edema, and significantly more increased pressure. If the cycle is not interrupted the patient may die. Common causes of increased ICP are high altitude, suffocation, head trauma, and stroke.

Nerve Problems

Two mechanisms damage nerve fibers: pressure and cutting. *Pressure* on any nerve may interrupt its signals and may cause numbness, pain, and decreased function. Pressure applied for long periods of time may cause permanent nerve damage. The pressure may be internal due to tissue damage and subsequent swelling from an injury or external from the poorly adjusted shoulder strap of a backpack to a splint that is too tight. The *cutting* of a nerve will effectively stop any communication beyond that point. Damage to the spinal cord is permanent while peripheral nerves often regenerate or heal.

Autonomic Stress Response (ASR)

The autonomic nervous system responds to stress by stimulating either its sympathetic or its parasympathetic division. If the sympathetic nervous system is engaged, the body prepares for "fight or flight." Pupils dilate to increase vision. Pulse, respiratory, and blood pressure rates rise to meet an intense physical demand. Awareness, often seen as anxiety, increases. Sweating increases and vasoconstriction leaves the skin pale, cool, and moist. Endorphins are released to block pain. *A patient experiencing sympathetic ASR cannot give accurate information about their injuries. In most cases the patient is unaware of any physical problems and may not exhibit abnormal signs or symptoms upon examination. Their vital sign pattern may mimic or mask volume shock.*

If the parasympathetic nervous system is stimulated, the patient becomes nauseous and/or faints. Blood pools centrally as their pulse, respiratory, and blood pressure rates fall. Their skin is pale and cool. Afterward, the patient is often confused. *Parasympathetic ASR may mimic the signs and symptoms of a concussion and make accurate assessment of a head injury difficult.*

ASR, regardless of the type of response, is not life-threatening. Given the removal of the stressful incident, time, and reassurance, its signs and symptoms will disappear. The danger lies not in the ASR but in the possibility that a serious problem will go unrecognized and untreated because of a lack of physical signs and symptoms in the patient. *Assume that all patients involved in a stressful incident, especially major trauma, have ASR. Treat all patients under these situations as if they have the worst possible injuries indicated by the MOI.*

Anatomy and Physiology 16

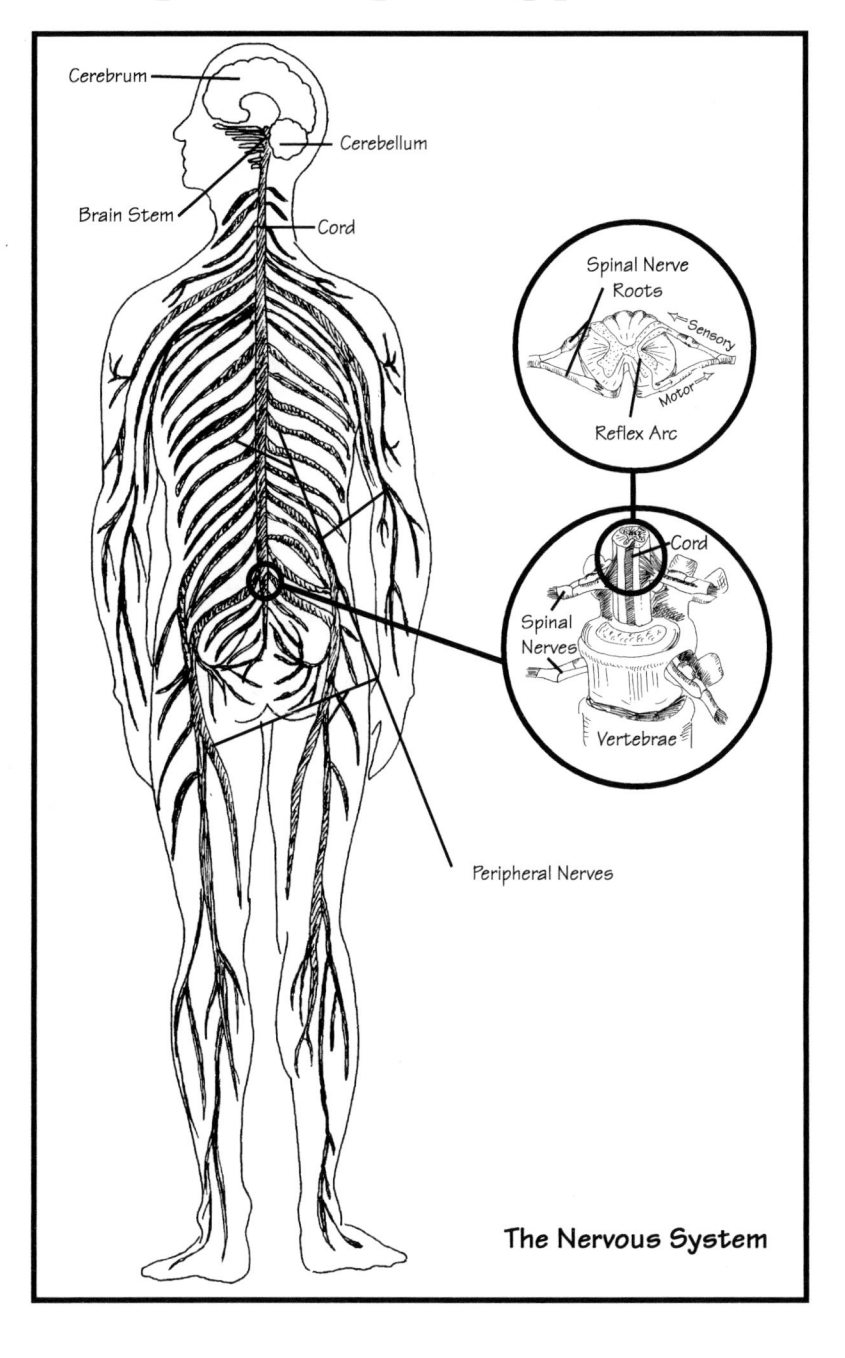

Cerebrum

Cerebellum

Brain Stem

Cord

Spinal Nerve Roots

Sensory

Motor

Reflex Arc

Cord

Spinal Nerves

Vertebrae

Peripheral Nerves

The Nervous System

The Endocrine System

The endocrine system works with the autonomic nervous system to maintain homeostasis. Once stimulated by nerve impulses, its ductless glands release **hormones** into the circulating blood. In contrast to the short quick nerve impulses generated by the nervous system, body responses to hormones are both slower and longer lasting. Hormones regulate metabolism, fluid and electrolyte balance, blood pressure, blood sugar levels, digestion, growth and repair of tissue, and stress responses. Damage to any of the glands of the endocrine system is usually due to a medical mechanism and generally has serious consequences.

The Digestive System

The digestive system is a series of interconnected hollow organs, connecting tubes, and solid organs. Many of the hollow organs are muscular tubes themselves and collectively form a "main" digestive tube. This main tube begins with the mouth and continues down to include the pharynx, esophagus, stomach, and small intestine. From the end of the small intestine it continues past the appendix into the large intestine and rectum before ending at the anus. This central tube is connected via other tubes (portal vein, bile duct, and pancreatic duct) to the liver, gall bladder, and pancreas.

The digestive system mechanically and chemically breaks down food, absorbs nutrients and water, and eliminates unusable material. Mechanical breakdown is accomplished initially by chewing and then through the coordinated muscular contractions of the stomach and small intestine. The chemical breakdown of food requires the presence of specific **enzymes** that are released as food travels through the digestive system. Enzymes chemically break down food into amino acids, simple sugars, and fats. These simple substances are then prepared for absorption. The process begins when **saliva** is released in the mouth and the enzymes contained in the saliva digest starch. In the **stomach**, gastric juices containing hydrochloric acid are released to initiate protein digestion. Food leaves the stomach as a thick liquid and enters the first part of the **small intestine** (duodenum) where the **gallbladder** releases bile and the **pancreas** releases pancreatic juice. **Bile** emulsifies fats while the **pancreatic juices** continue to break down proteins, fats,

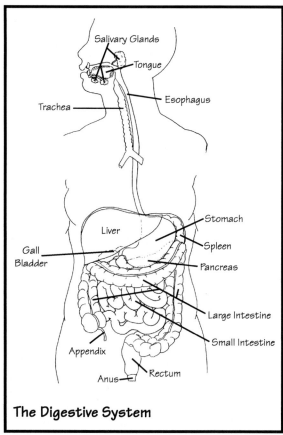

The Digestive System

Anatomy and Physiology 18

and starches. In addition to secreting digestive enzymes, the pancreas secretes *insulin* and *glucagon*. Insulin and glucagon are hormones that act to balance blood sugar levels. Insulin lowers blood sugar levels by increasing glucose (sugar) transport into cells while glucagon acts to increase blood sugar by stimulating the liver to release glucose. The primary purpose of the small intestine is absorption. Nutrients pass directly through the intestinal mucosa into the bloodstream and are immediately transported to the *liver* for filtering before entering general circulation. In addition to acting as a filter the liver functions as a storage chamber for glucose and vitamins. The *large intestine* removes water and solidifies fecal matter. Once formed, fecal matter is eliminated through the *anus*.

While the digestive organs are susceptible to disease, most problems with the digestive system are associated with the structure and function of its tubes. These tubes can become blocked, kinked, cut, ruptured, irritated by toxins, or infected.

The Urinary System

The urinary system is a collection of tubes and solid filter organs. It removes waste products from the blood and eliminates them from the body. A mucus membrane lines the urinary tubes in both men and women. The *kidneys* are the primary filtering organs of the urinary system. They lie in the rear of the abdominal cavity separated from the other abdominal organs by a strong membrane (*parietal peritoneum*) and are somewhat protected by the floating ribs. In addition to blood filtration the kidneys balance blood pH, fluids, and electrolytes. As the kidneys remove waste from the blood, urine is formed and carried via tubes (*ureters*) to the *bladder* where it is collected prior to elimination. Urine is eliminated from the bladder through another tube (*urethra*). In women the urethra is quite short and emerges as a small opening in the anterior vagina. In men it travels a significantly longer route through the penis.

Normal urine is clear or pale yellow in color. *Cloudy urine usually indicates bleeding or infection. High doses of B vitamins will produce a dark yellow or orange color.* The pH of urine is usually acidic but it may become basic with a predominantly vegetable diet. A high-protein diet increases its acidity. Normal urine does not contain sugar.

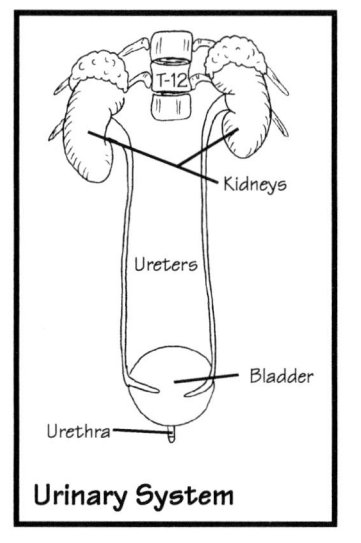

Urinary System

While the kidneys can be injured through trauma or by infection, the most common problems with the urinary system are associated with the blockage of its tubes from kidney stones in both sexes, to bacterial infections in women, and sexually transmitted diseases in men.

The Reproductive System

The reproductive system is a series of interconnecting tubes and sex glands. The function of the system in both men and women is reproduction of the species and the secretion of hormones necessary to develop and maintain secondary sex characteristics.

In men the sex glands (*testes*) are carried outside the body in the *scrotum* with tubes connecting to the urethra. In women the sex glands are internal (*ovaries*) with tubes leading to the pear shaped *uterus*. The uterus is where the fertilized egg attaches and the fetus develops. The cervix a muscular opening that separates the uterus from the vagina and functions to preserve its sterility. A relatively short muscular tube (**vagina**) leads from the **cervix** to the outside. Under normal conditions the mucus lining of the vagina contains a balanced mix of yeast and bacteria.

While both sexes may suffer from sexually transmitted diseases, yeast and bacterial infections are primarily female problems. Women may also suffer from problems arising during pregnancy and delivery.

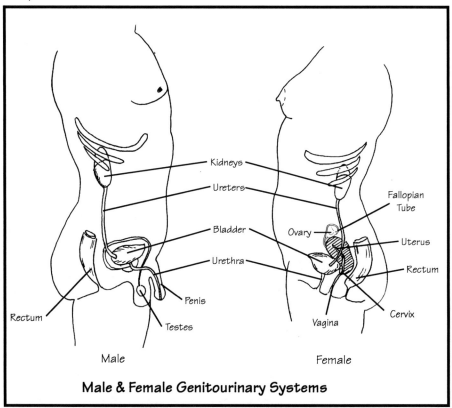

Male & Female Genitourinary Systems

The Musculoskeletal System

The musculoskeletal system is made up of bones, joints, cartilage, ligaments, tendons, and muscle. It provides the basis for support and movement. All components of the system require both perfusion and communication to develop, function, and heal. Arteries, veins, and nerves combine in the extremities to form neurovascular bundles that travel medially beside the body's long bones to carry nerve impulses and blood to the hands and feet.

Bones form the rigid structure of the system and are highly vascular. They provide support and protection, are reservoirs for calcium and other minerals, and it is in the bone marrow that blood cells are formed. Bones are surrounded by a highly vascular and innervated stuffsack (periosteum) that contains special bone forming cells (osteoblasts). These bone cells, together with others (osteoclasts), regulate the density and strength of each bone. Continued stress on bones (walking,

Anatomy and Physiology 20

running, exercising) causes an increase in both density and strength. Conversely, a decrease in stress producing exercise causes a decrease in bone strength and density. *Joints* hold bones together and permit movement.

There are three basic types of joints in the human body: fibrous, cartilaginous, and synovial. *Fibrous joints* are formed when fibrous tissue securely binds the surfaces of the bones so tightly that no movement is possible (e.g.: skull sutures, teeth, radius/ulna, tibia/fibula). *Cartilaginous joints* have a limited amount of movement and are created when cartilage binds the bones together (e.g.: sternum to ribs, symphysis pubis). *Synovial joints* are very mobile and extremely complex; they make up the majority of the joints in the body (e.g.: elbow, knee, ankle, spine, etc.). In synovial joints the articulating bone ends are covered with cartilage and the entire joint is encased with a sleeve-like extension of the periosteum (bone stuffsack) that forms the joint capsule. Each capsule is lined with a slippery membrane that both contains and secretes a lubricating fluid.

Synovial joint

Ligaments are strong bands of fibrous tissue that complete the joint structure by firmly tying the bone ends together. Ligaments, like door hinges, help define the movement of synovial joints.

**Muscles
Tendons
Ligaments**

Muscle tissue composes about half of the body's total weight, is highly vascular, provides additional glucose storage, and produces most of the body's heat. Muscles and tendons work together to create movement. Tendons are fibrous bands of tissue that connect muscle to bone. While tendons do not cause movement they must be intact for movement to occur. When stimulated, muscle fibers contract and pull on the tendon. The tendon transfers the energy of the muscles to the bone, creating movement. Since muscles can only contract and relax they must work in pairs through opposition to produce movement in two or more directions. *While both bone and muscle are highly vascular, tendons, ligaments, and cartilage have decreasingly less perfusion.*

Problems with the musculoskeletal system are usually those associated with traumatic injury and classified as stable or unstable. Significant musculoskeletal damage may indicate life-threatening internal injury.

The Integumentary (Skin) System

The skin is the ultimate body stuffsack. It varies greatly in thickness offering both physical protection from minor traumatic injury and denying access to potentially dangerous micro organisms. *Melanin* offers protection from prolonged exposure to sunlight. Blood vessels within the skin layers aid in thermoregulation as they contract to conserve heat or dilate to release it. Sensory nerves transmit environmental messages to the brain. Medically, skin color is not related to pigmentation but to its perfusion status; hence, normal skin color is considered pink regardless of race. Glands within the skin excrete water, electrolytes, and oils.

The outer layers of skin (*epidermis*) are extremely tough and contain melanin while the more sensitive underlying layers (dermis) contain both blood vessels and nerve endings. **Connective tissue** (superficial fascia) lies directly underneath the dermis and ties it to underlying structures. A subcutaneous fat layer separates the layers of the skin from underlying muscle.

Numerous mechanisms may damage the skin. Any break in the integrity of the stuffsack may expose underlying structures to injury. Trauma may cut or abrade the skin causing bleeding, tenderness, and pain. Extreme cold or heat may freeze or burn it. Infection may destroy cells locally then move systemically.

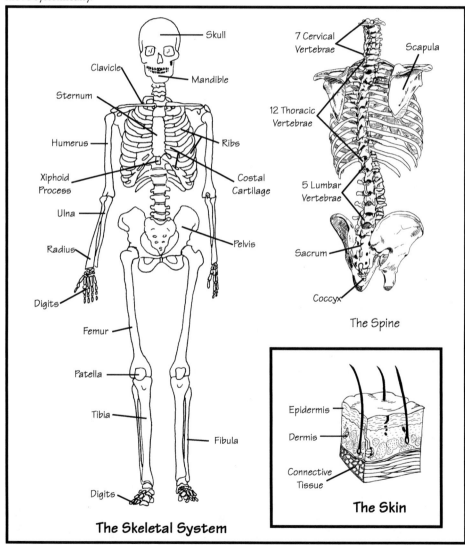

Skull
Clavicle
Mandible
Sternum
Humerus
Ribs
Xiphoid Process
Costal Cartilage
Ulna
Radius
Pelvis
Digits
Femur
Patella
Tibia
Fibula
Digits

The Skeletal System

7 Cervical Vertebrae
Scapula
12 Thoracic Vertebrae
5 Lumbar Vertebrae
Sacrum
Coccyx

The Spine

Epidermis
Dermis
Connective Tissue

The Skin

Anatomy and Physiology   22

The Patient Assessment System 23

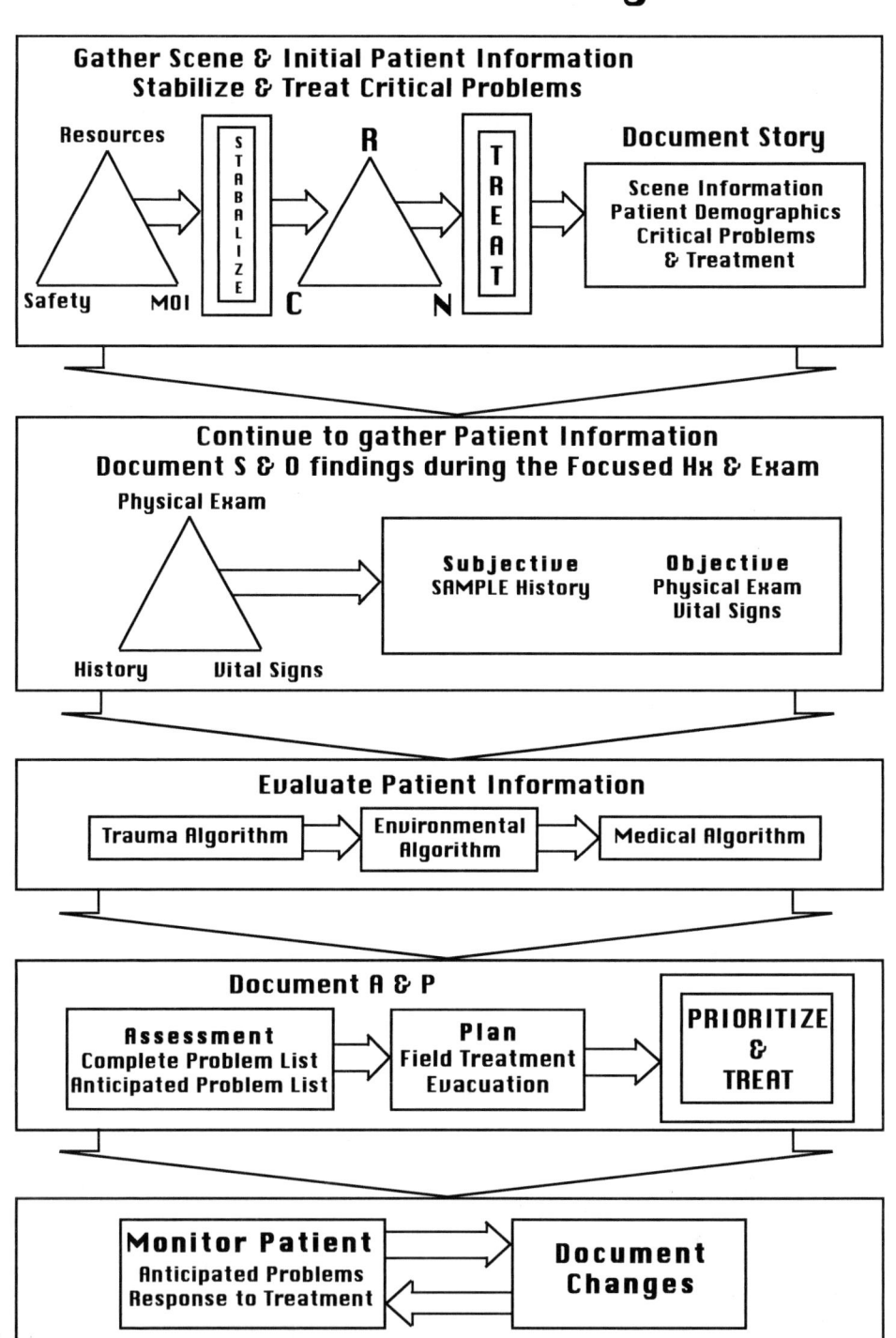

The Patient Assessment System

Overview

The Patient Assessment System (PAS) contains three interdependent components required for accurate patient assessment: surveys, patient SOAP notes, and an evaluation process. It is required for effective field treatment, evacuation (when necessary), and ongoing patient monitoring. The *three surveys* (scene size-up, initial assessment, and focused history & exam) are done sequentially and gather both scene and patient information in an organized and highly efficient manner. Information from the surveys, and later the completed assessment and treatment plan, are recorded in the patient's SOAP note for easy reference. The *evaluation process* is based on a clear understanding of the Mechanism of Injury (MOI). Together the components of the PAS offer an integrated and systematic approach to gathering, organizing, and evaluating patient information. Each is necessary for accurate treatment.

To complete an accurate assessment and efficiently treat your patient, first size up and stabilize the scene. Then complete your initial assessment and treat your patient's life-threatening problems. Next document your observations and treatments. After recording the information you gathered during the scene size-up and the initial assessment, begin a second, more detailed, patient exam. Focus on the patient's history, physical exam findings, and their vital signs. Record, evaluate, and prioritize your findings before continuing to treat your patient. During a prolonged evacuation, monitor your patient by repeating both patient surveys. Revise and update your notes as necessary. Refer to the flow chart on page 23 and the SOAP Notes located in the back of the manual as you read the remaining text. Case studies that will help you develop your evaluation and recording skills are available in workbook form from the Wilderness Medicine Training Center.

SOAP Notes

The general story and scene information, relevant patient demographics, subjective information, objective information, the patient's problems, their anticipated problems, and your proposed treatment plan (including evacuation) are recorded in the patient's SOAP note. SOAP stands for *Subjective* (what you are told), *Objective* (what you see), *Assessment* (what you think is wrong), and *Plan* (what you're going to do about it). The SOAP format is the medical profession's way to document your findings. Two complete sets of SOAP notes are located at the end of the manual.

Once you become used to it, you will find the SOAP format both efficient and helpful in assessing and treating your patients. *Record* the story, scene, subjective, and objective information you gathered during the three patient surveys in the first three sections of the SOAP note then begin the evaluation process. Once you have completed the evaluation process, record your assessment (the patient's current problems and their anticipated problems) and your treatment plan (including evacuation) under the Assessment and Plan headings in the SOAP note. During prolonged treatment, repeat the two patient surveys, as needed, to monitor the patient for changes, the development of any new and/or anticipated problems, and how they are responding to your treatment. *Revise* your SOAP note as it becomes necessary. Transfer a copy of your SOAP note with your patient and keep one for your records.

Patient Surveys

The **three surveys** gather the information you will need to evaluate and treat your patient. *Each survey has three components.* While you always complete the surveys sequentially, the order of their components varies with each patient and situation. Follow each survey with a treatment phase to address any problems you encountered. Record all your findings in the patient's SOAP note.

Scene Size-up

The Scene Size-up is the first of the three surveys. It is divided into three components: mechanism of injury (MOI), safety, and resources. *Complete the Scene Size-up BEFORE you enter the scene.*

Safety: The safety of yourself, other rescuers, bystanders, and your patient is critical. Danger may present itself in numerous ways: rockfall, avalanche, flood, lightning, hazardous materials, violent people or animals, poisonous insects, etc. Address these **physical dangers** immediately without endangering yourself or others. If there are potentially **dangerous environmental factors** present (e.g.: extreme heat, cold, etc.) remove the patient from them as soon as possible while protecting yourself and others. **Medical mechanisms** (illness and disease) require additional protection. Your minimum precautions for all patient contacts should include protective clothing, rubber gloves, and glasses. Wear a mask if you suspect a respiratory disease. Wash yourself and your clothing thoroughly after treating a patient. Contaminated materials must be deposited in a sealed plastic or metal container and clearly marked for proper disposal. It is imperative you do not enter a scene without first assessing and addressing both its real and potential dangers.

MOI: MOI is divided into three broad categories: trauma, environmental, and medical. If during the Scene Size-up you suspect **major trauma**, assume that the patient's spine is unstable and immediately immobilize it. If movement is necessary, support their spine in the "in-line" position throughout the movement. Immediately address obvious environmental and medical mechanisms that may place you or your patient at risk. Address subtle environmental and medical problems after the focused history and exam.

Resources: Quickly assess the available resources in light of the scene dangers, MOI, and number of patients. If possible, assess the number and training of the rescuers; the medical, rescue, and evacuation equipment immediately available; the closest medical and rescue assistance, their training and response time; and, all communication options. It may be appropriate to "call for help" before entering the scene.

Initial Assessment

The Initial Assessment is the first of two patient surveys. Begin the Initial Assessment after the scene has been stabilized. **Quickly check your patient's three critical systems (respiratory, circulatory, and nervous) then treat any immediate life-threatening problems.** Treatment for Initial Assessment problems is covered under "Basic Life Support."

Respiratory System Check: Assess your patient's airway and breathing. Their **airway** should be open with air moving freely in and out. **Breathing** should be adequate enough to perfuse the body tissues with oxygen. If absent, restore their airway and breathing.

Circulatory System Check: Feel for a pulse and do a complete body survey looking for external bleeding. If necessary, cut their clothing. They should have a palpable **pulse** and no **severe bleeding**. If they do not have a pulse, consider CPR. If severe external bleeding is present, stop it with direct pressure.

Nervous System Check: Patients with a normal functioning nervous system should be awake and cooperative. If the patient's is not **awake** consider, "calling for help" now. If there is evidence of major trauma during the scene survey immobilize the patient's *spine* and maintain in line stability during any patient movement.

Treat all problems found in the Initial Assessment BEFORE continuing on to the Focused History & Exam. Record all the information gathered during the scene size-up and initial assessment, including patient demographics and treatments rendered, in the first part of the patient's SOAP note BEFORE beginning the Focused History & Exam.

Focused History & Exam

Begin the Focused History & Exam after the Initial Assessment has been completed, the patient's critical systems stabilized, and the findings documented. Record the information gathered during the Focused History & Exam as you find it in the appropriate spaces in the patient's SOAP note. The three components of the Focused History & Exam are: a SAMPLE history, a detailed physical exam, and the patient's vital signs. The sequencing of the components will vary depending upon the individual patient and situation.

SAMPLE History: The patient's history is extremely important in identifying and treating illness and disease. The history may be subdivided into components and identified by the acronym SAMPLE. SAMPLE stands for Symptoms, Allergies, Medications, Last food and fluids, Past medical history, and Events leading up to the illness or injury. The patient's history is considered *subjective information* because it is told to you (by the patient or someone else). Some information for the SAMPLE history may be prerecorded in a medical form. Ask questions relating to the onset, provocation, quality, and severity of their *symptoms*. Ask questions related to the type of allergy (drug, insect, food, contact, etc.), the severity of their response, and what type of treatment was required. When asking questions about *medications*, consider prescription medications, over-the-counter medications (OTC), herbal remedies, homeopathic treatments, and recreational drugs or alcohol. If the patient is currently taking any "medication," follow-up with additional questions (e.g.: what is it for, dose, location, when did they last take it, who prescribed it, etc.). Relate questions about their *past medical history* to a suspected MOI. When asking questions about the patient's *last food and fluids*, focus on assessing their available calories, electrolytes, and water. Include questions about the frequency and color of their urine. Ask the patient to describe in as much detail as possible all the *events* leading up to the illness or injury. Try and identify any lapses in the patient's memory if you suspect head trauma as a MOI.

Physical Exam: Both the physical exam and vital signs are considered *objective information* because they have been directly observed by you during the Focused History & Exam. A detailed physical exam should reveal any skin, soft tissue, or musculoskeletal injures. A thorough exam should both **look** and **feel** for any abnormalities over the patient's entire body. Essentially you are looking for discoloration, swelling, abnormal fluid loss, and deformity. Feel for tenderness, crepitus, and instability. In most cases you will begin the physical exam at the patient's head and progress to their chest, abdomen, pelvis, back, and extremities. Pressure should be gentle but firm. Ultimately the depth and speed of the physical exam will depend on a number of factors: the overall severity of the patient's condition, the harshness of the environment, and the skill and resources of the rescuers.

Vital Signs: Take a complete set of vital signs as early as possible to establish a base line for further assessment. Vital signs assist in measuring the function of the three critical systems and are necessary aids in identifying clinical patterns specific to a particular injury or illness. Because you are concerned with identifying patterns, **the change in the patient's vital signs over time is more important than any single set.** Rather than take vital signs at regular intervals it is more efficient to use the patient's pulse, mental status, and level of consciousness as indicators of clinically significant change. You should continually monitor both the patient's pulse, mental status, and level of consciousness. If their pulse varies in either direction by ten or more points OR their mental status/

The Patient Assessment System 26

level of consciousness changes, record a complete set of vitals. Once you have identified a clinical pattern, treatment and evacuation should not be hindered to take further complete sets of vital signs UNLESS a change in the patient's vital signs would indicate a change in treatment. Because it is the changes over time that concern you, **record the time with every set of vital signs taken.** If you do not take a vital sign note that as well. The six vital signs are: pulse, respiration, blood pressure, skin, core temperature, and mental status. Record the patients vital signs in the vital sign chart in the patient's SOAP note.

- **Pulse:** Take your patient's pulse **rate** and **regularity** at their radial (wrist) or carotid (neck) arteries. Rate is measured over a minute. Limit the adjectives describing your patient's pulse to regular or irregular.

- **Respirations:** Take your patient's respiratory **rate** over a minute. You will probably find it easier to time the interval between respirations and divide the result into sixty than actually count each respiration. Describe the **quality** of their respirations. Limit your adjectives to easy or labored.

- **Blood Pressure:** Taking a blood pressure is often a luxury in a field situation. In emergency medicine the systolic (top number) pressure is the more important than the diastolic (bottom number) to measure the patient's perfusion status. Take their systolic blood pressure by **auscultation** (listening with a stethoscope) or **palpation** (feeling at the radial artery). If you don't have a blood pressure cuff, closely monitor the patient's mental status and level of consciousness.

- **Skin:** Document the **color, temperature,** and **moisture** content of the skin. Normal skin, regardless of race or pigmentation, is pink, warm, and dry.

- **Core Temperature:** The most accurate core temperature is measured **rectally. Axillary** (under the arm) and **oral** temperatures are one degree less than rectal temperatures. Use an oral or axillary temperature if your patient is alert, cooperative, and their injuries or illness is minor.

- **Level of Consciousness/Mental Status:** Level of Consciousness is measured using the AVPU scale. AVPU stands for Awake, Voice responsive, Pain responsive, and Unresponsive. A patient is **awake** if they are asking questions, volunteering information, and/or responding to their environment appropriately. A **voice responsive** patient responds to the stimulus of the rescuer's voice. Within the voice responsive range patient responses may vary from abbreviated sentences or words to moans to directed movement. A high voice responsive patient will respond verbally but will not ask questions or volunteer information. A voice responsive patient may respond with single words or groans. And, a low voice responsive patient will not respond verbally but may move an arm, leg, fingers, etc. upon request. A **pain responsive** person will respond to a painful stimulus by groaning and/or moving while an **unresponsive** person will not respond to any stimulus. **Mental Status is a more detailed measurement of an awake patient.** If your patient is awake, describe their behavior: cooperative, irritable, combative, drunk, anxious, tired, sick, etc. Changes in mental status usually indicate a mild "peeling of the onion."

Patient Evaluation

Once you have completed the surveys and recorded the information in the patient's SOAP note under the subjective and objective headings, you need to evaluate it. The evaluation process is algorithmic in nature. **An algorithm is a flow chart or decision making tree.** Begin the evaluation process by identifying the specific MOI within each of the three categories: trauma, environmental, and medical, then follow the algorithm for that category. Since mechanisms are often mixed it may be necessary to work through more than one algorithm. **Trauma and environmental mechanisms are easier to rule out than medical mechanisms;** therefore, begin with trauma, move to environmental, and finish with medical. Each mechanism will have a problem list associated with it; together, they form a complete list of your patient's problems and anticipated problems. Use this list to prioritize and develop a treatment plan, including evacuation. Continue treating your patient *after* you have recorded your assessment, evaluation, and treatment plan in their SOAP notes.

Trauma Algorithm

When you are evaluating traumatic injuries, first identify what *part of the patient's body* was impacted by the traumatic mechanism (head, chest, abdomen, spine, extremities). Next, for each part, identify the *major system(s)* housed within that part and its components. Each system *component* will have a limited number of problems associated with both the component and the specific mechanism. This is your possible problem list. *Use the patient's signs and symptoms to rule out problems from your possible problem list and create a new one.*

Environmental Algorithm

When you are evaluating the potential for environmental problems first examine the environmental conditions and mechanisms over the past few days to the present. *Environmental conditions or mechanisms* can only yield a few related problems. These problems form your possible problem list. *Use the patient's history, signs, and symptoms to rule out problems from your possible problems list and create a new one.*

Medical Algorithm

Medical problems are diagnosed based on the patient's signs, symptoms, and history. Accurate diagnosis requires an in-depth knowledge of specific illnesses and disease. Many medical problems cannot be diagnosed without the clinical procedures and knowledge available to a hospital. When evaluating the potential for medical problems a *thorough* history and physical exam, including all vital signs, is necessary. If flu-like signs and symptoms, eye pain, skin rash, or respiratory distress are present, review the patient's potential contact history for infectious diseases. Create a possible problem list based on your findings. *Rule out problems through specific diagnostic testing.* If a problem cannot be identified consider treating the patient's signs and symptoms. Closely monitor the patient for any anticipated problems, drug reactions, and improvement. *Rule out problems based on successful treatment.* Modify the problem list, anticipated problem list, and treatment plan as necessary.

Patient Monitoring

Monitor your patient for changes, the development of new problems, anticipated problems, and how they are responding to treatment. Monitor by repeating all or part of the two patient surveys. Evaluate and record any new information in the patient's SOAP note. Revise the treatment plan as it becomes necessary.

Guidelines for Evacuation

The need for evacuation depends on the severity of the problem and your resources. The type of evacuation depends on the mobility of the patient, the size of your party and its resources, the difficulty of terrain, and the distance involved. Any evacuation, regardless of the type (helicopter, plane, car, boat, horse, carry, etc.) should not endanger either your or your patient beyond your capacity to deal effectively with the risk. In most cases, your field treatment for minor non life-

The Patient Assessment System 28

threatening injuries will be effective and rapid evacuation will not be necessary. By contrast, your field treatment for most life-threatening illnesses or injuries will simply buy you and your patient some time. In these situations, focus on a quick accurate assessment and fast evacuation. The "medical window" for life-threatening problems is often specific to the particular illness or injury. If evacuation is not possible, your field treatment will usually be limited to supporting your patient's critical systems. This is often ineffective and your patient may die. In general any problem that causes a change in the patient's mental status is very serious. If a patient reaches definitive medical care (major hospital) while they are still awake they have a reasonable chance for complete recovery. If they reach definitive care with a significantly decreased level of consciousness (voice responsive, pain responsive, or unresponsive) their chances for a complete recovery, or a recovery at all are respectively reduced. A general guideline for making evacuation decisions follows: any problem that is persistent, uncomfortable, and not relieved by your treatment requires an evacuation. The speed of the evacuation depends on the degree of involvement, or potential involvement, of any critical system(s). The greater the degree or potential, the faster the evacuation.

Helicopter Use

Level 1 Life threat High risk

Helicopters serve two primary uses in wilderness medicine: 1) early treatment and rapid evacuation of the critically injured; and 2) the controlled evacuation of minor injuries where other methods of evacuation would be more difficult, more costly, and potentially dangerous to rescuers.

"Go" and "standby" requests are usually made via a radio or cell phone. Most aeromedical helicopters are dispatched directly from their base, by Search and Rescue (SAR) teams on the scene, or through local law enforcement (sheriff's office). Rescuers should immediately request a helicopter to standby if they suspect a critical need; in most cases there is no charge for a standby request. Map or GPS coordinates insure that the pilot will find you.

Helicopters have limitations. Most fly under "Visual Flight Rules" (VFR) and require a minimum of 1/2 mile of visibility and a 500 foot ceiling during the day; the visibility minimum increases to 3 miles at night. Larger helicopters often have greater VFR minimums. Some helicopters, usually military, are equipped with specialized instruments that permit them to fly in more difficult conditions. Even with a helicopter en route to your scene, weather and air turbulence at the landing site could pose a significant problem and prevent landing. Never assume that a helicopter dispatched for you will arrive; always have a backup plan.

While helicopters require less space than fixed wing aircraft to land they have their limitations here too. A safe landing zone should be flat and permit the chopper to land and take off into the wind; a light breeze is preferable to no wind, heavy wind, or gusts. At night use headlamps to illuminate the landing spot and any hazards. Rotors generate extremely high wind. You should hold down or anchor any loose gear. Direct everyone near the landing site to cover their eyes or look away. Most pilots circle the landing zone before landing. Avoid waving your hands above your head to attract their attention; this is the universal "wave-off" signal that tells a pilot NOT to land. While there are specific hand signals used to guide a helicopter to a safe landing you do not need to know or use them. Once the helicopter has landed wait for the rotors to come to a FULL STOP. Continue to wait until you receive a clear signal from the pilot (or crew member) before approaching any helicopter. Stay within the pilot's (or crew member's) line of site and follow their directions. Do not smoke within 200 feet of any helicopter.

The Evaluation Process

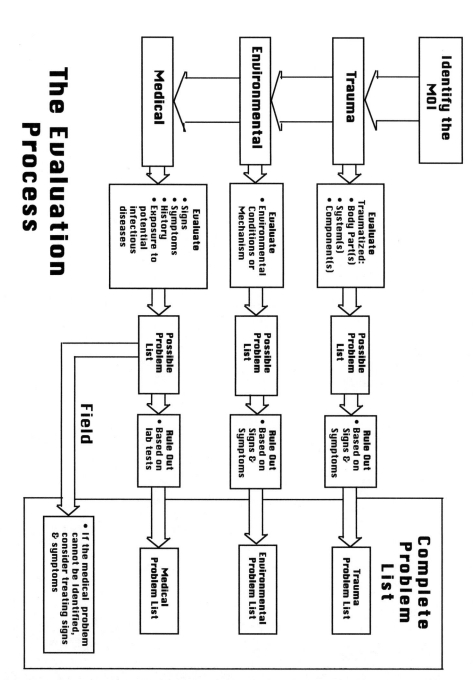

The Patient Assessment System 30

Overview

Basic Life Support (BLS) refers to non-invasive emergency assessment and treatment for problems encountered during the Initial Assessment (see PAS). You can learn the skills outlined in the following pages in CPR (cardiopulmonary resuscitation) courses offered by the American Heart Association or the American Red Cross. Advanced Life Support (ALS) refers to the more invasive types of treatment usually reserved for EMT intermediates, paramedics, nurses, and doctors.

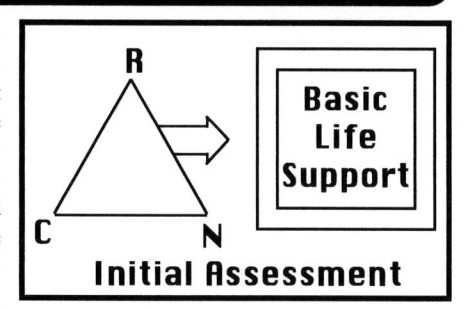

Obstructed Airway

Pathophysiology

Any blockage, partial or complete, that significantly reduces the patient's ability to exchange air requires immediate intervention. **There are four ways that a patient's airway can be blocked: corks, kinks, swelling, and fluid.** Corks are foreign objects that physically obstruct the upper airway. Common causes are food, gum, chewing tobacco, and teeth. If the patient's neck is twisted or flexed at an odd angle the airway may be kinked. In an unresponsive person the muscles that make up the tongue may relax, causing it to block the air passage. Trauma, anaphylaxis, or burns may cause local swelling of the soft tissue and subsequent blockage. Fluids (blood, vomitus, water) may block the airway and be aspirated.

Assessment

• If a patient is talking their airway is clear.
• In a patient with a severely depressed level of consciousness (low V, P, or U) it may be necessary to place a hand or cheek next to the patient's nose and mouth to determine if they are exchanging air.
• No air moving in or out may indicate a blocked airway. Closely examine the patient's upper airway for corks, kinks, fluids, and swelling.

BLS Treatment

Corks

• Do not intervene with an alert patient who is coughing and actively trying to clear their own airway.
• With **adults and children,** use abdominal or chest thrusts. With **infants** use alternating sets of back blows and chest thrusts.
• Be prepared for vomiting.

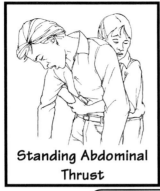

Standing Abdominal Thrust

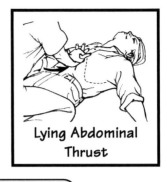

Lying Abdominal Thrust

Kinks

- *Align* the patient's head to open their airway. *Maintain spine stabilization if the MOI is major trauma.*
- Use a jaw thrust or similar maneuver in patients with a depressed level of consciousness (V, P, or U).
- Consider inserting an oral or nasal airway.
- If patient is on their back consider rolling them onto their side. *Maintain spine stabilization if the MOI is major trauma.*

Fluids

- *Reposition* the patient so that gravity assists fluid drainage. *Maintain spine stabilization if the MOI is major trauma.*
- *Finger sweep* for chunks. Look first. Use extreme care (you will want to keep your fingers).
- *Suction* for fluids. Suction from the patient's cheek.
- *Call ALS* for insertion of an endotracheal tube.

Swelling

- If *anaphylaxis* is the MOI, administer SQ or IM 1:1000 epinephrine immediately. Pediatric dose: 0.15 cc. Adult dose: 0.3-0.5 cc. Follow with an antihistamine to prevent rebound. (See Allergic Reactions).
- For trauma and burn patients: *align patient's airway and call ALS*. Advanced life support treatment includes the insertion of an endotracheal tube or emergency tracheotomy.

Absent/Inadequate Respirations

Pathophysiology

Even if a patient is moving air they may not be exchanging enough oxygen to maintain critical perfusion. Respiratory mechanisms for inadequate perfusion include respiratory infection, asthma, respiratory burns and toxins, damage to the respiratory center, and chest trauma. Under normal conditions brain cells die within six minutes without oxygen. *You do not need to know the specific mechanism to begin emergency treatment; however, the mechanism will effect the outcome of the treatment.*

Assessment

- A clear airway with no air moving in or out.
- A clear airway with moving air, cyanosis, and a severely depressed level of consciousness (low V, P, or U).

BLS Treatment

- **Positive pressure ventilations.** Ventilate until the patient's chest begins to rise. Do not over inflate. Mouth to simple face mask is both safe and efficient.
- Supplemental **oxygen** at high liter flow. Plug oxygen line into oxygen port on the face mask.

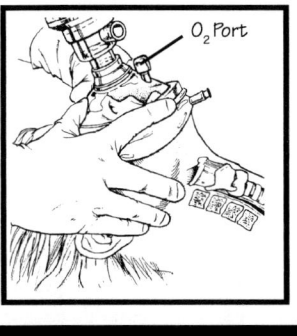 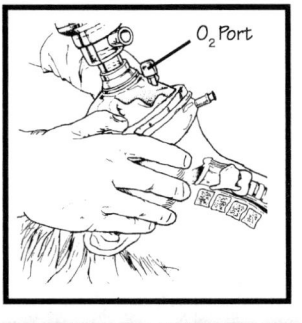

No Pulse

Pathophysiology

A patient with no pulse is not perfusing and their brain cells will die within six minutes without oxygen. Unlike the sensitive cells of the central nervous system, both striated and smooth muscle tissue can live up to two hours without oxygen. Because of this disparity in cellular survival times it is possible to restart a patient's heart after their brain has died. Numerous mechanisms may cause a cessation in pulse. All are extremely serious. A patient's chance of survival significantly increases if CPR is started within four minutes of the arrest and ALS intervention begins within four to eight minutes. Even with timely CPR and ALS intervention the majority of pulseless patients will die. In a wilderness context where ALS is rarely available most people that arrest will die. **The success of CPR independent of ALS intervention is limited to those patients with a healthy and intact circulatory system who have arrested due to a primary respiratory problem (e.g.: near drowning or lightning) where CPR has been initiated within the first few minutes after the arrest.** In those instances the pulse may return within the first few minutes. Even with ALS intervention statistics show that there is a 0% chance of recovery after twenty minutes without a pulse. All patients who remain pulseless for thirty minutes are dead regardless of the MOI.

Assessment

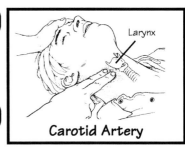

Carotid Artery

- No pulse. For the purpose of initiating CPR the patient's pulse is checked at the carotid artery for a maximum of ten seconds. The patient's neck should be in alignment during the pulse check.

BLS Treatment

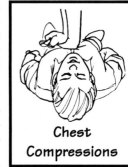

Chest Compressions

- *Call for ALS* support immediately if there is any chance that they will arrive within twenty minutes.
- *Begin CPR* unless contraindicated (see below). If indicated begin CPR (chest compressions and positive pressure ventilations) immediately. Ventilate until the patient's chest begins to rise. Do not over-inflate. The ratio of compressions to ventilations is generally five compressions to one ventilation. Use high flow supplemental oxygen if available. Be prepared for vomiting.
- *Do not begin CPR* if obvious signs of death are present (e.g.: dismemberment, rigor mortis, etc.), if the patient has a standing DNR (Do Not Resuscitate) order, and if initiating and continuing CPR puts rescuers at risk. Some protocols recommend not initiating CPR on arrest patients with blunt trauma. Follow your protocols.
- *Stop CPR* when authorized by your medical control. Consider stopping CPR after a documented thirty minutes of pulselessness.

Severe Bleeding

Pathophysiology

Assess all trauma patients for external bleeding that, if not immediately controlled, may rapidly lead to volume shock and death. Most life-threatening bleeding is arterial; however, severe venous bleeding is possible. Hemophiliacs and patient's taking anticoagulant medications may be at extreme risk from even small lacerations.

Assessment

- Closely examine all trauma patients for significant bleeding. Remove or cut clothing where appropriate and possible to *visualize* the wound. If necessary, wipe away excess blood. Feel for blood in areas that are difficult to see. *Maintain spine stabilization* throughout.

BLS Treatment

- Wipe away blood to identify source(s).
- Immediately *apply well-aimed direct pressure*. Use a trauma dressing to distribute the pressure if possible. Maintain the pressure until the bleeding has stopped. Normal clotting requires 10-20 minutes.

- Consider a **pressure bandage**. A wide elastic bandage (ace wrap) makes an excellent pressure bandage. Apply the bandage with enough force to stop the bleeding. Write the time applied on the bandage and remove the bandage within thirty minutes of application. **Monitor** the patient's circulation, sensation, and motor function below the injury site (distal CSM) and consider loosening the bandage earlier if it becomes severely compromised.

Unstable Spine

Pathophysiology

If you find or suspect major trauma as a MOI during the scene size up (see PAS), immediately **immobilize the patient's spine**. Movement of unstable vertebrae may cut the spinal cord causing irreversible loss of motor function and sensation below the injury site. A high cord injury may cause death. Unstable movement may be caused by the traumatic event, voluntary patient movement, or by the rescuers. Damage to the tissue surrounding the spinal cord may cause pain, tenderness, and swelling. Cord damage resulting from swelling may be temporary or permanent. When working with a patient with a suspected spine injury the treatment goal is to avoid all unstable spinal movement (See Trauma: Unstable Spine).

Assessment

- **Assume** all patients with an uncertain or positive mechanism (major trauma) for a spine injury to have an **unstable spine**.

BLS Treatment

- **Stabilize** the patient in the position found using your hands.
- If necessary during your initial treatment, you may safely align the patient's spine to anatomical position using traction. Once the movement has been completed traction is no longer required. Continue to stabilize and support the patient's spine.
- If rapid movement is necessary, you should maintain the patient's spinal alignment by firmly controlling their weight centers (head, shoulders, hips). Their head is best controlled using your hands or the patient's arms to form a "head sandwich." Their shoulders and hips are best controlled by using leverage and lots of hands.
- Attach a **cervical collar** to help prevent cervical flexion as soon as possible.

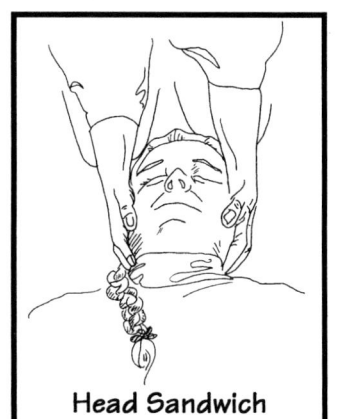

Head Sandwich

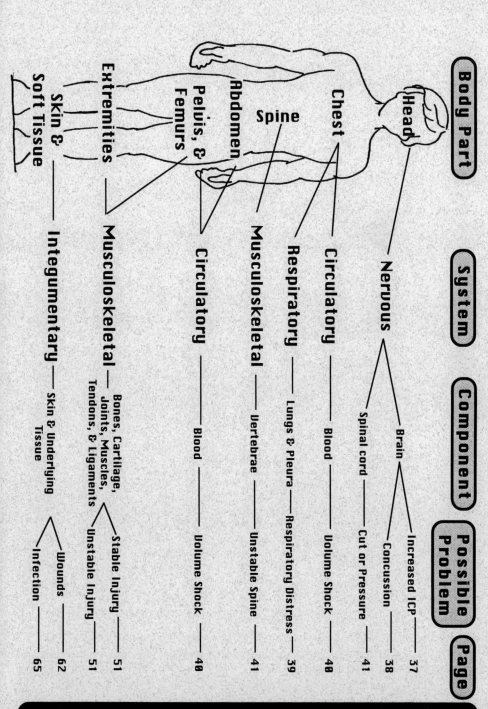

Body Part	System	Component	Possible Problem	Page
Head	Nervous	Brain	Increased ICP	37
			Concussion	38
		Spinal cord	Cut or Pressure	41
Chest	Respiratory	Lungs & Pleura	Respiratory Distress	39
	Circulatory	Blood	Volume Shock	40
Spine	Musculoskeletal	Vertebrae	Unstable Spine	41
Abdomen	Circulatory	Blood	Volume Shock	40
Pelvis, & Femurs	Musculoskeletal	Bones, Cartilage, Joints, Muscles, Tendons, & Ligaments	Stable Injury	51
Extremities			Unstable Injury	51
Skin & Soft Tissue	Integumentary	Skin & Underlying Tissue	Wounds	62
			Infection	65

Trauma Index

36

Increased ICP

Pathophysiology

Head trauma may injure brain cells or damage intracranial blood vessels and cause localized **bleeding**. Damaged brain cells activate the inflammatory response causing local vasodilation and **edema during the next 24 hours**. Any fluid, blood or plasma, leaking into the closed compartment of the skull causes an increase in pressure. Increasing pressure causes a decrease in perfusion and subsequent injury to otherwise healthy brain tissue. This, in turn, causes more leakage and progressively increasing pressure. This increasing intracranial pressure (ICP) may lead to a change in the patient's mental status, severe headache, persistent vomiting, decreasing level of consciousness, seizures, coma, and death. The body has no compensatory mechanism for increased ICP; field care is limited to early recognition and immediate evacuation to a major trauma center.

Prevention

- Wear a fitted well padded helmet designed for the specific activity (climbing, bicycling, paddling, etc.).

Assessment

- **The MOI is head trauma.** While positive signs and symptoms for musculoskeletal injuries to the head indicate head trauma they do not necessarily indicate increased ICP.
- Patients with increasing ICP are assumed to have a spine injury unless previously cleared.
- Patients may present with a late clinical pattern.

Early Clinical Pattern

- **Change in normal mental status** to: awake and lethargic, awake and irritable, or awake and combative.
- Patients with the early clinical pattern for increased ICP often appear drunk.
- Severe headache similar to a migraine.
- **Persistent vomiting.**

Late Clinical Pattern

- **Continued decrease in level of consciousness** to voice responsive, pain responsive, or unresponsive.
- Vomiting and headache continue.
- Seizures are common.
- Coma.
- Respiratory Arrest.
- Cardiac Arrest.

Field Treatment

- Support Critical Systems.
- Maintain spine stability unless previously cleared.
- Position patient on back or side with their head slightly higher than their feet.

- Maintain clear airway; suction as necessary.
- Ventilate the patient with supplemental oxygen. This may help slow the developing cerebral edema.
- Positive pressure ventilations as necessary.
- CPR as per protocols. Note: chest compressions and Advanced Cardiac Care not successful with patients suffering from increased ICP.
- *Evacuate with ALS to a major trauma center.*

Concussion

Pathophysiology

Trauma can disrupt the electrical signals within the brain, damage blood vessels, and injure brain tissue. A concussion is a *minor brain injury*. Because of internal bleeding or a developing inflammatory response, the concussed patient has the potential to develop increased ICP during the next 24 hours. Clinically, a concussion is defined as a temporary loss of consciousness or amnesia due to a blow to the head. A concussed patient is alert and cooperative. Many have headaches, are slightly nauseous, and wish to sleep.

Prevention

- Wear a fitted well padded helmet designed for the specific activity (climbing, bicycling, paddling, etc.).

Assessment

- *The MOI is head trauma.* While positive signs and symptoms for musculoskeletal injuries to the head indicate head trauma they do not necessarily indicate a concussion.
- *Patient is alert and cooperative* NOW following a period of altered mental status or temporary loss of consciousness.
- Amnesia is usually present. Most patients cannot remember the events prior to and/or following the injury. If you cannot determine if the patient has had an episode of altered mental status and amnesia is present, assume the patient has a concussion.
- A mild headache is common.
- Nausea may be present due to parasympathetic ASR. A single episode of vomiting is not uncommon.
- Many concussed patients are tired and wish to sleep.
- *Increased ICP may develop within 24 hours of the traumatic event.*

Field Treatment

- Rest. Sleep is healing; however, because of the potential for developing increased ICP, do not leave your patient alone during the first 24 hours and awaken them to an alert status at regular intervals during that time period. Every two hours during the first six hours and every 4-6 hours for the remaining 24 is reasonable. Closely monitor for vomiting while they are sleeping.
- *Monitor for the early clinical pattern for Increased ICP.*
- *Evacuate to close proximity of a major hospital;* some programs may require evacuation to a major hospital.

Trauma   38

Respiratory Distress

Pathophysiology

Chest trauma may disrupt the integrity of the pleura and permit air or blood to leak between them breaking their attachment and causing *delamination*. The delamination may grow as each inhalation forces more blood or air into the increasing pleural space. The loss of pleural attachment (delamination) prevents the lung from fully inflating (collapsed lung) causing decreased oxygen pickup and respiratory distress. Prognosis is good with damage to one lung. If both lungs are involved and ALS is not rapidly available, the patient may die.

The *bruising* of lung tissue may occur independent from or in addition to a pleural delamination if blood vessels and alveoli are ruptured during the traumatic episode. Blood leaking into damaged alveoli will usually cause productive coughing. The patient may issue pink foam as the blood is expelled.

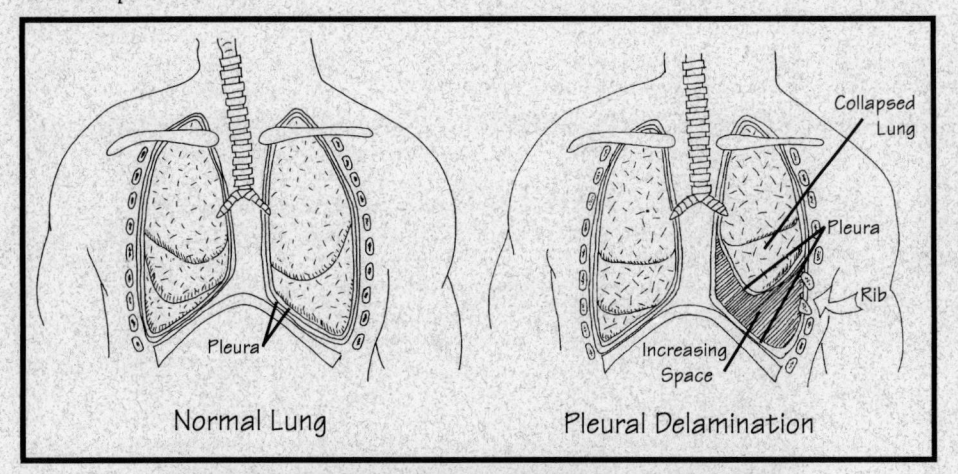

Normal Lung   Pleural Delamination

Assessment

- **The MOI is chest trauma.** While positive signs and symptoms for musculoskeletal injuries to the chest indicate chest trauma they do not necessarily indicate respiratory distress.
- Patient may present with a late clinical pattern.
- A pink foamy productive cough indicates bruised lung tissue.

Early Clinical Pattern

- *Change in normal mental status* to alert and anxious or alert and irritable.
- *Patient has difficulty breathing.*
- Increased respiratory rate.
- Increased pulse rate.
- Blood pressure may vary and is NOT clinically helpful in the assessment of pleural delamination. Consider the potential for volume shock.
- Prognosis is good with damage to one lung and rapid evacuation.

Late Clinical Pattern

- *Continued decrease in mental status* to voice responsive, pain responsive, and unresponsive.
- *Patient continues to have greater and greater difficulty breathing.*
- Respiratory rate continues to rise.
- Pulse rate continues to rise.
- Blood pressure may vary and is NOT clinically helpful in the assessment of pleural delamination. Consider the potential for volume shock.
- No lung sounds are present in the injured part of the lung.
- Cyanosis (blue color) may be present in mucus membranes and skin as the patient's condition deteriorates.
- A complete delamination of both lungs may result in death.

Field Treatment

- Support critical systems.
- Position Patient on injured side to help remove pressure from the undamaged lung.
- Provide rest and reassurance to the alert patient.
- Begin positive pressure ventilations if the patient becomes cyanotic and unresponsive. Note that positive pressure ventilations may not be effective as pressure in the pleural space increases.
- Administer oxygen.
- With penetrating trauma: cover wound site with occlusive dressing as soon as possible. Remove and reapply if the patient's respiratory distress dramatically increases after application. Hold dressing in place with an ace wrap.
- *Evacuate with ALS to a major trauma center.*

Volume Shock

Pathophysiology

Trauma to the chest, abdomen, pelvis, and upper leg may result in damage to large blood vessels, highly vascular organs (lungs, liver, spleen, kidneys), and large bones. Serious damage to any of these components may result in *severe internal bleeding* and a progressive loss of systemic perfusion ultimately affecting the brain and often leading to death. Occasionally internal bleeding may be contained within an organ stuffsack. In these cases the stuffsack is swollen and the area tender. With continued bleeding or rough handling the stuffsack may rupture leading to severe volume shock. *External bleeding* from any major artery may also lead to volume shock; however, external bleeding is easier to assess and successfully treat in the field.

Assessment

- *The MOI is trauma to the major vessels and vascular organs.* While positive signs and symptoms for musculoskeletal injuries to the chest, abdomen, pelvis, or femur(s) indicates trauma as MOI to a compartment large enough to bleed into, they do not necessarily indicate volume shock.
- Patient may present with a late clinical pattern.

Early Clinical Pattern

- **Change in normal mental status** to alert and anxious, alert and irritable, or alert and lethargic.
- **Increased pulse rate.**
- Increased respiratory rate.
- Patient's skin is usually pale, cool, and moist.
- Blood Pressure is within the normal range,
- A patient can show the early clinical pattern for volume shock and "stabilize" if the bleeding is contained within an organ stuffsack. These **patients MUST be handled gently** to avoid a rupture of the stuffsack and development of severe volume shock.
- Young, fit patients may appear to stabilize then deteriorate rapidly as their compensatory mechanisms are overwhelmed. **Monitor their pulse closely.** Consider taking a six second monitoring pulse at regular intervals during assessment and evacuation.

Late Clinical Pattern

- **Continued decrease in mental status** to voice responsive, pain responsive, and unresponsive.
- **Pulse rate continues to increase.**
- **Respiratory rate continues to increase.**
- Patients skin is pale, cool, and moist.
- Blood Pressure is decreasing.
- Progressive volume shock may lead to cardiac arrest and death.

Field Treatment

- Support critical systems.
- **Stop external bleeding** with well aimed *DIRECT PRESSURE*.
- Provide rest and reassurance to the alert patient.
- Position patient on back with legs and feet slightly elevated.
- **Handle the patient gently** to prevent rupturing a swollen organ stuffsack.
- Administer supplemental oxygen.
- CPR as per protocols. Note: CPR and Advanced Cardiac Care are rarely successful.
- **Evacuate with ALS to a major trauma center.**

Unstable Spine

Pathophysiology

Spinal trauma may fracture vertebrae and/or damage the tissue surrounding the spinal cord. Movement of unstable vertebrae may cut the spinal cord causing irreversible loss of motor function and sensation below the injury site. A high cord injury may cause death. **Unstable movement may be caused by the traumatic event, voluntary patient movement, or by the rescuers.** Damage to the tissue surrounding the spinal cord may activate the inflammatory response causing spinal pain, tenderness, and swelling. Swelling may cause cord damage if undue pressure accumulates within the closed space of a vertebrae. Cord damage resulting from swelling may be temporary or permanent.

Initial Spine Assessment & Patient Handling Guidelines

The MOI is direct trauma to the spine or trauma to any part of the body that may indirectly damage the spine. **INITIALLY, *because the anticipated problem is a cord injury, assume all patients with an uncertain or positive mechanism for a spine injury have an unstable spine. Immobilize their spine AS SOON AS POSSIBLE.*** Later, IF they meet the criteria for ruling out an unstable spinal injury you may remove the immobilization. Your initial spine stabilization is best accomplished with "hand stability" in the position the patient is found *UNLESS* there is immediate danger to the scene and/or the patient presents with a primary respiratory or circulatory problem. In either case you will need be move the patient quickly. ***RAPID MOVEMENT OF PATIENTS SUSPECTED OF HAVING AN UNSTABLE SPINE INCREASES THE RISK OF SPINAL CORD DAMAGE . AVOIDED RAPID MOVEMENT UNLESS THERE IS A LIFE THREATENING SITUATION THAT REQUIRES IT.*** Slow controlled movement of a spine injured patient into anatomical position is safe and necessary for patient comfort and packaging. The goal for moving a patient with an injured spine is to prevent any unstable spine movement. Movement towards normal anatomical position is considered safe. Adhere to the following guidelines:

- **Move the patient as little as possible** to get the job done.
- **Break down all movement into small increments.**
- **Axial pulling is better than axial pushing, lateral pulling, or lateral pushing.** Axial pulling in line with the patient's spine is considered safe; however, spinal compression, as a result of axial pushing, may damage the spinal cord. Avoid lateral movement (pushing or pulling); it is easily transmitted up to other parts of the spine and may cause cord damage.

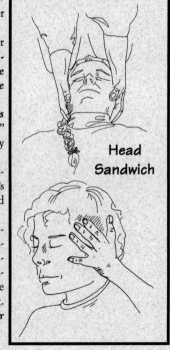

Head Sandwich

- If the movement is rapid, the rescuers limited in number, or the terrain extremely difficult you will need to **PRIORITIZE** focusing your attention and strengths on: **first the cervical spine, second the thoracic spine, and third the lumbar spine.**
- **Attach a cervical collar to help prevent cervical flexion as soon as possible.** Hand stabilization using a "head sandwich" must remain in place even when a cervical collar is securely applied. Cervical collars are not considered a splint.
- **Firmly control the patient's weight centers** (head, shoulders, hips). Control the head using your hands or the patient's arms to form a "head sandwich." Control the shoulders and hips through leverage and lots of hands.
- **Move one weight center at a time** into alignment while supporting the others. Once one weight center is in normal anatomical position with respect to another maintain that alignment throughout the movement process. The person controlling the patient's head *FOLLOWS* the movements of the patient's shoulders in order to maintain cervical alignment.
- When multiple rescuers are involved **there must be one leader and many supporters.**
- When using a litter or backboard **focus your attention on**

how to move the backboard closer to the patient rather than how to move the patient closer to the backboard. Avoid carrying a spine injured patient to a backboard or litter; a slip or fall could be fatal.

• *Axial loading is preferable to horizontal loading.* In most cases a patient may be lifted, the litter or backboard slid axially under them, and the patient lowered onto the litter or board. The entire procedure is quick with little rescuer or patient movement.

Assessment Criteria for Ruling Out Unstable Spine Injuries[8]

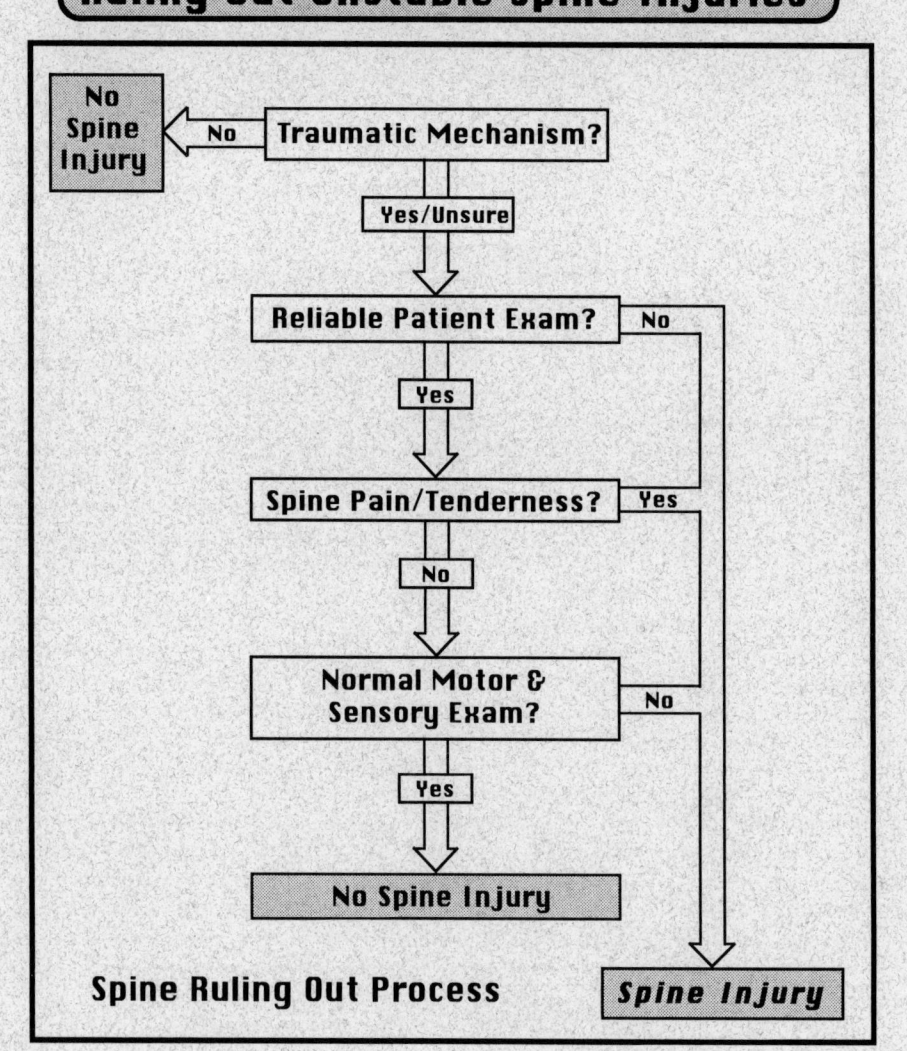

No Spine Injury

Traumatic Mechanism? — No →

Yes/Unsure

Reliable Patient Exam? — No →

Yes

Spine Pain/Tenderness? — Yes →

No

Normal Motor & Sensory Exam? — No →

Yes

No Spine Injury

Spine Ruling Out Process

Spine Injury

- *Patient must have a reliable mental status. They must be alert, calm, and cooperative.* A spine injury cannot be ruled out in patients who present with ASR, other major or painful injuries, intoxication, or an altered mental status.
- A patient's spine cannot be cleared if, when questioned, they complain of spine pain.
- A patient's spine cannot be cleared if, upon a through spinal exam, they indicate any spinal tenderness. During the spinal exam *each spinous process must be individually palpated.* This is a safe procedure as long as gross spinal movement is prevented.
- *The patient must have a normal motor and sensory exam* as described below. An abnormal finding in either exam indicates a possible injury to the patient's spinal cord and the patient must be immobilized. Incomplete cord damage is possible (anterior cord syndrome, central cord syndrome, Brown-Sequard Syndrome) and picked-up through the following motor/sensory examinations.

Normal Motor Exam

The motor examinations described below test motor nerve roots in the cervical and lumbar spine; a normal exam indicates intact motor function at the level of the cervical and lumbar spine. There are two motor exams for each hand and foot. If a local injury limits movement in a hand or foot, the motor exam may be considered normal with a minimum of one normal test at each hand and foot. If neither exam can be conducted because of local injuries on a hand or foot, the motor exam is considered abnormal and the patient's spine must be immobilized.

- First have the patient spread the fingers of both hands and offer resistance by trying to keep them spread as you squeeze the index and ring fingers together (1st and 3rd). With a normal exam their resistance should be equal and feel "springy." This exam tests the T-1 nerve root.
- Next, while holding the patients wrist with one of your hands, have them extend the supported hand and offer resistance as you push downward on the extended fingers. Repeat on the other hand. Again with a normal exam their resistance should be equal and feel "springy." This test can be performed on a patient with a local wrist, hand, or digit injury in the following manner: for a wrist or hand injury support the hand and push down on the fingers. For a digit injury support the wrist and push down on the hand. *Support and testing must be done in the same manner on each upper extremity.* This exam tests the C-7 nerve root.

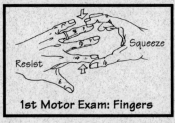

1st Motor Exam: Fingers

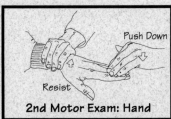

2nd Motor Exam: Hand

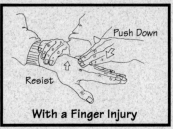

With a Finger Injury

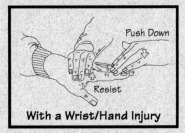

With a Wrist/Hand Injury

- Moving to the patient's feet, place your hand against the bottom of the patients foot and ask them to push against it. Repeat with the other foot. With a normal exam the pressure will be strong and equal. This exam can be performed in the presence of a local injury to the ankle or foot by using the patient's big toe in place of their foot. *Support and testing must be done in the same manner on each lower extremity.* This exam tests the nerve roots controlled by S-1, 2.

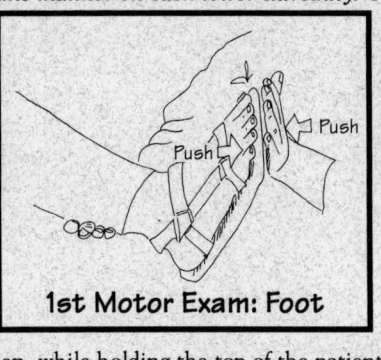

1st Motor Exam: Foot

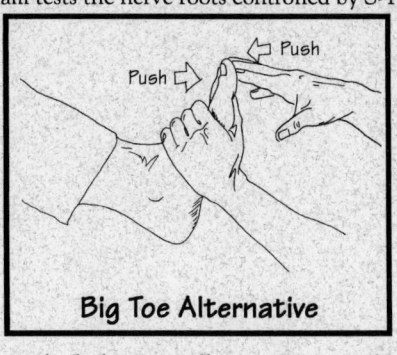

Big Toe Alternative

- Then, while holding the top of the patient's foot, and ask them to pull up against your fingers. With a normal exam the pressure will be strong and equal. This exam can also be performed in the presence of a local injury to the ankle or foot by using the patient's big toe in place of their foot. *Support and testing must be done in the same manner on each lower extremity.* This exam tests the L-5 nerve root.

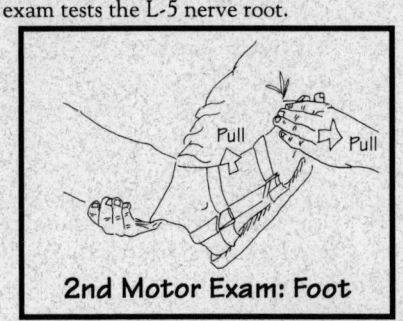

2nd Motor Exam: Foot

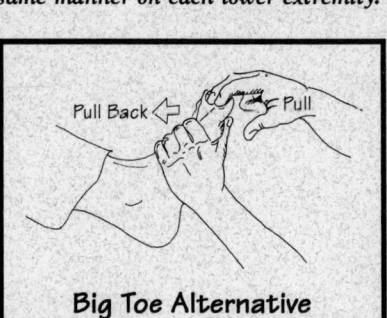

Big Toe Alternative

Normal Sensory Exam

The sensory examinations described below tests the sensory nerves located in the front (anterior) of the spinal cord. It would be extremely unusual to have an abnormal sensory exam without an abnormal motor exam.

- Ask if the patient feels any unusual sensation in any extremity. If the patient reports weakness, numbness, tingling, electric or shooting pain, or no sensation in any extremity the exam is considered abnormal.
- Ask the patient to close their eyes and using a sharp object prick the skin on the back of the patient's hands (avoid drawing blood); use the same testing site on both hands. Using a dull or soft object again touch each of the patient's hands; again use the same testing site. Ask the patient to compare each test. Repeat both steps for each foot; use the same testing site on each foot. The sensation for pain, unlike light touch, is only carried in lateral (spinothalamic) tracts of the anterior cord. *It is extremely important for the patient to distinguish between pain (pin prick) and light touch.* The exam is considered abnormal and the patient immobilized if they are unable to tell the difference.

Field Treatment for an Unstable Spine & Spinal Cord Injury

- The treatment goal is to immobilize all potentially unstable vertebrae to prevent spinal cord injury. Field treatment for a spinal cord injury is the same as the field treatment for an unstable spine injury.
- Patients with unstable spines MUST be handled very carefully during the splinting process to avoid causing a spinal cord injury or causing additional damage to those patients who are already cord injured. When the potential (or actual) injury site can be localized, spine splints (back boards, litters, KED, etc.) may be applied by using conventional splinting principles: with an unstable "long bone," immobilize the "long bone", the "joint" above and below. With an unstable "joint," immobilize the "joint", the "long bone" above and below. When the spine is involved the patient's head is considered a "long bone"; their cervical vertebrae a "joint"; their thoracic vertebrae a "long bone"; their lower lumbar vertebrae, pelvis, and hip a "joint"; and both their femurs "long bones."

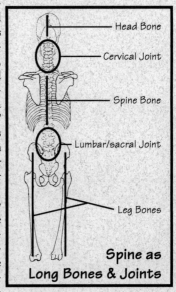

Spine as
Long Bones & Joints

- In alert and reliable patients the potential (or actual) injury site may be localized using the information gathered in the ruling out process. Pain *or* tenderness at a specific site indicates potential instability at that site. When in doubt immobilize the entire spine. If the suspected injury can be localized to the lower lumbar spine (L-4, L-5), hip, or pelvis the patient's head may remain free during the evacuation, significantly increasing their comfort. If the injury can be localized to the cervical spine, the lower lumbar spine (L-4, L-5), hip, or pelvis may be extended or flexed (avoid lateral movement because it is easily transmitted up to other parts of the spine); this small freedom also increases patient comfort during a long evacuation. Injuries to the thoracic spine require complete spinal immobilization.
- *In all other patients the complete spine must be immobilized.*
- All litters or back boards should provide a lightweight rigid platform for the patient to be attached to. Because improvising effective spine splints is extremely difficult and the consequences severe if the improvised splint fails during use, use commercial litters, commercial back boards, or pretested homemade back boards specifically designed for that purpose. There are numerous commercial litters available; the most common are the SKED litter (a lightweight flexible plastic litter that rolls and fits into its own backpack), the Stokes litter (a steel wire basket litter), and the Thompson litter (a fiberglass or plastic shell with aluminium rails). In addition, there are numerous fiberglass litters designed for ski evacuation. The most common is the Cascade toboggan. With the exception of the SKED litter, it is unnecessary to use both a litter and backboard in combination. Little support is gained for the added weight. The most versatile and easiest to transport is the SKED; it is used in conjunction with a thin lightweight backboard, a KED or OSS, or total body vacuum splint. It excels in all technical evacuations and carry-outs; unfortunately it is expensive and rarely available. Both the Stokes and Thompson litters are

Trauma 46

more common. The Stokes works well in technical situations while the Thompson slides easily over snow; both work equally well in a carry-out. Back boards are commonly used with commercial ski toboggans to facilitate the transfer of the patient into a waiting ambulance or clinic. The practical (and visual) difference between a litter and backboard are huge. A litter has sides offering the patient increased stability and comfort over difficult terrain; a backboard doesn't. If the evacuation is technical and/or the carry out long and arduous it is infinitely preferable to use a litter rather than a backboard. Unfortunately back boards, especially poorly designed ones, are much more common. If an improvised backboard is truly needed, one may be built by lashing poles together to form a strong, lightweight, axially rigid "board." It should be 12-18 inches wide and cut to the length of the patient. Its serviceability will depend upon the choice of materials (choose strong lightweight ones) and the lashing ability of the builder. Always test improvised spine splints on an uninjured person before using.

Litter/Backboard Packaging Guidelines

- The long term care of a spine injured patent is extremely difficult. Rescuers must provide for food, water, and waste elimination. Psychological problems related to claustrophobia or immobilization may arise with alert patients at any time. All packaging systems must be constructed with these issues in mind. The following guidelines apply to all litter packaging techniques regardless of the style of litter or backboard.
- The packaging system should immobilize the spine injury in all directions (side to side, up and down) without compressing the spine. Spinal compression can be easily avoided if padding is NOT placed directly above the patient's head.
- In the absence of severe environmental conditions that demand immediate protection for the patient, packaging material should be assembled and prepared before the patient is moved onto it.
- The packaging system should be well padded and protect the patient from the rigors of the evacuation. A minimum of two sleeping pads should be used to line the bottom of the litter. Rolled and taped blankets, sleeping pads, or sleeping bags should fill the spaces between the patient's side and the straps. Head blocks should secure and protect the patient's head from lateral movement. If a litter is used they should also prevent axial movement towards the patient's head if the head of the litter is tilted down. They may be made from taped blanket rolls, semi-rigid sleeping pads, soft material compressed into a stuffsack, etc. Foot stirrups or rigid padding should be used to prevent the patient from sliding towards the foot of the litter when the litter is tilted in that direction. The patient's knees should be slightly flexed and supported with soft firm padding (jacket roll, etc.).
- The packaging system should provide adequate thermoregulation. *Consider a hypothermia package for all patients immobilized in a litter regardless of the environmental conditions.* Restricted movement, traumatic injury, illness, available calories, hydration, etc. all contribute to the ability of patients to self-regulate their temperature. When in doubt monitor their core temperature.
- Consider diapering patients in preparation for waste elimination.
- To help prevent vascular damage from long term immobilization massage the patient's limbs, especially their legs, for a few minutes each hour.
- The attachment system should be simple, strong, and easily adjustable. It should provide easy access to the patient's airway. There are only two attachment systems effective enough to be •

used in a long term evacuation: the "X" and "Shoe Lace" attachment systems. In the *"X" system* individual straps with sturdy quick release buckles (seat belt buckles or cam straps) are used to create an X over the patient's shoulders, hips, thighs, and lower legs. Two inch straps are preferable. The center of the "shoulder x" should be over the center of the patient's sternum with the upper edges above the patient's shoulders. The center of the "hip x" should be midline between the patient's pelvic bones. The "thigh x" should be midway between the patient's knees and hips. The "lower leg x" should be midway between the patient's knees and ankles. With small people a single horizontal strap may be used in place of the "x's" over the legs. All the straps should be attached to the litter as low as possible to help eliminate lateral space and decrease the amount of padding. In the *"Shoe Lace" system*, six inch loops of one half inch to 1 inch webbing (quick draws) are either girthed or tied every 4-6 inches along both sides of the litter creating "eyelets." A second piece of rope or 1 inch webbing 30 feet long is then laced through the eyelets beginning at the patient's feet and the slack carefully "milked" out until the patient is secure; the ends are tied off at the patient's shoulders. In *both systems* the head is secured last and with separate straps. Use the go beyond principle and secure the head blocks to the litter or back board above the head; avoid compressing the patient's spine. Care should be taken to assure easy access to the patient's airway. In lieu of head straps, use duct tape; it works extremely well if applied across the patient's forehead and eyebrows. Wrap multiple times.

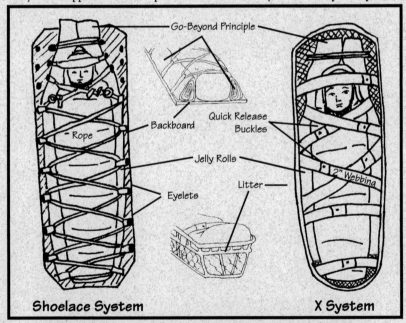

Shoelace System   X System

Guidelines for Litter Loading

- When loading a spine injured patient into a litter **ALL the Patient Handling Guidelines apply.** Additional guidelines appear below.
- When using a litter or backboard *focus your attention on how to move the backboard closer to the patient rather than how to move the patient closer to the backboard.* Avoid carrying a spine injured patient to a backboard or litter; a slip or fall could be fatal.

Trauma

Axial loading is preferable to horizontal loading. In most cases a patient may be lifted, the litter or backboard slid axially under them, and the patient lowered onto the litter or board. The entire procedure is quick with little rescuer or patient movement.

- All patients suspected of a cervical or thoracic spine injury should have a cervical collar in place prior to loading. *Hand stabilization using a "head sandwich" must remain in place while loading and packaging even when a cervical collar is securely applied.* Cervical collars are not considered a splint.

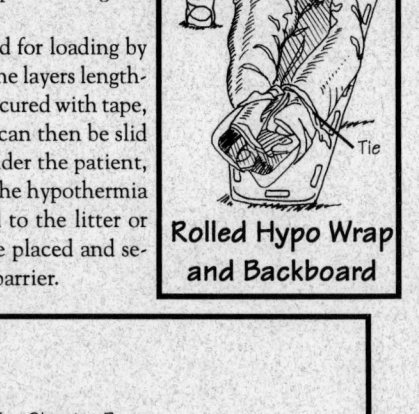

Rolled Hypo Wrap
and Backboard

- *The patient's body MUST be completely secured prior to strapping their head* in case vomiting occurs during packaging. It is easier to support the patient's head during a roll than their body thus offering less chance for unstable movement of the cervical spine during the roll.

- If a *hypothermia package* is used it should be prepared for loading by pre-assembling the individual layers, then rolling all the layers lengthwise into two connected jelly rolls, and temporarily secured with tape, cravats, or a quick release strap. The entire package can then be slid (either with the litter or backboard or separately) under the patient, the rolls quickly released, and the patient lowered. The hypothermia package can then be sealed and the patient secured to the litter or backboard. Head blocks and lateral jelly rolls can be placed and secured either inside or outside of the external vapor barrier.

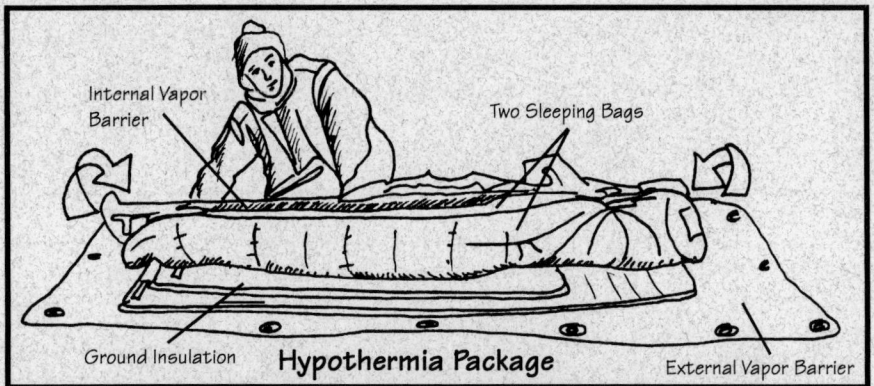

Hypothermia Package

Guidelines for Nontechnical Litter Use

- Nontechnical litter use is defined according to the steepness of the terrain. If a rescuer falls and is both quickly and safely able to arrest their fall without prior training or equipment then the terrain is considered nontechnical. Even on nontechnical terrain a litter may require a belay if it cannot rest securely without support.

- Once the strapping process is complete, *carrying straps* may be added along the sides of either a litter or backboard to facilitate long distance carrying. Three per side is common. To decrease the possibility of dropping the litter rescuers should not tie into the litter or attach themselves to the carrying straps in any way.

- *Passing the litter* is the fastest way to move a litter though short stretches of difficult or unstable terrain. Rescuers form two opposing lines facing one another and pass the litter slowly along the aisle between them. As the litter passes by them, pairs of rescuers peel off and move to the front of the line to await the litter once again. Each rescuer must assume a stable position upon reaching the front of the line. The process continues until the litter is past the difficult or unstable terrain. At any time a rescuer should be able to call "STOP!" to reassess a situation or give time for the line to reform. Rescuers may choose to alternate sides as they move to the front of the passing line. *Rescuers MUST remain secure and immobile in their position when in contact with the litter.* Litter passes are also a quick, safe, and easy way to change litter bearers. This is the most efficient method of litter travel especially during long evacuations. It is desirable to have a minimum of 36 people for most litter carry outs.
- *"Toe Nailing"* is a carrying method used in steep or rugged terrain where litter passes are impossible or the number of rescuers is limited. It involves resting the uphill end of the litter securely against the hill, on a rock, etc. while the down hill end is supported on the knees of one or two rescuers. The four remaining litter bearers step slightly uphill to a secure new but comfortable and stable position. On command they lift up and forwards to a new "Toe Nail" position. The process is repeated until the obstacle is past and litter carrying or passing can begin again.
- A *belay* for the litter should be considered if it cannot rest securely by itself on the terrain being crossed without support. A belay is most effective when it is directly above the litter; avoid traversing with a belay. A *tree wrap* is the simplest and most efficient form of litter belay; choose a strong healthy tree. Simply tie one end of the rope to the head (or tail) of the litter using any traditional climbing knot; the rope should be "rolled" a few times around the chosen rail to help maintain an even pressure to the litter and prevent rotation when in use. Then wrap the other end once or twice around the tree and you're ready to belay or lower. Use a static rope designed for rescue. Given the same size tree, the more wraps increase the friction. The bigger the tree the less wraps needed for the same amount of friction. It is often easier to manage the belay if you stand on the downhill side of the tree. If you leave a long tail when tying the belay rope into the litter the tail may be used to secure the litter when you need to raise or lower the belay (this is usually referred to as "tailing off" the litter). Consider all the patient's problems when deciding which end of the litter to tie the belay rope into. An alert and cooperative patient is most comfortable with their head pointing uphill. If a tree wrap is used to lower a litter be prepared to add or subtract wraps depending upon the friction required to support both the litter and its attendants. During a lower the attendants should face uphill and lean backward using the belayed litter for support; their legs should be perpendicular to the slope as if repelling.
- The simplest way to assist litter bearers in climbing a "steep" hill and belay the litter at the same time is to use a *"counterweight" raising system*. Although the counterweight raising system does require a rescue pulley it is not considered a true haul system because there is no mechanical advantage; HOWEVER, it does make climbing a slippery hill much easier and safer. It is also easy to remember, set up, and use. The principle is identical to the system used to raise old fashioned windows or heavy garage doors. Simply run the "haul" rope uphill and through a well anchored rescue pulley, then have three or four rescuers haul on the rope as the litter attendants "carry" the litter uphill. An additional rescuer can act as a belayer using a tree wrap located as directly below and near to the anchor and pulley as possible. It's amazing how much help is possible by using this simple system.
- *Rescuers who are unfamiliar with the use of the litter and rope systems described above should not try to use them during a real evacuation without prior training.*

Trauma   50

Stable & Unstable Musculoskeletal Injuries

Pathophysiology

Trauma may damage bones, cartilage, ligaments, tendons, and muscles. It may also damage nearby nerves and blood vessels resulting in a loss of distal perfusion and innervation. Musculoskeletal injury to the extremities rarely involves enough damage to blood vessels to cause volume shock, although with a severely angled femur fracture it is possible. Musculoskeletal damage to the head, chest, and pelvis often indicates the possibility of critical injuries. Damage done to the musculoskeletal system itself heals according to the development of its vascular bed. Bones and muscles are highly vascular and heal quickly, tendons more slowly, and ligaments and cartilage very slowly if at all. With open wounds the healing process begins with clotting to control bleeding. As with all tissue injuries the local inflammatory response is stimulated. After a few days the process of rebuilding the damaged structures begins and in most cases proceeds without serious complications. Complications occur when a large amount of tissue is damaged, the swelling is severe, and distal perfusion is compromised. If not restored within a few hours the cells lacking perfusion will die, gangrene may follow within days, and the limb will require amputation to save the patient's life. Deep wounds associated with underlying structural damage are high risk for infection. Field assessment of musculoskeletal injuries is based on distinguishing between "Stable Injuries" and "Unstable Injuries" rather than between types of fractures and degrees of sprains or strains. All stable injuries and many unstable injuries may be successfully treated in the field and may not require an emergency evacuation for medical reasons. Since musculoskeletal injuries are extremely common in wilderness settings great detail is given to their assessment and treatment in the following pages.

General Assessment Criteria for Long Bones and Joints

Signs & Symptoms	Stable Injuries	Unstable Injuries
Bruising	Possible	Possible
Pain	Mild	Moderate to Severe
Tenderness	Mild	Moderate to Severe
Swelling	Late & may be severe	Early & Severe
Decreased CSM	No	Possible
Decreased ROM	No	Yes
Early ability to bear weight or use normally	Yes	No
Crepitus	No	Possible
Angulation or Deformity	No	Possible
When in doubt...treat as an unstable injury.		

Field Treatment for Stable Injuries

- The goal is to prevent additional damage. Provide rest (see below) and allow time for healing. Field treatment is the same as hospital treatment.
- **Rest: SPLINT** Stable Injuries to the extremities IF it will help prevent additional damage; the splint may be removed when there is no further chance of additional injury. Refer to improvised splint section.
- Over the counter (OTC) pain and anti-inflammatory medications: aspirin, ibuprofen, naproxen sodium. These medications help reduce local swelling and improve circulation. They promote faster healing by increasing the delivery nutrients and the removal of waste.
- **Ice:** 20-30 minutes on to help reduce swelling then 90 minutes off to allow local reperfusion.
- Herbal remedies include arnica and comfrey. Comfrey contains allantoin and helps promote the growth of connective tissue; it is easily absorbed through the skin. Arnica appears to stimulate the circulatory system and help reabsorb internal bleeding. Other herbs useful in the treatment of stable musculoskeletal injuries include rue and witch hazel. The herbs are used externally in salves or as compresses over intact skin. Do not take internally.
- **Pain Free Activity** without medication after swelling goes down. Pain medications may mask pain during use and should be avoided. If swelling and pain return during or after exercise the pain and anti-inflammatory medications may be resumed; exercise should be discontinued and the limb rested until the swelling subsides once again.

Field Treatment for Unstable Injuries

General Guidelines

- The goal is to **immobilize the injury site** for protection and to permit healing; surgery may be necessary in difficult cases.
- **Open wounds** associated with unstable injuries are considered at high risk for infection and should be cleansed prior to realignment if possible (see Wounds, page 62).
- Pain and anti-inflammatory medications are indicated. OTC: aspirin, ibuprofen, naproxen sodium. Perscription (Rx) pain medications are usually opium derivatives.
- Ice: 20-30 minutes on to help reduce swelling then 90 minutes off to allow local reperfusion.
- **Monitor** the injury site for swelling and decreased distal CSM during the next 24 hours.

Evacuation Guidelines

- In-line closed fractures are not considered an emergency.
- **Open fractures should be evacuated to a major hospital within 24 hours due to possible infection.**
- Closed dislocations are best reduced within six hours but are not considered an emergency.
- **No CSM distal to the injury site for a period greater than two hours should be considered an emergency.**
- **Ligament repair** may be done at anytime and is not considered an emergency.
- **Tendon repair** is best done within 5-10 days but is not considered an emergency.
- **Muscle repair** is best done within 6 hours or 4-5 days later after inflammation has subsided. Muscle repair is not considered an emergency.

Trauma

Guidelines for Unstable Injuries to the Extremities

- Traction angulated long bones into anatomical position. Traction deformed joints or joints with decreased distal CSM into mid-range position of function. **STOP traction if patient complains of severely increased pain or physical resistance is felt during realignment.**
- *Stabilize the limb and the injury with hands* (as many as necessary) until splint is in place.
- *Immobilize in a splint.* Refer to improvised splint section.
- *Monitor the CSM distal to the injury* and adjust the splint as necessary to maintain good local perfusion.

Guidelines for Unstable Injuries to the Head, Chest, Hip, Pelvis, & Femur(s)

- *Rule out* increased ICP secondary to head trauma.
- *Rule out* respiratory distress secondary to chest trauma.
- *Rule out* volume shock secondary to trauma to the chest, abdomen, pelvis, and femur(s).
- Consider immobilization on backboard or in a litter. (see Litter Packaging, page 47)
- Isolated **rib fractures** may be stabilized using an ace wrap if it increases patient comfort. Patients with musculoskeletal injuries to the chest wall should be encouraged to inhale deeply at regular intervals to maintain air exchange in the entire lung to help prevent the development of a respiratory infection while healing.
- **With an extremely painful, isolated, and angulated unstable injury to mid-shaft femur(s) AND a total evacuation time less than six hours**, a femur traction splint with a backboard or litter is indicated. With a total evacuation time greater than six hours a sandwich style splint in combination with a backboard or litter is usually a better choice since all models of femur traction splints eventually cause a loss of distal perfusion to the injured leg. Refer to improvised splint section.

Guidelines for Unstable Joint Injuries

- Unstable joints should be splinted in the position they are found *UNLESS* the deformity is severe enough to impede safe packaging and transport or if the distal CSM is impaired.
- Joints with severe deformity or impaired distal CSM should be tractioned towards mid-range position and splinted as soon as the deformity is corrected or the distal CSM has returned. Traction should be discontinued and the joint splinted if physical resistance or extreme pain are encountered during the repositioning process.
- *Monitor the CSM distal to the injury* and adjust the splint as necessary to maintain good local perfusion.

Tx: • Reduce if possible — If it will reduce pain
• splint in mid-range pos. — If CSM compromised
STOP If ↑↑ PAIN meet resistance.

Simple Dislocations

Unstable

Pathophysiology

The immediate reduction of all dislocations helps prevent additional damage by returning the joint to its anatomical position and greatly assists the healing process. *The MOI for simple dislocations is INDIRECT TRAUMA.* Direct trauma causes complicating fractures that usually require surgery and classify the dislocation as complex. Complex dislocations are treated in the field as an unstable joint injury (see above). The field reduction of simple dislocations to digits, patellas, and shoulders is relatively simple and therefore encouraged. If reduction is successful the joint should be splinted for a minimum of 10 days and then treated as a stable injury. If reduction is unsuccessful *or* CSM is not restored following a successful reduction, treat the dislocation as an unstable joint injury. In either case follow-up care with a physician is recommended.

Assessment of Simple Digit Dislocations

- *The MOI is indirect trauma* often resulting from a fall out of a tight finger crack.
- Compare the injury with the same digit on the opposite (uninjured) hand or foot.
- Patient presents with an angulated/displaced finger or toe.

Field Treatment

- *Isolate* the injured joint between the index fingers and thumbs of the rescuer's hands.
- *Support* the injured appendage against your chest and traction the joint quickly into anatomical position.
- *Splint* the digit in mid-range position of function for a minimum of 10 days and then treat as a stable injury. Refer to treatment for stable injuries.
- Administer OTC pain and anti-inflammatory medications: aspirin, ibuprofen, naproxen sodium.
- *Ice:* 20-30 minutes on to help reduce swelling then 90 minutes off to permit local reperfusion.

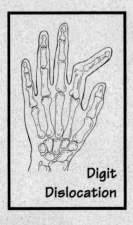

Digit
Dislocation

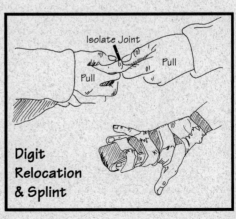

Isolate Joint

Pull   Pull

Digit
Relocation
& Splint

Assessment of Simple Patella Dislocations

- *The MOI is indirect trauma usually as a result of a sudden twist or pivot.* Dislocations of the patella are common while walking in deep snow or on slippery talus and occasionally occur while telemark or alpine skiing in breakable crust or heavy show.
- Patient commonly presents on side or back holding the injured knee; the knee is bent slightly and the patella displaced laterally.

Field Treatment

- During the relocation process *maintain a right angle between the patient's thigh and their hip/pelvis.*
- *Support* the injured leg at the knee and ankle. Encourage the patient to breath deeply and RELAX.
- *Guide the patella* into anatomical position with your thumb as you *straighten the injured knee*. Some range of motion should now be present in the knee joint; however, it may be slightly decreased and painful.
- *Splint* the knee in mid-range position of function for a minimum of 10 days and then treat as a stable injury. Refer to treatment for stable injuries.
- OTC pain and anti-inflammatory medications: aspirin, ibuprofen, naproxen sodium.
- **Ice:** 20-30 minutes on to help reduce swelling then 90 minutes off to permit local reperfusion.

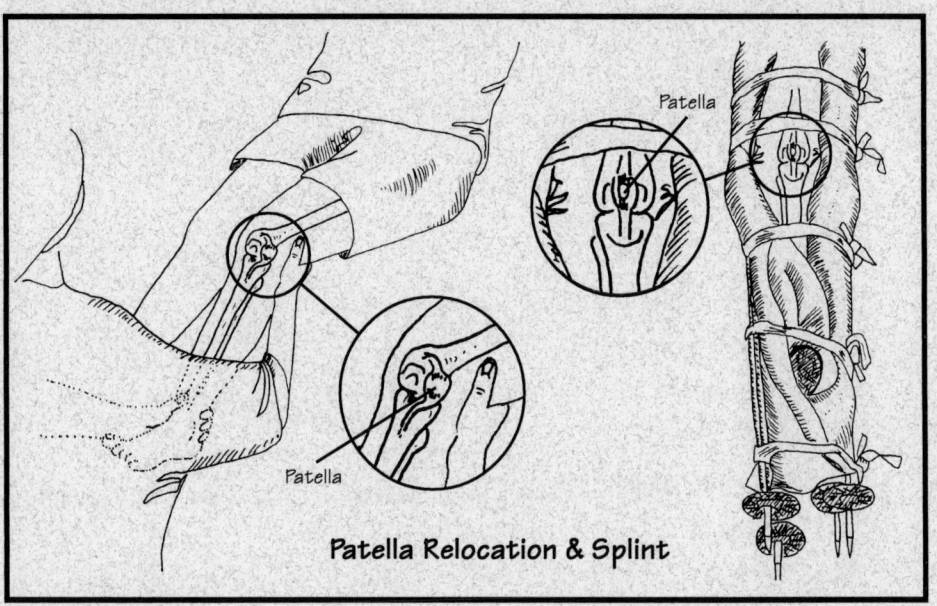

Patella

Patella

Patella Relocation & Splint

Assessment of Simple Shoulder Dislocations

- *The MOI is indirect trauma.* Shoulder dislocations often occur while paddling a canoe or kayak in whitewater (from rolls, hole riding, or eddy turns and peel outs in strong current), during a fall from a fist jam, during a fall while ice climbing onto a single tool, while bump skiing, or any fall to an outstretched arm.
- The patient usually presents sitting with the injured "arm/elbow" held away from their body. The patient is usually supporting the arm, often with self-traction.

Field Treatment

There are two widely accepted methods for reducing simple dislocations of the shoulder. The *baseball method* (below) is active while the *hanging traction method* is passive.

"Baseball" Method

- Assist patient in moving to a flat padded area.
- *Check distal CSM* in the hand on the injured side.
- *Check sensation of the axillary nerve* by pinching the deltoid muscle on the patients "injured" arm.
- Help position patient on their back.
- *Apply traction* at elbow to relax the shoulder muscles and relieve pain. *Maintain traction* throughout the treatment process until the reduction is successful or the unstable shoulder splinted. Use one of the following hand positions.

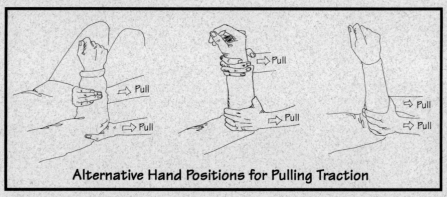

Alternative Hand Positions for Pulling Traction

- If the patient is on a slippery surface (snow, wet leaves, etc.) and likely to slide when traction is applied have an assistant hold onto their jacket (or a towel, sheet, blanket, sleeping bag, etc. wrapped around their chest).
- *While maintaining traction*, rotate the "injured" arm to "baseball" position and *WAIT*. If during this process the patient complains of severe pain while tensing their shoulder muscles, stop the rotation *while maintaining traction* and wait for them to relax once again. *While continuing to maintain traction*, resume rotation until patient is in "baseball" position. After a minimum of five minutes maintaining traction in "baseball" position move the arm to "high baseball" position.

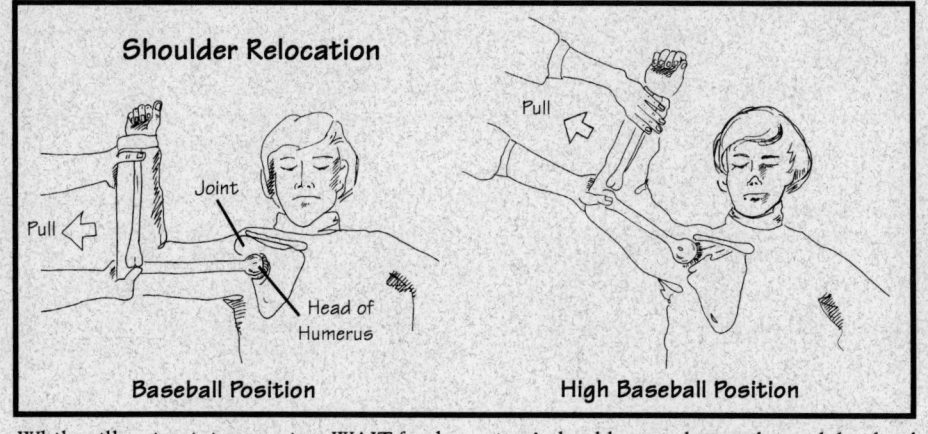

Shoulder Relocation

Pull

Joint

Pull

Head of Humerus

Baseball Position   High Baseball Position

- While still maintaining traction, *WAIT* for the patient's shoulder muscles to relax and the shoulder to relocate (reduce). This may be as short as 5 minutes or longer than one hour. If the patient's shoulder does not reduce within the hour, consider trying passive "Hanging Traction" method (see below) or splinting the shoulder in position for an evacuation.
- If you are able to get the patient to relax, most shoulders will reduce within 20 minutes. When the shoulder relocates you will feel a bump (or series of bumps) and the patient will smile.
- If the patient's shoulder has in fact relocated they will feel no pain as you *SLOWLY* release the traction. If pain is present, resume traction and wait for the shoulder to relocate. If the patient does not complain of pain as you release the traction, assist them in moving the arm to their side; the elbow should rest comfortably against the patient's body.
- *Recheck distal and axillary CSM* as above.
- *Splint* the injured shoulder against the patient's body for a minimum of 10 days and then treat as a Stable Injury.
- OTC pain and anti-inflammatory medications: aspirin, ibuprofen, naproxen sodium
- *Ice:* 20-30 minutes on to help reduce swelling then 90 minutes off to permit local reperfusion.

"Hanging Traction" Method

- *Check distal and axillary CSM* as discussed above.
- Assist patient to an padded "platform" tall and flat enough to permit their arm and a suspended weight to hang freely (a large rock, pile of coolers, etc.). Place patient face down on the "platform" with their "injured" arm hanging down.
- Attach duct tape to the skin of the "injured" arm to create an "eye hook" big enough for a carabiner or rope to pass though easily. Lightly wrap the taped arm with an ace bandage to increase the patient's venous return.
- Using a carabiner or rope, attach a slightly weighted container (stuffsack with rocks, bucket with water, etc.) through the taped "eye hook." Add weight (rocks, water, etc.) until the patient's pain is relieved. Use the smallest amount of weight possible to maintain pain free traction.
- If shoulder reduces (usually within one hour) continue treatment as discussed above.
- *If the patient's shoulder does not reduce within the hour consider splinting the shoulder in position for an evacuation.*

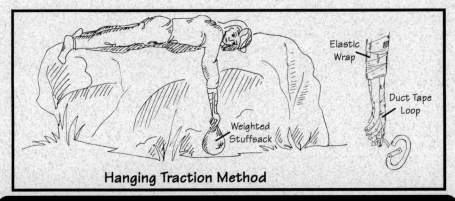

Elastic Wrap

Duct Tape Loop

Weighted Stuffsack

Hanging Traction Method

Improvising Effective Splints

The goal is to immobilize the injury in all directions. All splints should be:
- Well Padded
- Simple
- Strong
- Easily Adjustable
- Lightweight
- Multidimensional

The body part to be splinted and its most effective splinting principles are outlined in the following table.

Body Part(s)	Splinting Principle	Page
Fingers & Toes	Cast	59
	Buddy	59
Hand, Wrist, & Forearm	Cast	59
Elbow, Upper Arm, & Shoulder	Buddy	59
Neck, Back, & Hips	Backboard/Litter	47
Upper Leg	Sandwich	59
	Traction	60
	Backboard/Litter	47
Knee	Cast	59
	Jelly Roll with Go Beyond	59
	Sandwich with Go Beyond	59
Lower Leg	Jelly Roll with Go Beyond	59
	Sandwich with Go Beyond	59
Ankle & Foot	Cast	59
	Jelly Roll with Go Beyond	59
	Sandwich with Go Beyond	59
Splinting Principles are discussed in detail below.		

Improvising Extremity Splints

- **Cast:** Carefully mold, pad, and attach a SAM splint to the injured limb with numerous layers of roller gauze or vet wrap. Avoid elastic bandages because it is extremely difficult to control the pressure while wrapping. Too much pressure causes CSM problems while not enough permits unwanted movement. Padding should be thick and smooth; it may consist of the patient's heavy pile sleeve, wool sock(s), etc. This type of splint is best used to immobilize forearms, wrists, ankles, and knees.

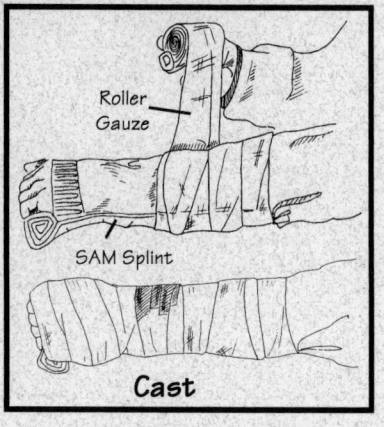

Roller Gauze

SAM Splint

Cast

- **Go Beyond:** This principle can be used with either a Jelly Roll or Sandwich splint (see below). It is effective *only* when used to immobilize the lower leg and ankle. To use this principle allow the splint to go past the end of the leg and "strap" immediately below the foot.

- **Sandwich:** (not a Taco) This splint has a rigid "board" on the outside, thick padding on the inside, and is held in place with "straps." When completed, the two "boards" are parallel (sandwich) rather than V shaped (taco) and distribute the compression forces evenly. A "board" may be a real board, snowshoe, etc. or one constructed with finger thick poles (tent poles, ski poles, green sticks, internal pack stays, etc.) taped together. Suitable "straps" can be webbing, cam straps, cravats, strips of strong cloth, rope, etc. Thick padding can be made from carefully folded and taped soft clothing, foam sleeping pads, sleeping bags, etc. Effective padding may also be made by filling a small stuff sack with soft objects. Sandwich splints may utilize the Go Beyond and Jelly Roll principles (see below). This type of splint is extremely effective for immobilizing leg injuries.

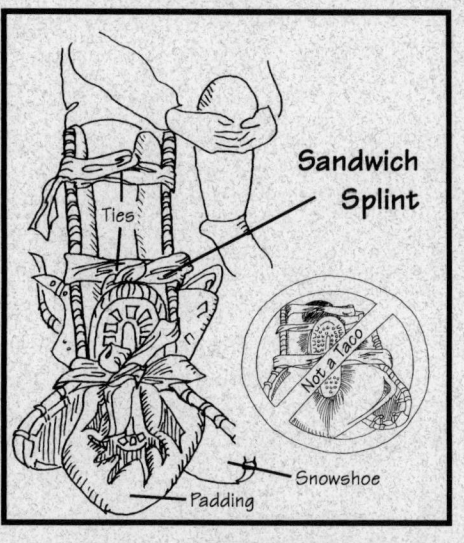

Sandwich Splint

Ties

Not a Taco

Snowshoe

Padding

- **Jelly Roll:** To use this principle you will need a long *FIRM* sleeping pad and thick padding. Roll the padding into the sleeping pad from both ends. Hold or tape each side to prevent the Jelly Roll from unrolling as it is attached; it is held in place using "straps." Jelly Rolls may utilize the Go Beyond principle. This type of splint provides effective immobilization of knees and ankles.

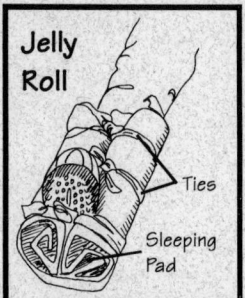

Jelly Roll

Ties

Sleeping Pad

- **Buddy Splint:** This kind of splint is simple and fast. The injured limb is simply splinted against another part of the body. For example, the shoulder, upper arm, elbow, and forearm can be splinted against the chest by rolling and knotting (or taping) the patient's shirt or jacket around the injured upper limb. A similar result can be obtained by pinning the sleeves of the patient's jacket to the body of the jacket or using cravats or cloth strips to tie the limb in place. Other common uses of Buddy Splints is taping two fingers together or tying two legs together. Both of the latter splints may be reinforced by adding a well padded "board."

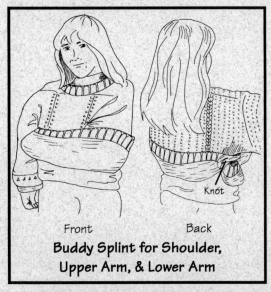

Front   Back
Knot

**Buddy Splint for Shoulder,
Upper Arm, & Lower Arm**

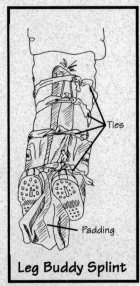

Ties
Padding

Leg Buddy Splint

Improvised Femur Traction Splint

All femur traction splints MUST be used with a backboard or litter. The improvised splint pictured below is easy to assemble and apply:

- First you must make an ***ankle hitch***. If the patient is wearing a boot with good padding around the ankle leave the boot in place, remove the laces, and tie the ankle hitch around the boot. If the patient is not wearing boots you will need to pad their ankle (wool socks work well) before applying the hitch. Hitches applied directly to ankle may cause local perfusion problems during a long evacuation. Use two 18-24 inch long pieces of strong cloth in the following manner:

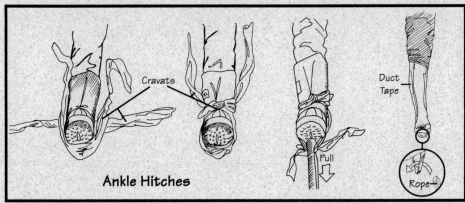

Cravats
Duct Tape
Pull
Rope

Ankle Hitches

- An ***effective alternative to an ankle hitch*** is to attach multiple strips of duct tape directly to the skin of the lower or upper leg to create a traction attachment point. This type of attachment generally does not create local perfusion problems and may permit traction directly from the knee. Keep the tape in-line with the leg bones.
- Next you'll need a ***rigid support*** for the leg strong enough to withstand the traction pressure without bending or breaking. Create a "board" or pole 1-3 inches wide and 6-10 inches longer than the patients leg as measured from the top of the pelvis to the sole of the foot; use the patient's uninjured leg to measure with. Multiple tent poles, a single Megamid pole, two ski poles, two paddle shafts, multiple green sticks, etc. can make good supports.
- Two sections of 1 inch webbing (or something of similar strength), each at least 30 inches long, will separately form the "proximal anchor" and the traction device. Tie an overhand loop in one end of both sections (or use cam straps). Using one section at a time, place the knot (or cam) as close as possible to one end of the rigid support, fold the other end over the top of the support, and tape in place creating a pocket for the support to rest in. Repeat the process on the other end of the support using the other section of webbing.
- **TO APPLY:** Pad and tie one section around the patient's upper thigh (proximal anchor). Make sure that it is resting snugly in their crotch with the rigid support on the outside of the patient's leg aligned with the axis of that leg. Pass the webbing on the other end of the rigid support through the bottom of the ankle hitch and back through the loop (or cam) to create a mini pulley system. Pad both the splint and between the patient's legs then tie cravats gently around both legs and the support. Slowly apply traction until the limb is aligned and the patient's pain is reduced. ***Use as little traction as possible to accomplish this task. The higher the traction pressure the faster the patient's distal CSM will decrease.*** Tighten the "straps" tying the patients legs and support together until snug.

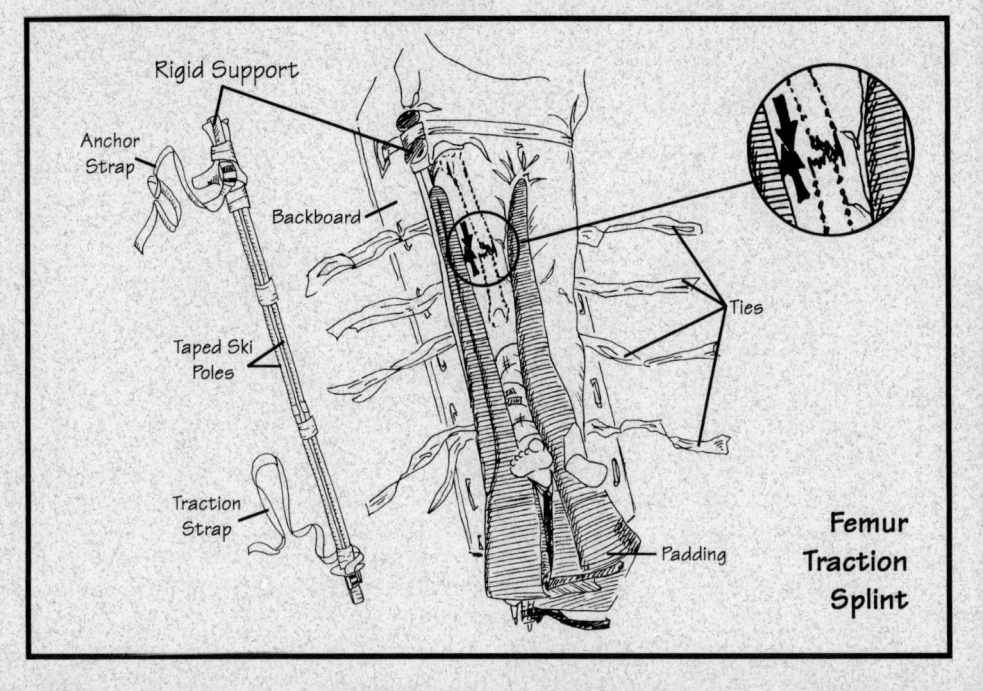

Rigid Support

Anchor
Strap

Backboard

Taped Ski
Poles

Ties

Traction
Strap

Padding

**Femur
Traction
Splint**

- The splint is finished when the patient's hip and legs are immobilized in a litter or backboard.
- *Monitor the patient's distal CSM.* When it becomes compromised loosen the traction until it returns or remove the traction splint and substitute a sandwich style splint OR immobilize directly to the litter.

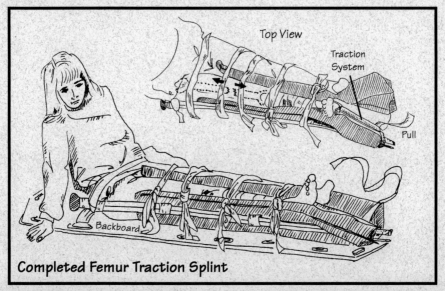

Top View

Traction System

Pull

Backboard

Completed Femur Traction Splint

Wounds

Pathophysiology

All wounds damage tissue, bleed, or ooze plasma. If bleeding occurs, arteries and arterioles constrict and the clotting cascade is activated. If it is successful, bleeding will stop within 5-15 minutes. Within hours cellular debris from the damaged tissue stimulates the inflammatory response to help prevent infection and begin healing. Local vasodilation permits white blood cells to leave the capillary beds, migrate into the local tissue, and form a protective barrier against invading bacteria. *The protective barrier is weak during the first five days and strong thereafter.* During the same period a scab is formed to seal and protect the wound while permitting drainage. With normal wound healing the local redness, pain, tenderness, heat, and swelling should subside after four or five days as the inflammatory response decreases and the protective barrier becomes strong. As days progress into weeks the wound heals from the inside outward and its edges migrate together to form a scar.

If the protective barrier is overwhelmed by invading bacteria a local infection will develop, increasing rather than decreasing the inflammatory response. The protective barrier may become overwhelmed by the presence of too many bacteria or through local movement. The chances for developing an infection are higher during the first four days after the injury and become low after the protective barrier is well established. A local infection may progress through the lymphatic system into the bloodstream and become systemic eliciting a low grade fever as the immune system responds. Fevers below 102 degrees F stimulate the immune system and create a hostile environment for the invading bacteria. As the fight continues and toxins build, the patient feels tired and sick.

Assessment

- Wounds are assessed according to their depth and potential for infection. **Partial thickness wounds** are superficial while full thickness wounds completely penetrate the skin layers. **Full thickness wounds** often damage underlying structures. The adjectives low, moderate, or high refer to the wounds potential for infection.

Low Risk Wounds

- Partial thickness wounds have a low potential for bacterial infection and include: abrasions, first and second degree burns, and friction blisters.

Moderate Risk Wounds

- Clean full thickness wounds with neat edges (laceration) have a moderate potential for infection.

High Risk Wounds

- Deep full thickness wounds with dirty ragged edges and damaged bones, ligaments, tendons, and/or muscles have a high potential for infection. Puncture wounds, animal bites, and wounds over joints are high risk wounds.
- Any wound that *becomes* infected is a high risk wound.

Field Treatment

General Wound Care

- Clean all wounds within two hours of the incident.
- Cover wound with a dry dressing and bandage. Monitor, reclean, and rebandage when both the dressing and bandage become wet.

Low Risk Wounds

- Wash both the wound and the surrounding skin with soap and clean water; OR a 10% providone-iodine (PI) solution; OR hydrogen peroxide. Remove all foreign debris by gentle scrubbing and/or by careful picking with a tweezers. **Vigorous scrubbing may cause minor bleeding and should be avoided.** Open closed blisters and remove dead skin prior to cleansing. Pat or air dry.
- If desired, silver sulfadiazine (a water soluble Rx ointment) can be used to help promote healing in partial thickness wounds; it is highly recommended for treatment on second degree burns. **Silver sulfadiazine is a sulfa drug and in rare cases may cause an allergic reaction.**

Moderate & High Risk Wounds

- **Begin the cleansing process after bleeding has stopped.** Do not clean a wound that is associated with severe life threatening bleeding.
- Wash only the skin surrounding the wound (not inside the wound itself) with soap and clean water; OR a 10% providone-iodine (PI) solution.
- Flush the wound numerous times with clean water. A 60 cc irrigation syringe is ideal but other delivery methods can work well: a bicycle water bottle, an old "Saline" container, a strong

plastic bag with a corner removed, etc. Flush using intense short bursts rather than one long stream. Avoid forcing material into tissue pockets by flushing along the axis of the wound. Pat or air dry.

- *Vigorous scrubbing may cause minor bleeding and should be avoided.* In the unlikely event of more severe bleeding, STOP the cleansing process and apply direct pressure until the wound has reclotted. Do not resume cleaning the wound until the bleeding has stopped; then, flush gently.
- Cover with a thick dressing (multiple layers of roller gauze, 4x4s, etc.) and bandage. *Monitor, reclean, and rebandage when both the dressing and bandage become wet from wound drainage, sweat, or environmental conditions.*
- While wound closure often speeds the healing process, it also increases the chance of infection by preventing drainage. Because of unsterile conditions and increased chance of infection, *avoid wound closure, regardless of the type (e.g.: sutures, Butterfly closures, tape, etc.) in most field situations.*

(High Risk Wounds Only)

- Remove dead skin and tissue that is poorly attached or turning blue or black. Use a clean sharp scissors or scalpel. *Do not cut or remove deep tissue or structures.*
- Remove the remaining foreign material with clean tweezers or hemostats. Gentle probing may be necessary. A large magnifying glass is often helpful.
- *Vigorous scrubbing, extensive probing, and excessive cutting may restart minor bleeding and should be avoided.* In the unlikely event of more severe bleeding, STOP the cleansing process and apply direct pressure until the wound has reclotted. Do not resume cleaning the wound until the bleeding has stopped; then, flush gently.
- Finish the cleansing process with multiple flushing of a 1% providone-iodine solution (diluted from a 10% providone-iodine solution or ointment). A herbal wash of echinacea tea may be substituted for the 1% PI solution.
- Because of the increased chance for infection *do not close high risk wounds in the field.*
- You may apply a 10% povidone-iodine ointment (or solution) or other petroleum based antibiotic ointments to the first few layers of the dressing. Do not apply directly onto or into the wound since they can cause damage to healthy cells.
- Consider immobilizing the limb (or wound site) with a splint to prevent mechanical disruption of the protective barrier especially if the wound is over a joint. All wounds associated with an unstable injury require splinting. If the limb is angulated or deformed it may also require realignment. Refer to unstable injuries on page 51.
- Evacuate all patients who have wounds associated with an unstable injury within 24 hours.
- *All patients with high risk wounds are at high risk for contracting Tetanus.* If they have not had a Tetanus vaccination or booster within the past five years they MUST receive shots containing the antitoxin (tetanus immune globulin) and vaccine within 24 hours of the incident.
- *All patients suffering from animal bites are at risk for contracting the Rabies virus* and require a 5 shot treatment series including the immune globulin and a vaccine. The first shot should be given within 72 hours of the bite. People who have been vaccinated against Rabies ALSO need the shot series. *ALL PEOPLE INFECTED WITH THE RABIES VIRUS DIE!*

Impaled Objects

Assessment

- Description: splinters, sticks, nails, ice axes, etc.
- In general, because of the high risk of infection and difficulty of transport, all impaled objects should be removed IF they are easy to remove and do no additional damage to the underlying structures as they are being removed.

Field Treatment

- It may be necessary when attempting to remove small impaled objects (splinters, nails, etc.) to make an incision through the skin following the axis of the object to gain solid purchase with a forceps, hemostat, or pliers to help prevent breakage. Use a clean sharp knife or scalpel. Do not cut underlying structures in an attempt to loosen any impaled object.
- Once the object has been removed, the existing puncture wound is a high risk for infection and treated accordingly.
- *If the impaled object cannot be removed easily and safely it must be stabilized in position and the patient carefully evacuated to a major hospital.*

Infection

Assessment

Local Infection

- Increased local redness, tenderness, and pain at both the site and surrounding tissue.
- Swelling increases and may pull the wound edges apart.
- The wound continually drains large amounts of pus OR the surface has sealed preventing drainage and forms a pus pocket beneath the skin.

Systemic Infection

- Pain, tenderness, and swelling continues to increase invading more of the surrounding tissue.
- Redness continues to increase and red streaks may appear radiating along the limb towards the trunk of the body.
- Patient complains of general achiness and feels tired.
- Fever and chills are common.

Field Treatment

Local Infection

- The treatment goal is to contain and reduce the infection through *aggressive cleaning.*
- The wound site and the affected tissue are either immersed in hot water or covered with hot compresses 105-112 degrees F (or as hot as the patient can bear) for 30 minutes, until the wound opens OR, in the case of an abscess, a pustule head develops and a small incision can be

made through the skin to expose the pocket and permit drainage.
- The wound edges are pulled apart and aggressively cleaned in the same manner as any high risk wound. *The wound should never be squeezed to remove pus pockets;* squeezing may force invading bacteria into healthy tissue and increase the infection.
- 10 % providone-iodine ointment should be applied to the first few layers of the dressing. The wound should then be bandaged and splinted to help establish a new protective barrier.
- *The wound should be soaked and recleaned on a regular basis* (4-6 times per day is not unusual) and the patient closely monitored for a developing systemic infection.
- *Consider evacuation if oral antibiotic therapy for a systemic infection is not an option.*

Systemic Infection

- The treatment goal is to contain and reduce the infection through aggressive cleaning and antibiotic therapy.
- The wound should be treated in the manner outlined under Field Treatment for a Local Infection (see above) AND:
- Give fever reducing medications (OTC: aspirin, ibuprofen, naproxen sodium, acetaminophen) IF patient's temperature is 102 degrees F or greater. The body's immune system functions efficiently in the temperature range between 99-101 degrees F; therefore, patients with a low grade fever should not be given fever reducing medications.
- *Rest* (no exercise) to decrease the production of metabolic waste.
- *Fluids* to increase the elimination of waste. Monitor the patient's urine color and output.
- The patient should be started on a *7-10 day oral course of one of the following systemic antibiotics:* cephalexin, adult dose 500 mg twice day (do not use with patients who are allergic to cephalosporins) OR erythromycin, adult dose 500 mg 4 times a day. [4,6]
- *Consider evacuation.*
- *If antibiotic therapy is not an option the patient MUST BE EVACUATED to a hospital.*

Notes

Environmental Conditions	Possible Problems	Page
VERY COLD! Temperatures below freezing	Frostbite/Frostnip	75
	Hypothermia	70
COLD! Moderate to low temperatures possibly with wind and/or humidity	Hypothermia	70
	Chilblains	73
Feet immersed in cold water greater than 10 hours	Immersion Foot (Trench Foot)	74
HOT! Moderate to high temperatures possibly with low wind and/or high humidity	Heat Related Problems (fainting, rash, heat exhaustion, heat stroke)	77
	Sunburn	83
	Dehydration	81
	Electrolyte Sickness	82
Sun Exposure	Sunburn	83
	Sun Poisoning	77
	Snow Blindness	145
Thermal, chemical, sun, & respiratory burns	Burns	83
Lightning strike	Lightning Injuries	86
Drowning	Near Drowning	88
Ingested or inhaled toxins	Wilderness Toxins	89
Bites & stings	Wilderness Toxins	89
	Allergic Reactions (local & systemic)	93
Allergies, including poison ivy, oak, or sumac	Allergic Reactions	93
Altitude	Acute Mountain Sickness (HAPE, HACE)	95

Environmental Conditions	Possible Problems	Page
SCUBA Injuries	Ruptured Alveoli (AGE, pneumothorax, subcutaneous emphysema)	98
	Nitrogen Narcosis	100
	Decompression Sickness (Bends)	101
	Squeeze	103
Free diving injuries	Squeeze	103
	Shallow Water Blackout	104

Hypothermia

Pathophysiology

Hypothermia occurs when you cannot maintain your normal body temperature in the face of a cold challenge. The cold challenge increases as you are exposed to progressively decreasing temperature, increasing wind, and increasing humidity. You respond to a cold challenge by increasing heat production through shivering and maintaining your core temperature through peripheral vasoconstriction. Any type of heat production requires an efficient metabolism and the burning of ingested or stored calories. As the availability of calories decreases so too does your ability to produce heat through shivering or exercise. Fitness, hydration, health, and injury all effect your metabolism and your ability to produce heat. If your heat production is inadequate your peripheral vascular bed will vasoconstrict in an effort to maintain a normal core temperature. Effective vasoconstriction is dependent upon a healthy circulatory system. The initial effects of vasoconstriction are readily apparent in a person exposed to a severe cold challenge. In a normal cold response skin becomes pale and cool as peripheral circulation decreases. The frequency of urination increases with the vasoconstriction. And, the urine is clear unless dehydration is present.

Eventually, as their core temperature drops, a normal response to cold becomes hypothermia and a cold person becomes a patient. Normal core temperatures range (including heat and cold responses) from 96-99 degrees F (35.5 to 37.2 degrees C). As a patient's core temperature drops below 96 degrees F (35.5 degrees C) their mental status becomes noticeably affected and they may become lethargic or irritable. Left untreated their level of consciousness may decrease on a downward spiral from awake and lethargic or irritable to voice responsive, pain responsive, and finally unresponsive. The patient's pulse rate, respiratory rate, and blood pressure drop respectively. Though still alive, the severely hypothermic patient often appears dead: unresponsive, with no visible respirations, no palpable pulse, and no measurable blood pressure. *At core temperatures below 90 degrees F (32.2 degrees C) the severely hypothermic patient's heart becomes extremely fragile and predisposed to arrest through abrupt trauma (dropping or chest compressions), exercise (returning cold toxic blood to the core), and peripheral rewarming (hot tub, sauna, etc. causes immediate vasodilation and a subsequent drop in blood pressure).* Patients with core temperatures below 90 degrees F (32.2 degrees C) may present as voice responsive, pain responsive, or unresponsive. When assessing hypothermic patients without a hypothermia thermometer all patients below an awake and alert status must be presumed to have severe hypothermia.

The *onset* of hypothermia is variable and depends on the severity of the cold challenge, the length of exposure, and the health of the patient. Acute hypothermia may occur in minutes to hours with cold water immersion regardless of the victim's health. Subacute hypothermia may occur in hours to days in a mountain or river environment where decreased calories predisposes the climber, hiker, or paddler to hypothermia from a moderate cold challenge. Expedition members with predisposing factors (poor health, inadequate nutrition, poor hydration, etc.) can develop a chronic cold response during prolonged exposure (days to weeks) to cool environmental conditions with limited calorie intake and no glycogen or fat stores. They may easily become hypothermic when presented with a slight increase in the cold challenge.

Environmental

Prevention

- Be prepared for environmental cold challenges with weather knowledge, good equipment, fitness, adequate nutrition, and good health.
- Balance intake and stored calories with the anticipated energy output. Provide rest days to resupply glycogen (sugar) and fat stores before a strenuous event involving a potential cold challenge.
- Keep hydrated.
- Avoid smoking; nicotine is a strong vasoconstrictor.

Assessment

Cold Response

- Exposure to a mild, moderate, or severe cold challenge.
- *Patient is alert and cooperative with a normal core temperature (above 96 degrees F or 35.5 degrees C).*
- Patient's skin may appear pale or white, cool, and moist.
- Frequency of urination increases; urine color is clear to pale yellow *unless* dehydration is present.
- Patient may be mildly shivering.

Mild Hypothermia

- Exposure to a mild, moderate, or severe cold challenge.
- *Change in normal mental status from Awake and cooperative to awake and lethargic, irritable, or voice responsive.* "Rule of umbles": patient is mumbling, fumbling, grumbling, tumbling, etc.
- *Core temperature is between 90 and 96 degrees F (32.2 to 35.5 degrees C).*
- Patient's skin may appear pale or white, cool, and moist. In temperatures below freezing frostbite may be present.
- Frequency of urination increases; urine color is clear to pale yellow *unless* dehydration is present.
- Patient may be shivering uncontrollably.

Severe Hypothermia

- Exposure to a mild, moderate, or severe cold challenge.
- *Patient's level of consciousness continues to decrease from voice responsive to pain responsive and unresponsive with pulse rates, respiratory rates, and blood pressure decreasing respectively.* Severely hypothermic patients are often unresponsive and appear dead with no visible respirations, palpable pulse or blood pressure.
- *Core temperature is below 90 degrees F (32.2 degrees C). When assessing hypothermic patients without a hypothermia thermometer, assume all patients below an awake status to have severe hypothermia.*
- Patient's skin may appear white or cyanotic (blue) and cold. In temperatures below freezing frostbite is usually present.
- The patient may no longer be shivering and urination has decreased or stopped.

Field Treatment

Cold Response

- Examine your resources and question your decision to continue in the face of the present cold challenge.
- Replace lost calories with simple sugars and carbohydrates. Consider providing rest days to resupply glycogen (sugar) and fat stores before re-exposure. Consider exercise if calories are in place.
- Replace lost fluids with hot liquids. Avoid caffeinated drinks.[1]
- Consider adding internal or external heat.
- Consider decreasing the cold challenge by providing dry insulation and shelter.
- Avoid smoking; nicotine is a strong vasoconstrictor.

Mild Hypothermia

- The treatment goal is to reduce the cold challenge and increase the body's ability to produce and retain heat.
- Reduce the cold challenge by creating a dry wind-proof shelter and add heat in any manner: fire, hot tub, sauna, heat packs, hot water bottles, body heat, etc. Increase the patient's ability to retain heat by removing any wet clothing and adding layers of dry insulation.
- One effective method of field rewarming is to place the mildly hypothermic patient into a sleeping bag, seal it completely around their face, and then place them (bag and all) inside two sleeping bags joined together with a warm person on each side. The bags should be well insulated from the ground and inside an effective shelter.
- Replace lost fluids with hot liquids. Avoid caffeinated drinks.[1]
- Replace lost calories with simple sugars and carbohydrates.
- Maintain treatment until the patient's body temperature returns to normal and they have replaced their calorie stores and fluids. This usually requires a few days.
- Avoid smoking; nicotine is a strong vasoconstrictor.

Severe Hypothermia

- The goal is to carefully reduce the cold challenge and evacuate with ALS to a major trauma center.
- At core temperatures below 90 degrees F (32.2 degrees C) the patient's heart becomes extremely fragile and predisposed to arrest. *AVOID dropping the patient, exercise, and peripheral rewarming* (hot tub, sauna, etc.).
- *Because field assessment of cardiac function in a severely hypothermic patient is extremely difficult and chest compressions may cause cardiac arrest in a perfusing patient DO NOT BEGIN chest compressions on a severely hypothermic patient.*
- Although chest compressions are controversial, they may be indicated with a sudden loss of pulse. *Follow your local protocols.*
- Begin chest compressions if a cardiac monitor shows asystole or ventricular fibrillation. Once initiated, continue chest compressions until the patient reaches definitive care.[1]
- Begin *positive pressure ventilations*. In addition to adding internal heat, forced ventilations increase the delivery of oxygen to the heart and help electrically stabilize it.[1]
- *Reduce the cold challenge* by creating a dry wind-proof shelter. Add external heat reluctantly, carefully, and slowly by using hot packs or hot water bottles *outside* an insulation layer. An effective method of packaging a severely hypothermic patient for litter transport (or for pre-

Environmental

venting hypothermia for litter patients in a cold challenge situation) is: first remove any wet clothes from the patient and seal them inside a vapor barrier (silver emergency blanket or bivy sack, garbage bags, sheet plastic, tarp, etc.). Follow with a sleeping bag (one you would be comfortable sleeping in that environment), then external heat packs on the patient's upper back and chest, and then a second sleeping bag. Multiple sleeping pads insulate the patient from the ground and a final vapor barrier seals the entire package

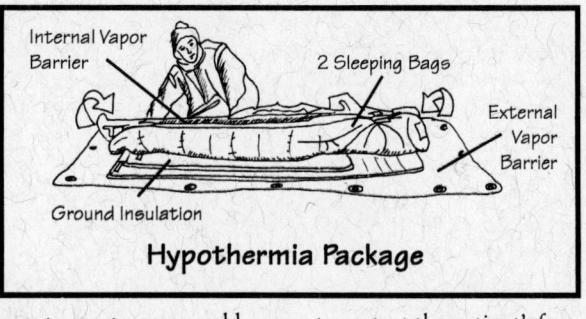

Hypothermia Package

from the environment. Make sure to create a removable cover to protect the patient's face. During long transports, the entire package may be placed into additional sleeping bags joined together and next to two warm bodies while in camp.

- *Evacuate with ALS to a major trauma center.*
- **Defibrillation and drugs are not effective when the patient's core temperature is below 86 degrees F (30 degrees C).**

Chilblains

Pathophysiology

Chilblains is believed to be caused by a pre-existing vascular abnormality in the extremities. It occurs with repeated exposure of bare skin to a cold (32-60 degrees F or 0-15.5 degrees C), wet, and often windy environment. During exposure the peripheral vessels constrict locally, denying perfusion to skin layers, with prolonged vasoconstriction even *after* rewarming has begun. Patient's complain of burning and itching in affected areas upon rewarming. The inflammatory response is activated and within 12-24 hours after rewarming the affected area becomes swollen and red with patches of cyanotic (blue) tissue or nodules. In severe cases small blisters may appear. Symptoms usually last 12-14 days. With continued exposure scarring and changes in skin pigmentation may occur. Chronic chilblains is often seasonal with complete healing during the summer months.

Prevention

- Wear protective clothing.
- People with Raynaud's disease are predisposed to chilblains.
- People with chronic and severe chilblains may need to avoid cold, wet, and windy environments.
- Herbal preventative include teas that stimulate circulation (fresh ginger, angelica, prickly ash) and those that promote vasodilation (yarrow, hawthorn, horse chestnut).
- Avoid smoking; nicotine is a strong vasoconstrictor.

Assessment

- History of skin exposure to cold (32-60 degrees F or 0-15.5 degrees C), wet, and windy conditions.

- Localized burning and itching upon rewarming.
- Appearing 12-24 hours after rewarming: localized blotchy patches and swelling, redness, tender blue nodules, and, in severe cases, small blisters or pustules.
- Signs and symptoms persist for 10-14 days.

Field Treatment

- Avoid continued exposure.
- Apply topical ointments containing the herbs aloe vera and rue.
- Elevate to reduce swelling.
- *The affected area is predisposed to a secondary bacterial infection and should be kept clean, warm, and dry.*
- Avoid smoking; nicotine is a strong vasoconstrictor.

Immersion Foot

Pathophysiology

Immersion foot or "trench foot" develops after prolonged immersion (greater than 10-12 hours) in cold water (32-50 degrees F or 0-10 degrees C). The constant immersion causes prolonged vasoconstriction and decreased local perfusion. Lack of oxygen to the local tissue causes increased permeability in the capillary beds resulting in local edema and swelling. The skin may be red, whitish, or cyanotic (blue). Initial symptoms include tingling and numbness. The extent of the injury is significantly increased when the limb is kept immobile below the heart (e.g.: sitting in a raft with feet immersed in cold water). Rewarming causes extreme pain and the extremity appears hot, red, and dry; small red blisters are common. This phase may last 4-10 days. *In appearance, damage to the limb is almost indistinguishable from frostbite and treatment is identical. Severe or repeated immersion can result in gangrene and extensive tissue loss. There is a high risk of infection during the healing process* and complete healing takes place over a period of months to years. A prolonged decrease or loss of sensation during this time is common and the patient remains predisposed to all forms of cold injury.

Prevention

- Avoid prolonged immersion in cold water. Keep feet warm and dry. In wet, cold environments consider a foot massage every 4 hours to maintain local perfusion.
- Maintain calorie stores.
- Avoid smoking; nicotine is a strong vasoconstrictor.

Assessment

- History of prolonged immersion (greater than 10-12 hours) in very cold water (32-50 degrees F or 0-10 degrees C) .
- Cold, numb, swollen feet.
- Skin color may be red, white, or cyanotic (blue).
- Decreased CSM in the affected extremity.

Environmental

Field Treatment

- *The treatment goal is rapid field rewarming and evacuation to a major trauma center.*
- Treat any existing hypothermia first.
- Rewarm limb in "warm" (104-108 degrees F or 40-42.2 degrees C) water for 30-40 minutes. Monitor the temperature constantly. Remove limb when adding additional hot water to prevent thermal burns.
- Administer pain medications prior to rewarming. OTC: ibuprofen. Rx: opium derivatives (e.g.: morphine).
- Treat as a high risk wound. Apply cotton between digits during healing phase.
- Avoid repeated exposure and use.
- Avoid smoking; nicotine is a strong vasoconstrictor.
- *Evacuate to a major trauma center.*

Frostbite

Pathophysiology

Frostbite occurs with exposure to temperatures below 32 degrees F (0 degrees C). If peripheral vasoconstriction occurs, it may reduce both distal perfusion and warmth to the patient's extremities enough to permit tissue to freeze (frostbite). Areas commonly affected by frostbite are the feet, hands, nose, cheeks, and ears. Hypothermia, traumatic injury, circulatory diseases, fatigue, illness, and high altitude may compromise peripheral circulation and predispose patients to frostbite. As perfusion decreases the extremity becomes cold and painful. With the freezing of surface tissue (frostnip) the skin takes on a white waxy appearance and feels numb; the affected area has a soft, doughy texture. As deeper tissue is frozen, ice crystals become visible within the skin layers, all sensation disappears, and the frostbitten area is hard and "wooden" to the touch. The longer an area remains frozen the greater the eventual damage. Rapid and controlled rewarming in "warm" water is essential to minimize the damage caused by the formation of ice crystals. Ultimately tissue damage due to frostbite may require amputation; however, *the depth and severity of the damage is not apparent until hours or days after the rewarming process has been completed.* Although tissue damage is exacerbated after rewarming by subsequent refreezing and use, walking on frozen feet prior to rewarming does no additional harm. There is extreme pain associated with the return of perfusion; the pain medication of choice is morphine. Within a few hours after rewarming the skin appears swollen and red, cyanotic, or mottled in color. It is usually accompanied by an intense itching and burning pain. Blisters commonly develop within a 12-24 hour period. The appearance of clear or pink distal blisters indicates less damage than the formation of dark proximal blood blisters. Early numbness is a poor sign and may be replaced later with a deep throbbing pain. In severe cases where tissue damage is extensive, early numbness will be followed by severe proximal swelling, leaving the distal frostbitten area cold, severely discolored, and *without* perfusion or blisters; mummification usually begins within a few days. *The healing tissue is predisposed to a secondary bacterial infection and must be treated as a high risk wound until the swelling subsides. It must not be refrozen or used.*

Prevention

- Prevent hypothermia.
- People with diseases of the circulatory system (Diabetes, Raynaud's, etc.) are predisposed to frostbite.
- Avoid alcohol; over one third of all frostbite cases involve alcohol.
- In mountaineering situations monitor protected extremities (feet, hands, etc.) subjectively for numbness or lack of sensation while traveling. *Only inspect feet visually when in camp.*
- Avoid local constriction (tight boots, wrist loops, etc.)
- Consider camping or changing route as environmental conditions deteriorate.
- Avoid smoking; nicotine is a strong vasoconstrictor.

Field Assessment

- Exposure to temperatures below 32 degrees F or 0 degrees C.

Frostnip

- Patient complains of numbness and lack of local motor skills.
- Affected area feels soft and dough-like upon palpation.
- Skin appears white and waxy.

Frostbite

- There is a complete loss of sensation with no movement.
- The affected tissue feels solid and "wooden" to the touch.
- On exam the skin is white with ice crystals visible within the skin layers.

Field Treatment

Frostnip

- *The treatment goal is rapid and early field rewarming.*
- *Treat any existing hypothermia first.*
- Consider spontaneous rewarming by increasing exercise and local perfusion.
- Consider rewarming skin to skin (warm noses, cheeks, and ears with warm hands, warm hands in groin or armpits, warm feet on a friend's stomach while in camp).
- Consider rewarming by immersing the extremity in "warm" (104-108 degrees F or 40-42.2 degrees C) water for 30-40 minutes. Monitor the temperature constantly. Remove limb when adding additional hot water to prevent thermal burns.
- Administer pain and anti-inflammatory medications. OTC: ibuprofen.
- Avoid smoking; nicotine is a strong vasoconstrictor.
- *If, after 24 hours, no blisters appear, the limb may be used.* Although the damage is minimal the limb is predisposed to refreezing and care should be taken to keep it warm.
- If blisters appear the damage is significant and the limb should not be refrozen or used.

Frostbite

- *Consider walking out on frozen feet if less than 24 hours from a major hospital. Consider field rewarming only if greater than 24 hours from medical care and subsequent use and refreezing can be avoided.*

Environmental

- *Treat any existing hypothermia first.*
- For controlled field rewarming: rewarm limb in "warm" (104-108 degrees F or 40-42.2 degrees C) water for 30-40 minutes. Monitor the temperature constantly. Remove limb when adding additional hot water to prevent thermal burns.
- Administer pain medications prior to rewarming. Rx: opium derivatives (e.g.: morphine).
- Treat as a high risk wound. Apply cotton between digits during healing phase.
- Avoid smoking; nicotine is a strong vasoconstrictor.
- Avoid refreezing and use.

Heat Related Problems

Pathophysiology

Most serious heat related problems occur as the heat challenge overwhelms your body's ability to cool itself. The heat challenge is a combination of exercise and environmental conditions; it increases as temperature increases, wind decreases, humidity increases, and exercise levels increase. Your body responds to an increasing heat challenge through systemic vasodilation to increase radiant and conductive cooling and by sweating to increase evaporative cooling. *Your ability to effectively dump heat is variable and dependant upon your health and your level of acclimatization.* As your body responds to a heat challenge the majority (80%) of the adaptive changes occur within the first 4-5 days after exposure. Complete acclimatization requires 2-3 weeks. During this time major changes occur in the thermoregulatory centers of your brain, within your peripheral vessels, and within your heart. Sweating, and therefore cooling, is increased and begun at a lower core temperature while electrolyte loss from both sweat and urine is minimized. Metabolic efficiency is significantly increased; essentially more usable energy is produced with less heat. Cardiac output and peripheral vasodilation are increased while the pulse rate is lowered. *Acclimatized individuals are predisposed to heat exhaustion while unacclimatized people are predisposed to heat stroke.* Dehydration and electrolyte imbalances play a large role in a person's ability to dump excess heat. *Urine, not the amount of fluid intake, is the primary evaluative tool when assessing water balance; it should be clear or pale yellow. Mental status is the primary evaluative tool when assessing severe heat injuries.* Any change from a normal mental status (alert and cooperative to alert and irritable, alert and anxious, dizziness, lethargic, etc.) is a significant finding. If vasodilation and sweating do not serve to maintain a normal mental status, heat injury has occurred; and, if left untreated, death will follow rapidly.

Prevention

- Allow time for the acclimatization process to occur.
- Maintain water and electrolyte balances. Cool oral fluids are more easily absorbed than warm or very cold ones.
- Minimize exercise in a heat challenge situation, especially with unacclimatized persons.

Assessment

- Exposure to a moderate or severe heat challenge. The heat challenge increases with increased temperature, decreased wind, increased humidity, and increased exercise. See diagram for the relationships between major heat illnesses.

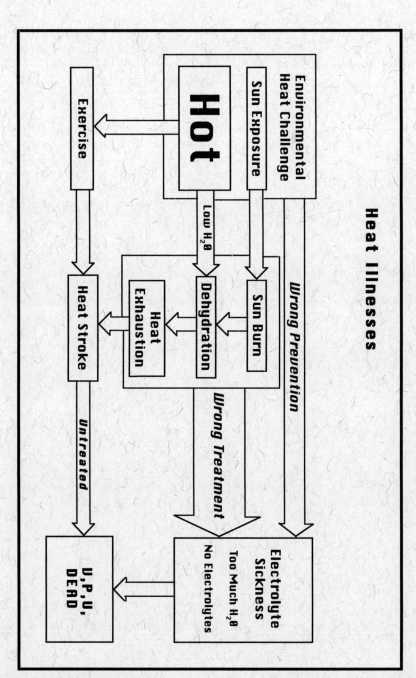

Heat Cramps

- Most common in the large muscle groups of the thigh and abdomen, they are usually the result of electrolyte imbalance and decreased volume.

Fainting

- Usually occurs when a person is standing with knees locked and minimal or no movement (belayers!) and decreased volume.

Heat Rash

- Usually occurs in a humid environment followed by prolonged sweating. The sweat ducts become blocked with sweat and skin cells activating the inflammatory response.
- The effected patient shows red swollen skin with small pustules.

Sun Poisoning

- A common dermatitis that appears in sun sensitive individuals. It usually presents as a rash or small pustules hours or days after increased exposure to ultraviolet radiation.

Heat Exhaustion

- Patient presents with a history of moderate to severe heat challenge and **limited or no fluid replacement.**
- Water balance is off and patient is dehydrated. Patient complains of headache and occasionally nausea. Vomiting is possible in more severe cases.
- Chills are common.
- **Urine output is decreased and the urine is concentrated and dark.**
- The patient's skin will usually be pale, cool, and moist from the volume loss and subsequent vasoconstriction.
- Core temperature is usually elevated but below 104 degrees F (40 degrees C).
- Patient looks and feels "sick".
- The patient's mental status may be normal, irritable, or lethargic.

Heat Stroke

- *Patient presents with an altered mental status in the presence of a moderate to severe heat challenge. Heat Stroke should be suspected with minor AVPU changes. If patient is anxious, irritable, lethargic, dizzy, exhibiting bizarre behavior, etc. in the presence of a heat challenge immediately begin treatment for heat stroke. Severe changes in mental status (voice responsive, pain responsive, unresponsive) are "later" signs and indicate more severe injury.*
- Core temperature is usually greater than 105 degrees F (40.5 degrees C).
- Seizures are common.
- Coma and death are possible.

Field Treatment

Heat Cramps

- Replace volume and electrolytes. Cool oral fluids are more easily absorbed than warm or very cold ones.
- Rest and massage are often helpful.

Fainting

- Consciousness returns quickly and spontaneously. Replace volume and electrolytes.
- Avoid standing with locked knees; regular movement, even if slight, maintains venous pressure and helps eliminate fainting.

Heat Rash

- Lightly scrub affected area to clear blocked sweat ducts.
- Monitor for infection.
- Decreased sweating may predispose the patient to heat stroke.
- Limit exercise and heat exposure.

Sun Poisoning

- *Protect the entire person from sun exposure* using both high SPF broad spectrum sun screens and protective clothing. The reaction will disappear in 7 to 10 days if continued sun exposure is avoided.

Heat Exhaustion

- *The treatment goal is to replace water and electrolytes as soon as possible and cool the patient as necessary.*
- Stop exercise and remove the patient from the hot environment as quickly as possible.
- Actively cool the patient to prevent heat stroke from developing. *Cold water immersion is very effective in humid environments while evaporative cooling on total body bare skin is up to four times faster in arid climates.* Use a combination of spray misting and fanning for effective evaporative cooling.
- Replace lost fluids and electrolytes slowly to avoid vomiting. Cool oral fluids are more easily absorbed than warm or very cold ones.
- Patient should be considered at risk for heat injuries and closely monitored.

Heat Stroke

- *The treatment goal is immediate and rapid cooling.*
- Stop exercise and remove the patient from the hot environment as quickly as possible.
- Actively cool the patient's brain as quickly as possible. *Cold water immersion (ice bath) is the treatment of choice.* Evaporative cooling is very effective and may be the only option in arid climates. Use a combination of spray misting and fanning for evaporative cooling.
- If patient remains alert replace lost fluids and electrolytes slowly to avoid vomiting. Cool oral fluids are more easily absorbed than warm or very cold ones.
- Alert patients who have not undergone a significant AVPU change (voice responsive, pain responsive, or unresponsive) may remain in the field but should be considered at high risk for heat injuries and closely monitored. If their environment cannot be modified (changing route, exercise levels, etc.) they should be evacuated.
- *Evacuate all voice responsive, pain responsive, or unresponsive patients to a major trauma center after cooling; maintain their critical systems enroute.*

Environmental

Dehydration

Pathophysiology

Water imbalances directly affect cellular metabolism. General perfusion is reduced and cellular function decreased. The body responds to water loss by vasoconstricting peripheral vessels to maintain perfusion pressure and by decreasing urine output to conserve existing supplies. The concentration of waste products in the patient's urine increases proportionally with decreasing urine output. Mental and physical performance may be significantly reduced. If the loss continues, systemic perfusion may be affected and the patient may show the clinical pattern for volume shock: progressively increasing pulse and respiratory rates followed by decreased blood pressure and AVPU levels. *Urine output and concentration are the primary evaluative tools; thirst is unreliable.*

Prevention

- Maintain fluid and electrolyte balances. Cool oral fluids are more easily absorbed than warm or very cold ones.
- Monitor urine output and concentration. Normal urine for a well hydrated person is clear or pale yellow.
- Thirst is unreliable; drink before you are thirsty.

Assessment

- Patient presents with a history of fluid losses and minimal or no replacement. Possible causes include heavy exercise, hot environment, severe vomiting or diarrhea.
- Urine output is decreased; urine is concentrated and dark yellow or orange in color.
- Patient may complain of headache or nausea. Vomiting is possible in severe cases.
- Mental and physical performance is significantly impaired. The patient's mental status may be normal, irritable, or lethargic.

Field Treatment

- *The treatment goal is to replace fluids and electrolytes.*
- Replace fluid loss with water; cool water is tolerated better than lukewarm water. Replace slowly with small sips to prevent vomiting.
- Replace electrolytes with foods high in simple sugars, potassium, and sodium (bananas, raisins, etc.). Electrolyte replacement drinks should be diluted to tolerable levels (usually 50%). Dilution increases the absorption rate.
- Monitor urine output and concentration.
- *Severe losses may require IV replacement.*

Electrolyte Sickness

Pathophysiology

All cells require information and direction from the brain to maintain normal body functioning. Water soluble minerals (electrolytes), especially sodium and potassium, are necessary for the brain to transmit its signals or commands to the rest of the body. The signals are electrochemical in nature and involve the ionization and transfer of electrical "current" between the sodium and potassium molecules across cell membranes. Because electrolytes are water soluble, they are easily available to cells as long as they are present in sufficient quantity within the blood and plasma. Potassium and sodium stores are limited and electrolyte balance is primarily maintained through oral intake. Sodium and potassium are transported across cell membranes by active transportation. Both are normally excreted in both urine and sweat. Normal consumption of food containing sodium is usually all that is necessary to maintain electrolyte balance. Drinking large amounts of water may upset the balance by requiring the kidneys to eliminate excess water that, by necessity, contains electrolytes. This effectively "dilutes" the electrolytes remaining in the person's blood and plasma. If the consumption of plain water continues without the addition of food or salt, electrolytes continue to be lost. Electrolyte loss is significantly increased by sweating. As blood sodium levels drop, tissue sodium levels within the body also drop respectively often produceing muscle cramps and tingling in the extremities. Because blood vessels within the brain are not permeable to sodium (blood/brain barrier), something different happens in the brain. In order to maintain the ion balance within the brain, water, instead of sodium, moves across the vascular membranes. The resulting cerebral edema causes significant mental status changes, nausea & vomiting, and eventually a decrease in AVPU, seizures, and coma. Death is possible. These progressive signs and symptoms are known as electrolyte sickness, hyponatremia (low sodium), or water toxicity. *Unfortunately the signs and symptoms of electrolyte sickness mimic, in its early stages, heat exhaustion and later, heat stroke. Treatment of these heat related diseases with water, without replacing electrolytes, is a primary cause of electrolyte sickness. Regardless of the cause, whenever replacing fluids replace electrolytes.*

Prevention

- Replace electrolytes by eating foods containing salts (sodium and potassium) and sugar (to help facilitate the absorption of the electrolytes from the digestive system). Electrolyte drinks work well but are less effective than foods high in sodium. Fruit juices, soda, and beer contain little sodium and are not effective replacement drinks. In the absence of electrolyte replacement solutions, a pinch of salt and a pinch of sugar per 8 oz. glass of water is all that is necessary. Salt tablets are too concentrated and often cause nausea and vomiting.
- Persons exercising in a hot environment (especially unacclimatized persons) should increase their dietary sodium intake.

Assessment

- *Patient presents with a history of drinking large amounts of plain water (or other drinks lacking in sodium) and not eating foods high in sodium.*
- *Their urine is clear and copious.* Most patients suffering from electrolyte sickness have urinated within the past two hours.

Environmental

- General weakness, dizziness, and fatigue are followed by nausea and vomiting is common. Diarrhea is possible.
- Patient looks and feels sick.
- They may exhibit mental status changes and eventually drop on the AVPU scale; bizarre or irrational behavior is common.
- Seizures, coma, and death are possible with severe sodium loss.

Field Treatment

- If the patient is awake, encourage them to **drink an electrolyte replacement solution sparingly AND eat foods high in sodium.** Eating foods high in sodium is more efficient at replacing lost electrolytes than drinking electrolyte solutions. Carbohydrates increase salt absorption while proteins and fats slow absorption. A pinch of salt and a pinch of sugar per 8 oz. glass will work if standard electrolyte replacement drinks and foods high in sodium are not available. Salted fruits are effective. Salt tablets are too concentrated and often cause nausea and vomiting. With aggressive treatment, symptoms usually resolve within several hours.
- Intravenous (IV) sodium replacement will be necessary for patients who are voice responsive, pain responsive, or unresponsive. Administering a small amount of concentrated electrolyte solution sublingually may be beneficial in a field situation if IV therapy is not available.
- *Evacuate all voice responsive, pain responsive, and unresponsive patients.*

Thermal, Chemical, Sun, & Respiratory Burns

Pathophysiology

First and second degree thermal, chemical, and sun burns activate the body's normal inflammatory response causing vasodilation and an increase in the permeability of the local blood vessels and capillary beds. Vasodilation causes local redness and heat while increased permeability allows fluid to leak into the surrounding tissue causing swelling and blisters. Swelling follows the generic swelling curve. It may begin immediately and continue to develop over the next 24 hours. Insensible fluid loss is increased as much as 15 times above normal. Fluid lost within the surrounding tissue to swelling is not available for general perfusion until the burn heals and it is reabsorbed. Fluid loss in patients who have serious first degree burns greater than 50% of their total body surface area (severe sunburn) and those with second degree burns greater than 20% of their total body surface area may show the clinical pattern for volume shock and require IV therapy to maintain their fluid balance. *Patients with large surface area burns in the backcountry often die from volume shock. Those with less serious first and second degree burns are predisposed to dehydration, heat exhaustion, and heat stroke because of the lost volume.*

Since the vessels in the burn area are vasodilated due to the inflammatory response they cannot constrict in the presence of cold and thermoregulation is severely compromised or lost. *Patients who have first and second degree thermal or sun burns greater than 10% of their total body surface area are predisposed to hypothermia* and should not be immersed in cool or cold water for more than a few minutes or not at all. Because of the high degree of efficiency of evaporative cooling they should also be careful when repeatedly soaking and wearing wet cotton clothing in a desert environment. Patients with thermal burns covering less than 10% of their total body surface area should immediately immerse the burned area in cold water to cool the burn and relieve pain. Chemical burns should be flushed with large amounts of water.

Third degree burns destroy the entire skin layer including capillaries, blood vessels, and nerves; therefore, there is no surface perfusion. Often underlying tissue is also affected. Third degree burns may appear less severe than first or second degree burns because with the nerves destroyed there is no pain and with no perfusion there is no swelling; the skin appears white or grey. Because there is no perfusion healing will be limited and slow. All dead tissue must be removed to prevent infection. **Third degree burns are at high risk for infection.**

The inhalation of steam or hot gases rarely damages the lung tissue directly. Swelling can occur in the upper airway within minutes to hours often completely obstructing the airway and leading to respiratory arrest. Toxins present in the inhaled gases may cause immediate muscular contraction of the smooth muscle lining of the lower airway and subsequent bronchial constriction. They may also activate the inflammatory response within the lining of the lower airway

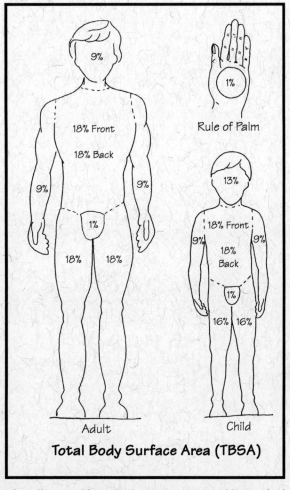

Rule of Palm

Total Body Surface Area (TBSA)

Adult

Child

causing vasodilation, fluid leaks, delayed swelling, and bronchial constriction. In addition, fluid may accumulate in the alveoli causing severe respiratory distress and arrest. Respiratory distress may appear at any time within the 24 hours following inhalation. **Patients developing severe respiratory distress from the inhalation of steam or hot gases in the backcountry often die.**

Prevention

- **SUNBURN is the most common burn seen in the backcountry.** The resulting first and occasional second degree burns directly predispose sunburn patients to hypothermia, dehydration, heat exhaustion, heat stroke, and indirectly to electrolyte sickness. Protection of the skin from over-exposure to the sun cannot be overrated. Use waterproof sunscreens with a high SPF factor or a complete sun block; apply on cool dry skin 30-40 minutes before sun exposure. Use enough to provide for adequate coverage (usually a minimum of 1 oz. per total body application). Dark clothing provides much more sun protection than light clothing just as dry clothing gives more

Environmental

protection than wet.
- Be extremely careful when lighting and cooking on portable stoves or fires. Avoid grease fires!
- Avoid using flammable liquids to start campfires.
- Be extremely careful pouring or walking near boiling water.

Assessment of Thermal, Chemical, & Sun Burns

- First Degree: Redness, pain, and tenderness.
- Second Degree: Initial redness, pain, and tenderness that develops into clear fluid filled blisters within 24 hours.
- Third Degree: No redness, pain, or tenderness. The patient's skin appears unnaturally white, grey, or black. The burned area may be deep and involve underlying structures which may also appear black. There will be little or no bleeding.

Field Treatment

- Immerse thermal burns in cool water to cool damaged tissue and reduce pain. Exercise extreme care in immersing patients in water if the burned area is greater that 10% of their total body surface area; they are susceptible to hypothermia.
- Flush chemical burns thoroughly with large amounts of water.
- *If patient is alert give oral fluids and electrolytes to help prevent dehydration.* Monitor the patient's urine; it should be pale yellow. Dark concentrated urine indicates a fluid imbalance and additional fluids and electrolytes are required.
- Aloe vera may be applied to all first degree burns to help ease pain and promote healing.
- With Second Degree burns: Remove all dead tissue and treat as a partial thickness wound. Apply silver sulfadiazine ointment to all second degree burns twice a day prior to dressing. *Silver sulfadiazine ointment is a Rx sulfa drug and may cause an allergic reaction in some patients with a history of sulfa allergies.* [6]
- Cover second degree burns with a breathable dry dressing (gauze, etc.) to reduce pain and fluid losses; reclean and replace every 24 hours. Occlusive dressings promote infection; *do not cover burn with occlusive dressings.* Spenco 2nd Skin may be used on small second degree burns. Since burns remain sterile for 24-48 hours burn treatment should not delay an evacuation.
- If no ointment or dressings are available a protective scab will develop if the burn is left open to the air.
- First and Second Degree burn patients have a limited ability to thermoregulate and are predisposed to hypothermia, heat exhaustion, and heat stroke.
- Third Degree Burns are at high risk of infection. Treat as a full thickness wound. Consider evacuation. If medical care is within 24 hours, cleansing should not delay the patient's evacuation.
- Burn patients are also at risk for contracting Tetanus. Check immunization history.
- Pain and anti-inflammatory meds may be given. OTC: aspirin, ibuprofen, naproxen sodium.
- *Evacuate with ALS to a major burn center: second degree burns over 20%, all burns totaling over 30% of the patient's total body surface area, all respiratory and third degree burns, and burns to the head, hands, or groin.*

Assessment of Respiratory Burns

- All patients who report having inhaled hot gases are at risk for delayed respiratory swelling and constriction even if they do not present with the early clinical pattern for respiratory distress. If respiratory distress does not develop within 24 hours respiratory problems associated with inhalation may be ruled out. All patients who have been exposed to hot gas inhalation who develop the clinical pattern for respiratory distress will need hospital care.

Early Clinical Pattern for Respiratory Distress

- Change in normal mental status to Alert and anxious or Alert and irritable.
- Patient complains of difficulty breathing.
- Wheezing sounds are present in both lungs.
- Respiratory rate increases.
- Pulse rate increases.

Late Clinical Pattern for Respiratory Distress

- Change in mental status to voice responsive, pain responsive, or unresponsive.
- In severe cases wet lung sounds are present with rales or gurgling.
- Clear or blood-tinged (rare) productive cough.
- Cyanosis (blue color) may develop in mucus membranes.
- Respiratory rate continues to increase; respiratory arrest is possible.
- Pulse rate continues to increase.

Field Treatment

- *The field treatment for respiratory burns is extremely limited and fatalities are high. Focus your attention on early recognition and fast evacuation.*
- All patients in respiratory distress should be supported in a sitting position.
- Administer supplemental oxygen.
- The effect of positive pressure ventilations may be limited due to the constriction of the patient's lower airway and developing pulmonary edema.
- *Evacuate with ALS to a major burn center.*

Lightning Injuries

Pathophysiology

Lightning, like all electrical current, travels the path of least resistance. Patients "struck" by lightning may come in contact with its electricity through a direct hit, splash, or ground current. The severity of lightning injuries is associated with the type of "strike" and its subsequent pathway. Splash and ground current are the most common forms of injurious strikes and patients struck in either manner are more likely to survive than those struck by a direct hit. Pathways through the head and chest commonly cause respiratory and cardiac arrest; and, even with successful resuscitation, permanent damage to the central nervous system is possible. General confusion and amnesia are common and may persist for several days. Heart dysrhythmias may occur immediately or be delayed for several days. Current following muscular pathways may cause immediate muscular con-

Environmental 86

tractions and subsequent unstable injures to tendons or bones; temporary paralysis is common. Entrance and exit wounds are rare. The most common pathway is peripheral causing temporary fernlike or star-burst burn patterns on the patient's skin. A peripheral pathway or "flashover" may also cause minor thermal burns as water is converted into steam. The patient's clothes may literally be "blown off" by expanding steam. Deeper thermal burns are possible if the patient is in direct contact with metal objects. Over 50% of lightning victims rupture one or both ear drums from the rapidly heated and expanding air associated with all lightning strikes.

Prevention

- Know local weather patterns (both frontal and diurnal).
- Stay away from high exposed places.
- Move away from open areas (fields, open water, etc.).
- Do not take shelter under trees.
- Remove all metal from contact with your body (climbing racks, ice axes, etc.).
- Seek shelter in dry areas not exposed to the storm's rain shadow (tents, buildings, tarps, etc.) and insulate yourself from the ground (dry sleeping pads, packs, etc.)
- Avoid shallow caves, gullies, and overhangs. Caves should be dry and big (at least twice as long as high).
- Avoid holding onto metal fences, wires, or shrouds.

Assessment

- Both respiratory and cardiac arrest are possible.
- Assume any person with a severely altered mental status in the vicinity of a lightning storm to have been struck by lightning.
- Fernlike or star-burst patterns on patients's skin indicate a positive lightning strike.
- If patient's clothes have been blown off check for thermal burns.
- Ruptured ear drums are common. Patients with damaged ear drums may be disoriented and deaf.
- Unstable musculoskeletal injuries are likely, especially if patient has been thrown by the blast. Temporary paralysis is possible. *Assume all lightning victims have an unstable spine.*
- General confusion and amnesia are common and may persist for several days.
- If a lightning victim is awake it is likely that they will remain so.

Field Treatment

- Immediate CPR is indicated for any lightning patient in cardiac arrest. *Recovery with CPR is possible.* Continue to breath for the patient if respirations are absent. It is common for lightning patients to require ventilations for hours before resuming breathing on their own. Heart dysrhythmias may occur immediately or be delayed for several days. Evacuate all patients who have suffered cardiac or respiratory arrest.
- Immobilize the patient's spine or "Rule Out" as the situation warrants.
- Treat all burns normally.
- Treat all musculoskeletal injuries normally. Associated paralysis is usually temporary.
- Treat ruptured ear drums normally (see Medical Index).
- Fernlike or star-burst patterns on patients's skin are temporary and will disappear in 24-48 hours.
- *Evacuate all lightning victims who have an altered mental status with ALS to a major trauma center.*

start CPR if Pts. have been submerged for ≤ 1 hr.

Drowning/Near Drowning

Pathophysiology

Drowning is the cause of numerous deaths in the outdoors each year. Upon submersion in water 85% of drowning victims involuntarily inhale, flooding their lungs with water; 15% will experience an immediate spasm of their larynx that prevents water from entering their lungs. In both cases, due to a systemic loss of oxygen, the victims will become quickly unresponsive, after a few minutes their hearts will stop, and, in most cases, after another 5 minutes they will suffer permanent brain damage. If not rescued, all drowning victims will die. If rescued the unresponsive patient who still has a pulse has an excellent chance for recovery if positive pressure ventilations are started immediately. A patient who has no pulse and no respirations may, with immediate CPR, recover completely. In rare cases, usually associated with cold water and young children, a few victims may also have a complete recovery if rescued within one hour and CPR started immediately. These "lucky" few will have experienced both a laryngospasm and an immediate shell/core response known as the "Mammalian Diving Response" or MDR. An MDR immediately slows their metabolic processes while preventing water from entering their lungs, thus giving protection for up to one hour. Therefore, **CPR should be initiated immediately with all drowning victims recovered within one hour of immersion who have no pulse and no respirations.** If a recovery occurs during CPR it will usually happen within the first few minutes. If pulse and respirations are not forthcoming continue resuscitation efforts for a full 30 minutes.

If a recovery is successful a patient may still die from delayed respiratory distress and arrest due to developing pulmonary edema within 24 hours of the near drowning incident. The incidence of pulmonary edema increases with the amount of particulate matter dissolved or suspended in the water (salt, dirt, sand, chemicals, etc.). Delayed infection is also a potential respiratory complication that may result in the patient's death due to bacteria in the aspirated water; seawater has an extremely high bacteria count compared to clean freshwater.

Prevention

- Wear a life-jacket.
- Know how to swim (rapids, surf, open water, etc.). For organizations this means training both your guides and your clients.
- Prevent hypothermia through judgement, equipment choice, and calorie intake.
- Wear protective equipment to prevent accidental trauma (helmets, etc.).
- Be trained in rescue.
- Avoid alcohol and drugs.

Assessment

- If a traumatic MOI is present the patient's spine should be stabilized during both rescue and treatment.
- If patient is in respiratory arrest and has a pulse their chances of recovery are good.
- If patient is in both respiratory and cardiac arrest recovery with CPR is possible.
- Decreased water quality increases the chance for delayed pulmonary edema over the next 24 hours and subsequent respiratory infections.

Environmental

Field Treatment

- Begin immediate resuscitation efforts if documented immersion time is less than one hour.
- Immediately begin positive pressure ventilations if respirations are absent.
- **Begin CPR immediately (regardless of core temperature) if pulse is absent.** Consider stopping CPR after 30 minutes.
- If Trauma is a potential MOI immobilize the patient's spine or "Rule Out" depending upon the situation. Treat other injuries as usual.
- Monitor all near drowning patients for delayed respiratory distress over the next 24 hours.
- Continue to monitor all near drowning patients for 3-7 days for a secondary respiratory infection.
- **Evacuate with ALS to a major trauma center.**

Wilderness Toxins

General Pathophysiology

Although toxins may be introduced into the body through inhalation, absorption, injection, and ingestion, the common mechanisms for most wilderness toxins are bites and stings. Bites and stings may be further broken down according to the individual type: insects, mammals, marine life, and reptiles. Ingested toxins may be either plant or animal in nature. The most common inhaled toxin is smoke. Plant saps and "hairs" may produce skin irritations.

Toxins may effect any or all of the body's systems. Toxic reactions may roughly be broken down into hemotoxic, neurotoxic, and proteolytic effects. **Hemotoxins** target the circulatory system and may cause increased swelling by interfering with the clotting mechanism and destroying microvascular beds (anticoagulants, hemorrhagic factors), cardiac dysrhythmias or arrest by damaging the heart directly (cardiotoxic), or vascular shock by damaging the intravascular control mechanism (vasotoxic). **Neurotoxins** target the nervous system and may cause muscle spasms, tingling or paralysis, respiratory arrest, seizures, coma, headache, hypertension leading to stroke or cardiac arrest, anxiety, hallucinations, altered mental status, fever, and generalized weakness. **Proteolytic** (protein destroying) effects are primarily associated with bites or stings and usually limited to the destruction of local tissue. Dead tissue predisposes the injury site to infection. **Some toxins also cause an immediate or delayed allergic reaction.** In addition, many insects or animal bites transmit serious infections or diseases. If the type, time, and amount of toxin are unknown assessment and treatment are difficult.

Prevention

- Most insect bites and stings may be prevented by wearing protective clothing, shaking out all clothing and bedding before wearing or sleeping, wearing a repellent, and avoiding confrontation through habitat awareness. Insect repellents containing DEET are the most effective; however, concentrations of DEET greater than 35% are considered toxic to humans. Clothing and nets may be soaked in (or sprayed with) permethrin, an insect repellent specifically designed for that purpose; a single application is good for several weeks.
- Most mammal, marine life, and reptile bites and stings may be prevented by avoiding confrontation through habitat awareness.
- Avoid handling all poisonous or toxic plants and animals.
- Avoid ingesting unknown substances.

Assessment

General

- A specific history of the toxin detailing what, where, when, how much and the size/weight of the patient is necessary for treatments using specific antidotes or antivenin.
- When dealing with an incomplete history, follow the general treatment guidelines outlined below.
- All wounds associated with any bite or sting have a high potential for infection.
- *Monitor for anaphylaxis.*
- Depending upon the method of delivery, contracting an infectious disease is possible. Refer to the Infectious Disease Index in the Medical section.

Insect Bites and Stings

- Multiple unknown bites rule out most spider bites; spiders rarely bite more than once.
- Multiple stings from aggressive bees, yellow jackets, etc. may produce serious or fatal toxic reactions.
- Local burning pain and itching are common with all insect bites and stings.
- All blood sucking insects are potential vectors for the transmission of infectious diseases. Those associated with a high incidence of transmission are bites from fleas, mosquitoes, and ticks.
- Fleas are associated with the transmission of Bubonic Plague.
- Mosquitoes are associated with the transmission of Malaria, Yellow Fever, Encephalitis, and Dengue Fever.
- Ticks are associated with the transmission of Rocky Mountain Spotted Fever, Lyme disease, and Colorado Tick Fever.

Mammal Bites

- All mammal bites, especially those associated with dog bites, cat bites or scratches, and human bites, have a high potential for infection.
- Bites from bats, skunks, foxes, coyotes, raccoons, bobcats, and other carnivores are at high risk for rabies transmission. Bites from rodents (chipmunks, mice, rats, squirrels), rabbits, and domestic animals have a lower risk factor.
- All mammal bites and scratches are at risk for Tetanus and Diptheria.

Poisonous Snake and Reptile Bites

- *Crotalid envenomation (pit vipers: copperheads, rattlesnakes, cottonmouths)* is characterized by immediate local pain and swelling within 10-15 minutes; one third to one half of pit viper bites do not envenomate. The venom is usually hemotoxic with local proteolytic effects. Death is unusual and is confined to young children (under 30 pounds) and the elderly. Necrotic damage and subsequent infection can be severe.
- *Elapid envenomation (coral snakes, cobras, kraits, mambas, etc.)* is assumed to be present if bitten since local reactions are often minimal and most systemic reactions are delayed 3-4 hours. The primary reaction is neurotoxic. Death is possible, and in some cases likely, with untreated elapid envenomation.
- The bites of some *lizards (Gila Monster and the Mexican Beaded Lizard)* contain neuro and vasotoxins. Bites from these lizards are rare, painful, and not fatal.

Environmental

Absorbed Toxins

- *Saps and plant juices* may contain chemicals that act as skin irritants (buttercups, cortin plant, mustard seed plants, stinging nettles, wood nettles, etc.). Skin reactions are usually immediate following contact with the irritating plant.
- *Poison ivy, poison oak, and poison sumac* produce antigenic resins that cause delayed allergic reactions in 50% of the population.

Ingested Toxins

- The ingestion of *mushrooms and plants* may be fatal.
- The ingestion of *newts, salamanders, and toads* is usually fatal.
- *Food poisoning* usually follows ingestion of contaminated meats (often bought from street venders in hot third world countries).

Inhaled Toxins

- *Smoke* is the most common inhaled toxin in a wilderness environment. The more chemicals in the smoke the greater the damage it will do in the lungs.
- If respiratory distress is present it will often get worse during the next 24 hours as constriction increases in the lower airway and pulmonary edema develops.
- An increasing respiratory rate and difficulty breathing indicates respiratory distress. Wheezing usually indicates constriction in the lower airway; clear productive coughing, rales, and/or gurgles indicate developing pulmonary fluid. A bloody froth indicates severe damage to the patient's alveoli.

General Field Treatment

All Toxins:

- *Treat for Anaphylaxis if present.*
- Support critical systems.
- Remove and dilute all toxins by limiting their absorption (washing, activated charcoal, etc.) and enhancing elimination (fluids, oxygen, etc.) where appropriate.
- Treat signs and symptoms as they develop.
- Evacuate serious or potentially serious reactions with ALS to a major hospital.

Insect and Marine Animal Bites and Stings

- *Antivenin* is available for many specific toxins resulting from insect or marine animal bites or stings and is best given as soon as possible after envenomation. (Centruroides scorpion, black widow, sea snakes, Box Jellyfish) *Anaphylaxis and serum sickness are specific problems associated with the use of most antivenins and usually prohibit their use as a field treatment.* If a known antivenin is available the injury site should be immobilized with a splint and patient transported as soon as possible to the antivenin.
- Toxins are made up of proteins. *Local pain* may often be relieved by disassociating the protein using one of the following methods: *enzymes* (meat tenderizer) work well with bees, wasps, hornets, yellow jackets and scorpions; *a weak acid solution* (vinegar) works well with nematocyst stings (unfired nematocysts should be removed by scraping); *heat* (hot water soaks between

105 and 112 degrees F or 40.5 and 44.4 degrees C) works well with marine animal spiny injuries; **weak base solutions** (ammonia, baking soda) may work with red ants and other insect stings.
- OTC pain and anti-inflammatory medications: aspirin, ibuprofen, naproxen sodium may relieve pain associated with bites or stings.
- Calcium gluconate may help stop or prevent muscle spasms associated with some neurotoxins (Black Widow bites, etc.).
- Antihistamines may reduce the itching associated with insect and marine animal bites and stings.
- All wounds associated with insect and marine animal bites (whether immediate or delayed) are considered at high risk of infection and should be treated accordingly.

Mammal Bites

- All wounds associated with mammal bites are at high risk of infection and should be treated accordingly (See treatment for high risk wounds in Trauma section)
- All patients with mammal bites are at high risk for contracting Tetanus. If they have not had a Tetanus booster with in the past five years they **MUST** get a injection of tetanus toxoid promptly within the next 24 hours. Patients who have never completed a tetanus vaccine series (all 3 injections) **MUST** receive both the immune globulin and vaccine within 24 hours of the bite. *MANY PEOPLE WHO CONTRACT TETANUS DIE!*
- All patients suffering from animal bites are also at risk for contracting the Rabies virus and require a 5 shot treatment series including immune globulin and a vaccine. The first shot should be given within 72 hours of the bite. People who have been vaccinated against Rabies also need prompt treatment but only require a three shot series. *ALL PEOPLE INFECTED WITH THE RABIES VIRUS DIE!*

Poisonous Snake and Reptile Bites

- **Antivenin** is available for all poisonous snakes and is best given as soon as possible after envenomation. *Anaphylaxis and serum sickness are specific problems associated with the use of most antivenins and prohibit its use as a field treatment. If a known antivenin is available the injury site should be immobilized with a splint and patient transported as soon as possible to the antivenin.*
- Within the United States consult the Antivenin Index at the Arizona Poison Control Center for advice on antivenin and exotic snake envenomation. *(602-626-6016)*

Absorbed Toxins

- Remove contaminated clothing and flush the patient's skin with large amounts of water.
- Treat any wounds normally.
- Skin irritations from contact with poison ivy, oak, or sumac are due to delayed allergic reactions. Poison ivy, oak, and sumac are not considered toxins. See allergies for pathophysiology, assessment, and treatment.

Ingested Toxins

- If an **antidote** for an ingested poison is known the patient should be transported as soon as possible to the antidote. Contact a Poison Control Center.
- Increased fluid consumption and activated charcoal (1 ml per kg of patient's body weight) are recommended for alert patients with an ingested toxin. Both may cause vomiting.

Environmental

- Vomiting is rarely indicated but may be useful if the toxin has been ingested within 30 minutes, the toxin is not corrosive, and the patient is alert and cooperative. *Do not induce vomiting if the patient is drowsy or lethargic, voice responsive, pain responsive, or unresponsive.* To induce vomiting use 1-2 tablespoons of syrup of Ipecac and follow with 16 oz. of water. Vomiting will begin within 20 minutes and continue for 20-40 minutes.

Inhaled Toxins

- Remove the patient from the smoky (or toxic) environment. If respiratory distress is present (mild, moderate, or severe) the patient should be evacuated with ALS to a major hospital as soon as possible; delayed swelling and pulmonary edema are likely. Monitor and treat developing respiratory problems enroute.
- Reassure and calm the patient to slow their breathing rate.
- Place the patient in a comfortable position, usually sitting or semi-reclining, to facilitate their breathing.
- Administer oxygen during transport.
- Ventilate with positive pressure ventilations as needed. If the patient develops respiratory arrest during treatment, PPV may be inadequate to maintain life.

Allergic Reactions

Pathophysiology

Allergies are an abnormal response of the human immune system. While both local and systemic allergic reactions are common, systemic reactions are responsible for numerous patient deaths. Most of these deaths could have been avoided with prompt assessment and treatment. Allergies both develop and fade over time. Repeated contact with specific allergy causing agents (allergens) tends to sensitize people to that agent. A sensitized person produces antibodies to the specific allergen and positions them in localized tissue on mast cells or on circulating basophils. Both mast cells and basophils release histamine when stimulated. The introduction of the antigen causes an antigen/antibody reaction that stimulates either the stationary mast cells or circulating basophils to release histamine, producing either a local or systemic reaction respectively. Histamine is a vasodilator and leads to increased permeability and subsequent edema. The signs and symptoms of allergic responses are due to increased permeability and edema. A *local reaction* is characterized by severe local swelling that may become progressively worse during the next few hours. A *systemic reaction* (anaphylaxis) occurs when the antigen reaches the blood; the time varies with the delivery route (injection, ingestion, inhalation, absorption). Swelling associated with severe anaphylactic reactions produces a variety of signs and symptoms and may be life-threatening. The most common methods of delivery in a wilderness setting are injection (from insect bites and stings), ingestion, and absorption (poison ivy, oak, and sumac).

Prevention

- Immunotherapy may be helpful in eliminating serious allergies.
- People with known allergies should practice avoiding the responsible allergen.
- People with known allergies to poison ivy, oak, and sumac should carry and wash with Technu (or similar soap) any time they suspect contact. Washing must occur within 30 minutes of contact to prevent the development of a reaction.

- People with a past history of anaphylaxis should carry some form of injectable epinephrine and oral antihistamine on or near their person when exposure is possible.

Assessment

Local Allergic Reactions from Bites, Stings or Contact Allergens

- Local pain, itching, and swelling radiating from the site of the bite or sting.
- Contact allergens often produce localized dermatitis with itching, burning, and occasional blisters. The itching, burning, and blisters from poison ivy, poison oak, or poison sumac may appear within a few hours or be delayed for up to 72 hours.

Systemic Allergic Reactions (Anaphylaxis)

- Minimal or no local reaction occurs with most systemic reactions.
- Onset is dependant on the mechanism: Insect bites and stings may cause anaphylaxis within seconds or up to 20 minutes. Ingested allergens may cause anaphylaxis within a few minutes or up to 4 hours. Inhaled allergens often cause anaphylaxis within seconds. Anaphylaxis is rare with contact allergens.
- Itching, redness, and hives appear, usually near the groin, armpits, and flanks. The reaction is away from the site of the bite or sting. It may follow the ingestion or inhalation of an allergen.
- Nausea is common. Vomiting and diarrhea are possible.
- Respiratory distress may develop from the swelling and subsequent constriction of the upper airway and/or from bronchial constriction. Signs and symptoms of respiratory distress are: increased respiratory rate and difficulty breathing, wheezing, and changes in the patient's mental status. Respiratory distress may progress to respiratory arrest and death.
- Vascular shock may develop from progressive vasodilation and the patient is no longer able to maintain systemic perfusion; pulse and respiratory rates continue to rise followed by a drop in blood pressure and AVPU levels. Vascular shock may progress to cardiac arrest and death.

Field Treatment

Local Allergic Reactions from Bites Stings, or Contact Allergens

- For **mild local reactions** from bites, stings, or contact allergens administer an oral antihistamine until reaction subsides: 50-100 mg of diphenhydramine (Benadryl) every four to six hours.
- For **severe local reactions** from bites, stings, or contact allergens administer a Rx course of oral prednisone (corticosteroid) 60 mg the first four days, 40 mg the next four days, 20 mg the next four days, and 10 mg the last four days). [1,2]
- For contact allergens (poison ivy, poison oak, and poison sumac) wash the affected area with soap and water as soon as contact is suspected. The irritation is usually self-limiting and will heal once the toxic sap or juice has been removed. The resins are deposited upon contact with the plant and remain active for long periods of time. Consider washing the patient's entire body and anything that may have come into contact with the "poison" (clothing, gear, dogs, etc.). **The resin will bind with the skin within 30 minutes and washing will no longer be effective.** Technu is an effective soap specifically designed for poison ivy, oak, and sumac.

Environmental

- The sap from crushed flowers and stems from Jewelweed neutralizes any remaining toxin. Jewelweed often grows in close proximity to both poison ivy and oak.
- In addition to oral antihistamines, skin irritations from delayed allergic reactions due to contact with poison ivy, oak, or sumac may be treated with topical oat meal paste and calamine lotion.

Systemic Reactions (Anaphylaxis)

- When the mechanism is a bite, sting, or inhalation, treatment should begin at the first sign or symptom of a systemic allergic reaction (usually with red and itchy skin and/or the development of hives).
- Give 0.3 cc of epinephrine subcutaneously or intramuscularly (usually in the deltoid or the large muscles of the upper leg) followed by an oral antihistamine: 50-150 mg (estimate dose: 2 mg per kg of body weight) of diphenhydramine (Benadryl) every 4-6 hours for a 24 hour period.
- The pediatric dose of epinephrine is 0.15 cc. (for children 75 pounds or less).
- When the mechanism is a suspected ingestion of an possible allergen the oral antihistamine should be given and the patient monitored. Epinephrine should be administered immediately with the development of the first signs and symptoms of respiratory distress.
- The patient should be closely monitored and a second dose of epinephrine should be given if the signs and symptoms do not disappear within five minutes or if they reappear at any time. In rare cases additional doses may be required to reverse and control developing signs and symptoms.
- Consider evacuation if a limited amount of epinephrine is available and the possibility of re-exposure to the allergin exists. The patient will remain hypersensitive to the responsible allergen for an undetermined period of time.
- A general recovery period of 24-72 hours is usually required for all patients treated with epinephrine.

Acute Mountain Sickness

Pathophysiology

Acute Mountain Sickness (AMS) poses a serious threat to climbers around the world. As altitude increases the amount of available oxygen decreases until at 8,000 feet it is 25% less than at sea level and at 18,000 feet it is 50% less than at sea level. Unless there is pre-existing respiratory damage most altitude related problems occur above 8,000 feet. The body initially responds to decreasing oxygen levels by increasing both respiratory and pulse rates in an effort to maintain oxygen perfusion to its tissue. One of the functions of the respiratory system is to facilitate pH balance; if respiratory rates remain abnormally high for a prolonged period of time (usually 24-48 hours) the normally neutral blood pH becomes basic (alkalotic). The kidneys respond by dumping base (bicarbonate) into the urine. In most cases the kidneys take one to three days to balance blood pH. Full acclimation takes 2-3 weeks as red blood cell production and general metabolic efficiency increases.

If the kidney's attempt at balancing the blood pH fails, respirations cannot continue at a rate high enough to perfuse the body's tissue with oxygen (hypoxia). In response to the increasing cellular hypoxia and changing blood pH the microvascular bed in tissues throughout the body vasodilate. This systemic vasodilation causes edema to build within all body tissues. It is most noticeable in the swelling of the hands and feet, in the subsequent respiratory distress (from pulmonary edema), and in the subsequent increased ICP (from cerebral edema). The signs and symptoms

↑ in altitude = ↓ O₂ in tissue → ↑resp. → shift in pH
↑acid ↑kidney ↓resp.

Increase in altitude = ↓ Barometric pressure = lack of Pulmonary Pressure

of Acute Mountain Sickness are progressive and identical to those of increasing respiratory distress and increasing intracranial pressure. With the development of severe AMS death can occur within six hours.

Prevention

- **Slow ascent.** Allow the kidneys to maintain normal blood pH balance. Above 10,000 feet, ascend 1,000 to 3,000 feet per day with a rest day every 3,000 to 5,000 feet. This is a conservative pace that avoids High Altitude Pulmonary Edema (HAPE) and High Altitude Cerebral Edema (HACE) in most people by permitting the kidneys time to adapt to changing blood pH levels.
- Carry high, sleep low helps avoid sleep hypoxia.
- **Increase fluid intake** (including electrolytes) to maintain efficient kidney function.
- Avoid respiratory depressants (sleeping pills, alcohol, etc.).
- Restrict exercise levels during the first 24 hours at a new altitude to permit faster acclimation. Exercise increases oxygen demand.
- High carbohydrate diet facilitates acclimation; fats and proteins require more oxygen during the digestion process.
- Avoid smoking.
- Consider administering **acetazolamide (Rx)** to increase urinary excretion of bicarbonate thus aiding in the balance of blood pH. Increase fluid and electrolyte intake when using acetazolamide. Common adult dosage is 125-250 mg twice a day beginning on the day prior to ascent and continuing throughout the climb or until acclimatization is reached. **Acetazolamide is a sulfa drug and may cause allergic reactions in sensitized individuals.** [1]

Assessment

- **When assessing the severity of AMS it is important to remember that not all signs and symptoms may be present.**

Mild AMS

- Usually above 8,000 feet; onset is variable.
- Headache ("hangover" feeling).
- Increased respiratory rate with shortness of breath during exercise.
- Insomnia due to decreased respiratory drive and associated hypoxia while sleeping.
- Decreased appetite often accompanied by nausea.

Moderate AMS

- Usually occurs at new altitudes above 10,000 feet; onset is variable.
- Severe headache ("migraine").
- Episodes of vomiting are possible.
- Change in normal mental status to alert and irritable or alert and lethargic.
- Increased respiratory rate with shortness of breath during mild exertion.
- Rales or minor "crackling sounds" in the lungs.
- Increased fatigue.

Severe AMS: HACE/HAPE

- Usually occurs at new altitudes above 10,000 feet.
- Onset is variable; however, death may occur within 6 hours of developing signs and symptoms.

Environmental

- Severe headache ("migraine").
- Decrease in general coordination (ataxia).
- Lowered mental status to voice responsive, pain responsive, and unresponsive.
- Persistent vomiting.
- Increased respiratory rate with shortness of breath at rest.
- Respiratory distress with a productive cough, rales (crackling sounds), and/or gurgling.
- Extreme exhaustion.

Field Treatment

Mild AMS

- **Rest days** to allow kidneys to balance blood pH.
- Administer pain medications to reduce symptoms *during rest days*. OTC: aspirin, ibuprofen, naproxen sodium.
- Consider administering **acetazolamide (Rx)** to help increase acclimation process: adult dosage is 125-150 mg twice a day for up to 48 hours. *Acetazolamide is a sulfa drug and may cause allergic reactions in sensitized individuals.* [1]
- Increase fluids and electrolytes to **maintain hydration** status; monitor patient's urine.
- Diet high in carbohydrates; avoid proteins and fats.

Moderate AMS

- **Stop ascent.**
- **Consider 1,000 to 2,000 foot descent to relieve AMS and prevent possible progression to HACE/HAPE. Drug therapy is adjunctive in nature and does not substitute for descent.**
- Decrease and limit exercise.
- Consider administering supplemental oxygen.
- Consider using a Gamow Bag (a portable hyperbaric chamber) if descent is not immediately possible.
- Consider administering **acetazolamide (Rx)** orally: adult dosage is 125-250 mg twice a day for up to 48 hours. Increase fluids and electrolytes to maintain hydration status; monitor patient's urine. *Acetazolamide is a sulfa drug and may cause allergic reactions in sensitized individuals.* [1]
- As **adjunctive treatment** for HACE consider administering steroids as anti-edema medications if descent is not possible. **Rx: dexamethasone** adult dose 4 mg four times a day by mouth or intramuscular injection. [1]
- Administer pain medications to reduce symptoms during rest days. OTC: aspirin, ibuprofen, naproxen sodium.

Severe AMS: HACE/HAPE

- **Descend immediately 2,000 to 4,000 feet.** Carry or lower the patient in a litter. **Drug therapy is adjunctive in nature and does not substitute for descent.**
- Use supplemental oxygen if available *during descent.*
- Use a Gamow Bag (a portable hyperbaric chamber) if descent is not immediately possible.
- As **adjunctive treatment** for HAPE consider administering **Rx: nifedipine** 10 mg sublingual immediately and repeated as necessary (or 30 mg slow release every 12-24 hours). Nifedipine is a strong vasodilator that decreases pulmonary atrial pressure, vascular resistance, and edema. Continue until symptoms subside. [1]

- As *adjunctive treatment* for HACE consider administering steroids as anti-edema medications during descent. *Rx: dexamethasone* (adult dose) 4 mg four times a day by mouth or intramuscular injection until symptoms subside (usually within 12-24 hours); descent is still mandatory. [1]
- Support patient in sitting or semi-reclined position to help facilitate their breathing.
- Positive pressure ventilations may be helpful but difficult during an evacuation.

Scuba Diving Injuries
Ruptured Alveoli

Pathophysiology

As a diver descends, the increasing weight of the water above increases the pressure on the diver's body and respectively decreases the volume of air inside the alveoli (Boyle's Law). Conversely, as a diver ascends the water pressure is reduced and the air inside the alveoli expands.

SCUBA (Self Contained Underwater Breathing Apparatus) is necessary for a diver to breathe normally under water. SCUBA is compressed air contained within a steel tank. The regulator adjusts the pressure of the air delivered to a divers lungs during each breath permitting the diver to inflate their lungs normally regardless of the outside water pressure.

If a diver holds their breath while ascending they may rupture their alveoli as the air inside each sac expands. It takes very little pressure to rupture alveoli once the lungs are fully inflated; often only a few feet of ascent is all that is required. Tiny air bubbles may leak into the pulmonary capillaries, travel back to the heart, and enter general circulation. The bubbles may become lodged in small arteries anywhere in the diver's body, subsequently blocking blood and thus perfusion to that portion of the body. If the air bubble (*arterial gas embolism or AGE*) is in the brain the diver will present with the signs and symptoms of a stroke; if in their heart, they will present with the signs

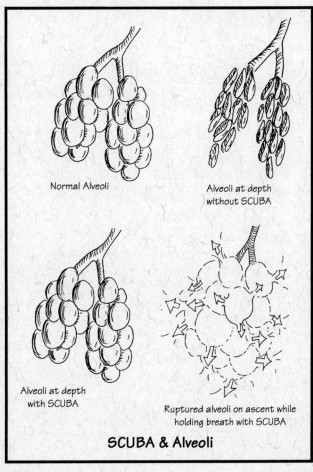

Normal Alveoli

Alveoli at depth without SCUBA

Alveoli at depth with SCUBA

Ruptured alveoli on ascent while holding breath with SCUBA

SCUBA & Alveoli

Environmental

and symptoms of a heart attack; if elsewhere in their body they will present with localized pain and a subsequent loss of function. AGE is a major cause of death in sport diving. Escaping air may also leak into the middle compartment of the chest cavity (mediastinal emphysema). If it exerts undue pressure on the heart, the diver may present with the signs and symptoms of a mild heart attack. Usually, it continues to leak through the surrounding muscles and emerge as small bubbles beneath the skin of the diver's chest and neck (subcutaneous emphysema). While *mediastinal and subcutaneous emphysema* are the most common result of alveoli ruptures and often resolve without invasive medical treatment the patient may, within a few hours, develop complications that do. Rarely air may leak between the lung and the chest wall causing a delamination of the pleura (collapsed lung, pneumothorax) and respiratory distress leading to arrest. *In a field setting, regardless of how the leaking air presents, the diver should be transported immediately with ALS for decompression in a hyperbaric chamber and adjunct medical care.*

Prevention

- Ascend slowly and breathe normally.
- Do not hold your breath while ascending with SCUBA.

Assessment

- The MOI is a rapid ascent while breath holding.
- Onset may occur while the diver is surfacing, upon surfacing, or within seconds to 10 minutes of surfacing.
- Signs and symptoms include: heart attack, stroke, respiratory distress, seizures, localized pain, air bubbles beneath the skin, and bloody froth at the mouth.

Field Treatment

- *The treatment goal is to support critical systems and evacuate with ALS to the closest decompression chamber. Early recognition and evacuation is essential to successful treatment.* Many cases initially present with mild signs and symptoms that progress into life-threatening conditions within a few hours.
- Within the United States call the Diving Alert Network (DAN) for the nearest decompression chamber: *1-919-684-8111 (24 hour emergency number).* DAN also maintains a non-emergency phone Monday through Friday, 9 AM-5 PM EST: 1-919-684-2948. Multi-place decompression chambers are preferred to mono-place chambers in the treatment of serious diving injuries because they permit medical help without decompressing the patient.
- Ideally a patient should not be flown unless the cabin is pressurized at sea level. Unpressurized aircraft (usually helicopters) must stay below 100 meters. Commercial aircraft are usually pressurized to 8,000 feet and should be avoided.
- *Place the patient in a neutral position on their back or on their left side.* A head down position will increase intracranial pressure while a head up position encourages the movement of air bubbles to the brain.
- Administer supplemental oxygen at high liter flow.
- Reassure alert patients.
- Positive pressure ventilations and chest compressions as necessary.
- *Evacuate with ALS to the closest decompression chamber as soon as possible; decompression is helpful even after long delays.*

SCUBA Diving Injuries
Nitrogen Narcosis

Pathophysiology

Normal air is a mixture of gases containing 21% oxygen, 78% nitrogen, and 1% other gases (including carbon dioxide). Oxygen is required for normal metabolism; rising carbon dioxide levels stimulate the respiratory center to begin a new breathing cycle; and, nitrogen at normal or slightly increased pressures remains inert. The percentage of gases in air remain the same while SCUBA diving (Dalton's Law) but the amount of gas dissolved in the blood increases as pressure increases (Henry's Law). This may become a problem when diving at depths near or greater than 100 feet using SCUBA with normal air; the problem becomes progressively worse with increased depth. As large amounts of nitrogen accumulate in the blood it begins to have a narcotic affect on the brain similar to alcohol intoxication. The sensation is generally pleasant and may affect the diver's judgement, leading to serious secondary problems; often the afflicted diver fails to recognize the developing condition and *recognition is dependent on an unimpaired diving partner.*

Prevention

- Avoid diving at depths near or greater than 100 feet while using SCUBA with compressed air. 130 feet is usually considered the maximum safe limit for experienced divers.
- Dive with a friend. Unaffected divers can easily recognize those that become impaired.
- A helium/oxygen mixture is safer than compressed air for deep dives. Although expensive it eliminates the problems associated with nitrogen.

Assessment

- The MOI is SCUBA diving at depths near or greater than 100 feet. *The results of nitrogen narcosis occur underwater.*
- Onset is within minutes at depth but varies with individuals.
- Diver's judgement becomes affected while using SCUBA with compressed air at depths near or greater than 100 feet. There is a change in normal mental status to alert and confused or alert and lethargic; the diver may develop bizarre behavior. It is common for an affected diver to forget to check their air supply, depth gauge, bottom time, etc. and a secondary life-threatening problem may develop.
- The condition deteriorates as the depth increases.

Field Treatment

- Reduce the pressure and the problem by ascending to shallow water; there are no after affects.

Environmental   100

SCUBA Diving Injuries
Decompression Sickness (The Bends)

Pathophysiology

When diving with SCUBA and compressed air, large amounts of nitrogen may become diffused into the diver's blood. Numerous factors increase the amount of nitrogen diffused into an individual diver's blood and tissue. Deep dives expose the diver to greater amounts of pressure and increase the nitrogen content proportionately. The longer the time a diver spends underwater the greater the accumulation of nitrogen. Exercise increases perfusion and gas solubility in both blood and tissues. If the nitrogen remains in solution it will diffuse back out of the blood and tissue through the diver's lungs as pressure is decreased "slowly." Nitrogen diffuses out of blood and tissue at roughly the same rate it entered; however, different tissues have different rates of absorption and the time required for nitrogen to come out of solution is dependent upon the specific type of tissue. More than 12 hours is required for nitrogen to diffuse out of fat. Residual nitrogen is the limiting factor for the number of deep dives within a 24 hour period; divers are predisposed to decompression sickness if too many deep dives are taken within that time frame. When a diver exercises at depth and then ascends without exercise the rate of diffusion is slower during ascent than descent (because of the lack of exercise during ascent), and the diver is predisposed to decompression sickness. This is the reason for stage decompression. When an ascent is too rapid to permit the nitrogen to be diffused and expelled during normal exhalation the diver's blood will become supersaturated with nitrogen and decompression sickness will occur. If a diver travels in an unpressurized aircraft within 24 hours after surfacing nitrogen bubbles may also form.

Once a diver's blood becomes supersaturated, the nitrogen will come out of solution as small bubbles in the bloodstream. Since the bubbles are too big to move across the membranes into the alveoli and be removed during exhalation, they travel through the circulatory system until they become lodged in small arteries or capillaries. Once a vessel is blocked, perfusion is cut off to all the tissue supplied by that vessel. The presence of nitrogen bubbles within the microvascular bed may activate the clotting process, causing permanent obstruction. *Minor cases* of decompression sickness cause fatigue, itching or burning skin, local discomfort, and pain. *Severe cases* involving vessels in the brain, the spinal cord, and the lungs may cause death. Signs and symptoms of serious decompression sickness are those of stroke, spinal cord injuries, and respiratory distress respectively. *It may be impossible to tell the difference between severe decompression sickness and the problems associated with ruptured alveoli.* The diver presenting with minor decompression sickness may, within a few hours, develop life-threatening problems. *Regardless of how decompression sickness presents the diver needs immediate decompression in a hyperbaric chamber* to force the nitrogen bubbles back into solution and reestablish perfusion to the effected areas before clotting problems develop. Adjunct medical care may be necessary before, during, and after decompression.

Prevention

• Avoid dives that require stage decompression.
• Plan dives according to the U.S. Navy diving tables and be conservative.

- Know how to convert the dive tables for high altitude diving.
- Avoid ascending at a rate greater than 60 feet per minute (1 foot per second).
- Avoid flying in unpressurized aircraft within 24 hours after a dive; allow surface time to fully decompress.
- Anyone with cardiovascular disease is predisposed to decompression sickness.
- Avoid smoking.
- Divers who have undergone minor decompression therapy should not dive for a minimum of 1-2 months following the therapy. Those who have undergone treatment for serious decompression sickness should not dive for 4-6 months. *Divers should not dive again if they have undergone repeated treatments for serious decompression sickness.*

Assessment

- The MOI is a rapid ascent.
- Onset is variable upon surfacing: 50% of cases occur immediately or within the first 30 minutes; 85% of cases occur within one hour; 95% of cases occur within three hours; and, **99% of cases occur within six hours.**
- Signs and symptoms include: heart attack, stroke, respiratory distress, localized pain, and/or paralysis; seizures and coma are possible.
- Minor, and often early, signs and symptoms that indicate the formation of nitrogen bubbles that may lead to life-threatening problems are: unusual fatigue; itching, burning, or mottled skin; deep aches or pain in the joints of the shoulder, elbow, or knees.

Field Treatment

- The goal is to support critical systems and *evacuate with ALS to the closest decompression chamber.* Early recognition and evacuation is essential to successful treatment. Many cases initially present with mild signs and symptoms that progress into life-threatening conditions within a few hours.
- Within the United States call the Diving Alert Network (DAN) for the nearest decompression chamber: *1-919-684-8111 (24 hour emergency number).* DAN also maintains a non-emergency phone Monday through Friday, 9 AM-5 PM EST: 1-919-684-2948. Multi-place decompression chambers are preferred to mono-place chambers in the treatment of serious diving injuries because they permit medical help without decompressing the patient.
- Ideally a patient should not be flown unless the cabin is pressurized to sea level. Unpressurized aircraft (usually helicopters) must stay below 100 meters. Commercial aircraft are usually pressurized to 8,000 feet and should be avoided.
- *Place the patient in a neutral position on their back or on their left side.* A head down position will increase intracranial pressure while a head up position encourages the movement of nitrogen bubbles to the brain.
- Administering 100% supplemental oxygen via a non-rebreathing face mask increases the gas gradient and rate of nitrogen excretion.
- Reassure alert patients and administer oral fluids, one liter within the first hour. IV fluids are preferred and required with voice responsive, pain responsive, and unresponsive patients. Increasing the patients's fluid volume increases the absorption of nitrogen bubbles.
- Administer aspirin (650 mg) to decrease the formation of intravascular clots. Chewable baby aspirin is absorbed faster than regular aspirin.

Environmental   102

- Positive pressure ventilations and chest compressions as necessary.
- *Evacuate with ALS to the closest decompression chamber as soon as possible; decompression is helpful even after long delays.*

SCUBA Diving/Free Diving Injuries
Pressure Imbalance (Squeeze)

Pathophysiology

Pressure increases as a diver descends; volume decreases. If the object surrounding the air is flexible, like a balloon (or alveoli), it shrinks as the air volume decreases. If the object is solid, like a ping pong ball (or sinus cavities, inner ear, etc.) it collapses as the air volume decreases. If pressure within the cavity can be equalized the cavity will not collapse. Most of the body cavities that contain air are either flexible (alveoli) and do not require equalization or have connecting tubes (inner ear, sinuses) that, with training, permit the pressure to be equalized. One exception is the teeth; if a filling is poorly packed there may be a small air cavity that causes pain and limits descent. Another unusual exception is when changing pressures cause temporary intestinal pain due to gas formation from partially digested or gas producing foods (beans, tofu, etc.). "Squeeze" problems are more common during descent. If the diver has a cold, allergy, flu, or sinus infection that causes swelling in the eustachian tubes or sinus passages equalization may be difficult or impossible. Local decongestants while offering short term relief may cause problems during ascent as they wear off. Eye squeeze is possible if the goggles worn do not permit equalization (exhaling through the nose into the air space).

Prevention

- Avoid diving (free diving and SCUBA) while congested from a cold, flu, allergy, sinus infection, or inner ear infection.
- Descend and ascend slowly allowing time for equalization.
- Avoid gas producing foods prior to diving.
- Do not wear goggles or ear plugs while diving.

Assessment

- The MOI is increased pressure on closed air spaces; onset is immediate.
- Immediate pain in the affected area usually while descending.
- Severe pain in the ear followed by a full feeling, dizziness, and/or disorientation indicates a ruptured ear drum.
- Severe vertigo (whirling dizziness and disorientation) followed by tinnitus (high pitched whining or ringing) or hearing loss indicates inner ear damage. Vertigo may be accompanied by nausea.
- Severe pain behind the forehead, eyes, or nose accompanied by a nose bleed indicates a rupture in the sinus lining.
- Intestinal pains due to gas are usually self-limiting and of short duration.

Field Treatment

- Upon experiencing "Squeeze" a diver should immediately stop their descent (or ascent) and attempt to equalize the pressure. If successful they should continue at a slower pace. If unsuccessful they should surface slowly.
- Injuries associated with "Squeeze" are treated as usual according to the type of injury.
- Patients suffering from ruptured ear drums who were diving in contaminated water may require systemic antibiotics to treat a subsequent infection.
- Persistent dizziness or vertigo may be relieved by administering systemic decongestants.

Free Diving Injuries
Shallow Water Blackout

Pathophysiology

Rising levels of carbon dioxide within the blood stimulate the respiratory center in the brain to begin a breathing cycle. During the cycle, carbon dioxide is exhaled and oxygen is inhaled. This causes a decrease in blood levels of carbon dioxide as oxygen levels rise. Oxygen is consumed during cellular metabolism and carbon dioxide is formed; rising carbon dioxide levels eventually stimulate the respiratory center and initiate another breathing cycle. Skin divers hold their breath to explore the underwater world when diving. Breath-holding interrupts the normal breathing cycle by limiting the oxygen uptake and permitting carbon dioxide levels to rise above normal. Eventually, before the diver runs out of oxygen, the respiratory center forces her to surface for a breath. If the diver hyperventilates before diving and succeeds in lowering her carbon dioxide level below normal, she will be able to hold her breath longer because her respiratory drive takes longer to stimulate. *BUT* the diver may run out of oxygen and loose consciousness before she surfaces to breathe because of her depressed respiratory drive. If this happens and she is not quickly rescued she will drown.

Prevention

- *Avoid hyperventilation prior to free diving.* A few deep breaths are acceptable to clear the lungs.

Assessment

- History of hyperventilation prior to diving.
- Free diver looses consciousness while diving and needs to be rescued.

Field Treatment

- Positive pressure ventilations (rescue breathing) and chest compressions as needed.
- Treat for near drowning and monitor for developing pulmonary edema over the following 24 hours. Consider evacuation.

Environmental   104

Notes

Major Signs, Symptoms, & History	Possible Problems	Page
• Altered mental status (A & disoriented, may appear drunk, V, P, or U) • History of diabetes	Hypoglycemia	136
• Altered mental status • Speech impairment and/or paralysis	Stroke	132
• Altered mental status • Clear copious urine • History of ingesting no food and lots of water • With or without nausea, vomiting, or diarrhea	Electrolyte Sickness	82
• Decreased mental & physical performance • Headache • Dark, concentrated urine • History of not balancing water intake with loss • With or without nausea or vomiting	Dehydration	81
• Seizures	Epilepsy & Other Causes	139
• Non-trumatic/non-tender chest pain	Heart Attack	133
• Acute respiratory distress	Asthma	138
	Infectious Disease	111
• Cold or flu signs and symptoms	Lower Respiratory Infection Throat Infection Sinus Infections	140
	Infectious Disease	111
• Abdominal pain • With or without nausea and/or vomiting	Gastrointestional Problems Genitourinary Problems	148 151
	Infectious Disease	111

Major Signs, Symptoms, & History	Possible Problems	Page
• Pain with urination (male)	Chlamydia Gonorrhea	151
• Pain with urination (female)	Vaginitis Urinary Tract Infection	151
• Vaginal itching or irritation	Vaginitis	151
• Vaginal bleeding	Miscarriage Ectopic pregnancy	151
• Ear pain	External ear infection Internal ear infection Ruptured ear drum	143
• Tooth and/or gum pain	Broken, damaged, or lost teeth Infection	147
• Eye irritation or pain	Non-specific Irritation Foreign Body Coreanal Abrasion Infection	145
	Infectious Disease	111
• Skin rash	Infectious Disease	111
	Environmental Problem: • Heat rash • Sun poisoning • Allergic reaction	77

General Information	Page
Infectious Disease Index	111
Drug Theory	154
Drug Table Index	154
Drug Tables	155–160
Herbal Theory	161
Herb Tables	162–165

Infectious Diseases

General Information

The following information on infectious diseases is offered to help you understand the importance and methodology of prevention. Pathophysiology of the disease is offered because definitive diagnosis often hinges upon a complete understanding of a patient's potential contact history, and that usually hinges upon your understanding of the disease. *UNLESS STATED OTHERWISE, THERE ARE NO EFFECTIVE FIELD TREATMENTS FOR THE INFECTIOUS DISEASES DISCUSSED IN THIS FIELD MANUAL.* Patients exhibiting the signs and symptoms of any infectious disease should be evacuated to the nearest medical facility. Specific treatments for adults are included for two reasons: first, to help you understand the significance of the disease and second, to assist with its treatment when hospital or clinic care is limited or not available. *TREATMENTS FOR CHILDREN AND PREGNANT WOMEN OFTEN DIFFER FROM THE NORMAL ADULT TREATMENTS AND ARE NOT INCLUDED IN THIS FIELD MANUAL.* Current treatment guidelines are available from the Centers for Disease Control in Atlanta, GA; phone **404-332-4555**.

The following general information together with the section on General Drug Theory (page 154) should be read and understood before referring to the index and a specific disease.

General Transmission

Most infectious diseases are caused by microbes (viruses, bacteria, protozoans, amoebas, etc.). They are transmitted through direct contact with the microorganism and through animal or insect vectors.

Patient's Body Fluids

Many infectious diseases are transmitted through direct contact with an infected patient's blood, mucus, genital secretions, saliva, feces, urine, sputum, and respiratory droplets. Prevention is possible by avoiding contact with "wet and slippery" body fluids. *Latex or nitrile gloves, masks, glasses, and clothing may act as a physical barrier and offer protection.* Latex surgical or exam gloves may be effectively carried in a wilderness setting by storing a pair inside a film canister. You should carry multiple pairs of gloves (and film canisters). Alernatively, you may use blue nitrile hazardous material gloves. They are significantly stronger than latex gloves and more appropriate to heavy field use. Hazardous material gloves may also be stored in film canisters one glove per canister. *Washing your body and clothing immediately after exposure with soap and water greatly reduces your risk.* Dispose of contaminated materials in a sealed and clearly marked container.

Animal Vectors

Animal bites may transfer disease. Rabies, tetanus, and plague are common examples. *Avoidance is protection*; become familiar with specific animal habitat and behaviors. Once bitten the wound should be thoroughly flushed with water and povidone-iodine. Thorough wound cleansing significantly reduces the risk of transmission.

Medical

Insect Vectors

Insect bites may also transmit disease. Common carriers are fleas, mosquitos, and ticks. Protection can be obtained by wearing **protective clothing** and **insect repellent** containing DEET. DEET is considered toxic in concentrations greater than 35%. A single application lasts about 4-6 hours. Clothing and nets may be soaked in (or sprayed with) permethrin, an insect repellent specifically designed for that purpose. A single application is good for several weeks.

Contaminated Water

Water-borne transmission of disease is both common and easily avoidable by one of the following treatment methods or a combination:

- **Filtering:** Allow dirty water to stand overnight to permit settling of particulate matter (sand, dirt, etc.) then pre-filter to prevent clogging of water filter. Clean bandanas, cheese cloth, coffee filters, etc. can be used for pre-filtering. Ceramic filters can be cleaned; most charcoal filters are disposable. A filter size of .2 microns effectively removes parasites, protozoans, and bacteria. *Viruses are not removed by filtration*.
- **Iodine:** Iodine is the most stable and effective of the chemical purification methods. A 2% tincture (alcohol solution) is the least subject to potency changes upon opening. The dose is 5 measured drops per liter followed by a 30 minute waiting period. The time is doubled for cold water. Dirty water may be pre-filtered and then treated as above or treated directly by doubling the dose. Treatment with iodine effectively kills all water borne organisms.
- **Boiling:** Boiling for 10 minutes plus an additional minute for each 1000 feet of elevation will completely sterilize contaminated water. Bringing water to a rolling boil, regardless of altitude, effectively kills all disease carrying organisms. Boiling does not kill spores but spores do not carry water borne diseases. Boiling does not remove minerals or debris; pre-filter dirty water to remove most particulate matter. Taste may be improved by pouring the treated water back and forth between two containers to aerate.

Contaminated Food

The Center for Disease Control (CDC) recommends that any **raw food** found in areas of poor sanitation should be assumed to be contaminated. Salads, uncooked vegetables and fruit, unpasteurized milk and milk products, raw meat and shellfish are considered high risk. Raw food that has been thoroughly washed with soap and rinsed in potable water, peeled vegetables and fruit, and food that is still hot is considered reasonably safe. **Tropical fish** should not be considered safe even when cooked because of the presence of toxins in their flesh. **Ice** made from contaminated water will also transmit disease.

Vaccinations

Effective vaccinations are available for many infectious diseases. Some are required for foreign travel or travel into endemic areas. The Centers for Disease Control and Prevention (CDC) located in Atlanta, Georgia maintain a Disease Hotline that provides current information on world wide infectious disease via phone or **FAX: 404-332-4555**. Since many immunizations require multiple doses over a potentially lengthy period of time and planning is necessary, complete your research as early as possible.

When vaccines are not available, preventive drug therapy is occasionally effective. The CDC also provides this information.

General Assessment

- Most infectious diseases have an *incubation period* of days to weeks before the onset of signs and symptoms.
- Most initial signs and symptoms are generic and *flu-like*.
- Severe AVPU changes usually indicate a severe infection and a poor prognosis.
- Specific diagnosis usually requires a blood serum test for antibodies or a culture and a detailed history of exposure.

General Treatment

In addition to specific treatments listed on the following pages:
- Provide bed rest and assist thermoregulation.
- Replace and force *fluids* and electrolytes. Monitor the patient's urine.
- *Herbs* that stimulate the immune system and have strong antimicrobial properties include: echinacea/golden seal in combination, ginseng/astragalus in combination, and hyssop.
- In most cases *vomiting* is self-limiting and should be permitted to run its course. Control persistent vomiting (greater than 12 hours) with promethazine (adults only). Oral dose 25 mg every 6-8 hours. Suppository: 12.5-25 mg every 12 hours. Alternately, 50 mg of diphenhydramine (Benadryl) may be given every six hours for 4 doses.
- In most cases *diarrhea* is self-limiting and should be permitted to run its course. Mild diarrhea may be controlled with teas made from five finger grass or the inner bark of slippery elm. Diarrhea should be controlled when you cannot maintain the patient's hydration status or it becomes persistent (greater than 24 hours). Control severe diarrhea with loperamide (Imodium): adult dose is 4-8 mg per day not to exceed 16 mg within a 24 hour period. Begin with the lowest dosage possible and repeat after each loose bowel movement. Constipation and abdominal cramps are possible.
- 50 mg of diphenhydramine (Benadryl) may be used every six hours to provide relief from the itching associated with *rashes*.
- *Fevers* above 102 degrees F may are best controlled with acetaminophen using the OTC dose. Yarrow tea is a strong fever reducing (antipyretic) herb.
- *Evacuate all patients suspected of contracting an infectious disease to a major hospital.*

Medical

Major Signs & Symptoms	Possible Disease	Tranmission Route	Page
• Acute respiratory distress	Hantavirus Pulmonary Syndrome	aerosolized rodent urine & feces	118
	Plague	flea bite	119
• Cold or flu signs & symptoms	Colorado Tick Fever	tick bite	126
	Dengue Fever	mosquito bite	123
	Diptheria	body fluids	113
	Japanese Encephalitis	mosquito bite	122
	Leptospirosis	swimming in contaminated H_2O	117
	Lyme Disease	tick bite	125
	Malaria	mosquito bite	120
	Meningococcal Meningitis	body fluids	113
	Rocky Mountain Spotted Fever	tick bite	124
	Plague	flea bite	119
	Yellow Fever	mosquito bite	121
	Typhoid Fever	ingestion of contaminated food/H_2O	130
• Abdominal pain • With or without nausea & vomiting	Bacterial Dysentery	ingestion of contaminated food/H_2O	128
	Cholera	ingestion of contaminated food/H_2O	127
	Giardia	ingestion of contaminated H_2O	131
	Hepatitis A	ingestion of contaminated food/H_2O	129
	Hepatitis B	body fluids	114
	Typhoid Fever	ingestion of contaminated food/H_2O	130
• Eye irritation or pain	Colorado Tick Fever	tick bite	126
	Dengue Fever	mosquito bite	123
	Leptospirosis	swimming in contaminated H_2O	117
• Skin rash	Dengue Fever	mosquito bite	123
	Hepatitis A	ingestion of contaminated food/H_2O	129
	Hepatitis B	body fluids	114
	Lyme Disese	tick bite	125
	Rocky Mountain Spotted Fever	tick bite	124
	Typhoid Fever	ingestion of contaminated food/H_2O	130

Infectious Disease Index by Transmission Route

Method of Transmission	Possible Disease	Page
Body Fluids	Meningococcal Meningitis	113
	Diptheria	113
	Hepatitis B	114
	Bacterial Dysentery	128
Animal Bites	Rabies	115
	Tetanus	116
Deep Wounds	Tetanus	116
Swimming in Contaminated Water Contact with Infected Urine & Feces	Leptospirosis	117
Aerosolized Rodent Urine & Feces	Hantavirus Pulmonary Syndrome	118
Flea Bites	Plague	119
Mosquito Bites	Malaria	120
	Yellow Fever	121
	Japanese Encephalitis	122
	Dengue Fever	123
Tick Bites	Rocky Mountain Spotted Fever	124
	Lyme Disease	125
	Colorado Tick Fever	126
Ingestion of Contaminated Water (including ice)	Cholera	127
	Bacterial Dysentery	128
	Hepatitis A	129
	Typhoid Fever	130
	Giardia	131
Ingestion of Contaminated Food	Cholera	127
	Bacterial Dysentery	128
	Hepatitis A	129
	Typhoid Fever	130

Meningococcal Meningitis

Pathophysiology

Meningococcal Meningitis is an *infection of the lining of the brain or spinal cord and can result from exposure to infectious bacteria*. Outbreaks of the disease have occurred in sub-Saharan Africa, India, Nepal, and China. Close contact to an infected patient is required to spread the disease since *primary transmission is by respiratory droplets*; 5-10% of the people infected are asymptomatic carriers. The disease moves from the respiratory system into the blood and from there to the central nervous system. The bacteria may cause septic shock, meningitis, or pneumonia.

Prevention

- **Vaccination:** one dose and a waiting period of 10-14 days; the vaccine is effective for one year.
- Avoid epidemic areas.
- Persons in close contact with the disease should receive oral prophylaxis: rifampin, adult dose is 600 mg twice a day for two days. [4]

Assessment

- *History of exposure to the respiratory droplets of an infected person within the last ten days.*
- Symptoms include a severe headache, nausea, vomiting, light sensitivity, fever, general weakness, and altered mental status.
- Patients often present with a stiff neck and complain of extreme pain when their chin is flexed toward their chest.
- Definitive assessment requires a positive culture from the patient's cerebrospinal fluid.

Treatment

- Treatment of choice is a 7-10 day course of penicillin G; IV adult dose is 300,000 units/kg/day given in divided doses every two hours (maximum dose is 24,000,000 units per day). Strains resistant to penicillin have been reported in both Africa and Spain. [1]
- For patients allergic to penicillin: 2 grams of ceftriaxone IM (adult dose) two times a day for 7-10 days. [1] Note: ceftriaxone treats all forms of bacterial meingitis.
- Immediately following the initial antibiotic course, rifampin is given to prevent relapse: adult dose is 600 mg twice a day for two days. [6]
- *Relapse* requires retreatment; consider alternative drug therapy.
- *Problems* associated with the treatment of the disease often require the invasive procedures available only to intensive care units.

Diptheria

Pathophysiology

Humans are a natural host for the *bacteria* that cause Diptheria. While transmission can occur from direct contact with infected persons, it usually occurs from *contact with people who have been previously infected or immunized* and have become asymptomatic carriers. There is a risk of Diptheria in the countries of the former Soviet Union and central Asia. The disease takes two forms. The most serious is associated with a respiratory tract infection and transmission occurs from contact with respiratory secretions. The disease may progress to include swelling of the pharynx and severe respiratory tract damage. In addition, the toxin directly injures the patient's heart and brain often causing congestive heart failure and paralysis. A second form associated with skin lesions is commonly seen in the tropics and is rarely fatal. Prevention is easier and more successful than treatment.

Prevention

- All persons should be immunized against the Diptheria toxin.
- *Vaccination* (usually includes tetanus vaccination) is available in three doses over 6-12 months. A booster is required every 10 years for persons at low risk and every 5 years for persons at high risk. Anyone working or playing in the outdoors is at high risk.
- Unimmunized persons who come into close contact with the respiratory form of the disease should receive the entire vaccine series and a 7-10 day oral course of erythromycin dosed at 1 gm per day. [3]
- Those who are immunized but who have not had a booster within the past 5 years should receive a booster as soon as possible.

Assessment

- *History of exposure to infected patients within the past week.*
- Initial signs and symptoms are nonspecific and flu-like. Symptoms include a sore throat, low grade fever, general muscle soreness, and fatigue.
- Definitive diagnosis is obtained through culturing.

Treatment

- An antitoxin is available. It is made from horse serum and associated with anaphylaxis. The antitoxin is given as a single IM dose 20,000-100,000 units depending on the duration and severity. [3]
- Additional treatment includes antibiotic therapy to destroy the bacteria and respiratory support. Antibiotics of choice are procaine penicillin G (PPG) *or* erythromycin. PPG is dosed IM at 1.2 million units per day in two divided doses <u>or</u> erythromycin dosed at 40-50 mg/kg/day until patient can swallow; then, oral penicillin VK dosed at 125-250 mg four times a day or oral erythromycin dosed at 250-500 mg four times a day for a total treatment of 14 days. [3]

Hepatitis B

Pathophysiology

Hepatitis B is a *viral disease transmitted through contact with the body fluids of infected persons* (especially blood and semen); it is a serious disease and easily prevented. 10% of the adults (and 90% of the infants) who survive the disease are carriers. In third world and developing countries 20% of the total population may be chronic carriers. Although this virus replicates in the liver and destroys liver cells, it is unrelated to the Hepatitis A virus. The disease is usually self-limiting within 4-6 weeks with a complete recovery after six months. The majority of patients recover completely, many become asymptomatic chronic carriers, and some develop chronic persistent hepatitis or chronic active hepatitis; very few die. Those that develop chronic active hepatitis develop progressive signs and symptoms and eventually die from cirrhosis of their liver.

Prevention

- All persons should be vaccinated against Hepatitis B.
- Avoid contamination through contact with body fluids.
- *Vaccination:* 3 injections given initially, at one month, and at six months.

Assessment

- *History of exposure to body fluids of a potentially infected person within the last six months.*
- The development of a rash, joint pain, arthritis, and fever is initially present in 20% of Hepatitis B patients.
- Loss of appetite, nausea, vomiting, abdominal pain, and fever soon follow.
- Enlargement of the spleen and liver usually accompanies the later signs and symptoms.
- Jaundice usually appears a short time after the onset of gastrointestinal symptoms.
- Definitive assessment is possible with a positive blood test for the Hepatitis B antigen.

Treatment

- Because the infection is viral, *treatment is supportive* in nature and focused on relieving the patient's signs and symptoms.

Rabies

Pathophysiology

Rabies is a *viral disease found in the saliva of infected animals and transmitted by their bite. The disease is possible in all mammals.* Common carriers are foxes, skunks, raccoons, bats, coyotes, cats, dogs, weasels, mongooses, wolves, and jackals. Rodents are unlikely carriers. Rabies may be also transmitted by inhalation in bat infested caves where there is a high concentration of bat guano and urine.

Once in the body it travels to the central nervous system via the peripheral nerves at an estimated rate of 3 mm per hour. The average incubation period is 20-60 days; although, a range from 9 days to 1 year has been documented. The virus establishes itself within the brain, multiplies, then spreads throughout the entire body. The progression of the disease produces one of two distinctive forms, either furious or paralytic rabies. The signs and symptoms of furious rabies include hyperactivity, aggressive behavior, and seizures alternating with calm periods. Persons infected with furious rabies may develop hallucinations, pharyngeal spasms, and excessive salivation ("foaming at the mouth"). They may also bite. With paralytic rabies the person becomes progressively uncoordinated and lethargic. Eventually *all people infected with the rabies virus die.* There is *no effective treatment* and attention is focused on prevention.

Prevention

- **Pre-exposure vaccination** is available and recommended for those traveling in endemic areas, countries with large dog populations, and those with a high risk of exposure. The vaccination is given in 3 doses over a 21 day period. Post exposure treatment is still required. Booster doses are given based on current antibody levels.
- Thorough **post-exposure wound cleaning** with soap and water and/or povidone-iodine may destroy the rabies virus and prevent infection.
- **Post-exposure vaccine** is given to all persons suspected of contracting the rabies virus (including those with Pre-exposure vaccination). The dose is given in the deltoid muscle to avoid to avoid absorption in local fatty tissue. Unimmunized persons should receive five 1.0 ml IM doses with the first dose on the day of exposure (day 0). Subsequent doses are given on days 3, 7, 14, and 28. Previously immunized persons should receive two 1.0 ml doses on days 0 and 3. Patients with severe head bites should receive a third dose on day 7.
- In addition to the post-exposure vaccine, **Post-exposure immune globulin** (HRIG) is given to all previously unimmunized persons suspected of contracting the rabies virus. It must be given at a different site than the vaccine to prevent neutralization of both the vaccine and the immune globulin. HRIG is dosed at 20 International Units (IU)/kg. Half the dose is infused into the wound site and the remaining half is given by IM injection. [3]

Assessment

- *History of exposure to the saliva of a potentially infected animal or inhalation of aerosolized bat urine. The incubation period varies greatly in humans ranging from 9 days to 1 year and averaging 20-60 days in most cases.*
- Assessment is focused on the type of bite and the behavior of the animal. Aggressive or unusual animal behavior increases the risk. *If the animal is suspected of carrying rabies post-exposure prophylaxis should begin immediately.*

Treatment

- There is **no effective treatment** for the rabies virus. Attention is focused on prevention. All persons suspected of exposure to rabies should begin prophylactic treatment within 72 hours. With the onset of signs and symptoms the disease is fatal.

Tetanus

Pathophysiology

Tetanus is *caused by a toxin produced by an anaerobic bacteria and is usually introduced via deep lacerations, puncture wounds, and animal bites.* The toxin travels to the central nervous system via the blood. Once established in the CNS, it interferes with normal muscle innervation and causes uncontrolled muscle spasms. The muscle groups surrounding the jaw are often the first to be effected; hence, the term "lockjaw." All muscles eventually become affected including the smooth muscle of the heart and vessels. Death is usually caused by a prolonged spasm of the intercostal muscles and diaphragm leading to respiratory arrest. Left untreated the disease has a 90% mortality rate among infants and 40% in adults. While treatment is possible prevention is much easier.

Prevention

- **All persons should be immunized against the tetanus toxin.**
- **Vaccination** (usually includes Diptheria vaccination) is available in 3 doses over 6-12 months. A booster is required every 10 years for persons at low risk and every 5 years for persons at high risk. Anyone who lives, works, or plays in the outdoors is at high risk.
- Thorough **wound cleaning** is essential for tetanus prevention.
- **Unimmunized persons with tetanus prone wounds** should receive a shot containing tetanus immune globulin (TIG) and begin the vaccination series within 24 hours of the incident.
- Those who are immunized but who have not had a **booster** within the past 5 years should receive a booster within 24 hours of the incident.

Assessment

- All persons with **deep lacerations, puncture wounds, and animal bites** are at risk for tetanus.
- There is **no test available** to confirm a diagnosis of tetanus.

Treatment

- **Field treatment** is limited to thorough wound cleaning and evacuation to a hospital or clinic.
- Specific treatment for tetanus includes surgical removal of infected tissue, 3,000-6,000 International Units (IU) of the immune globulin IM 3, antibiotic therapy, and respiratory support. The antibiotic of choice is metronidazole delivered IV at 500 mg every six hours for 7-10 days. [4]

Leptospirosis

Pathophysiology

Leptospirosis is **caused by a group of bacteria (spirochetes) with over 200 identified strains.** Cases range from asymptomatic or mild in areas where infections are endemic to severe depending upon the individual strain. Except for polar regions, leptospirosis is present worldwide and considered a hazard to all people active in the outdoors. It is transmitted through the urine and feces of infected animals usually via contaminated water. Carrier hosts include both domestic and wild animals. Common carriers are dogs, rats, swine, and cattle. **Humans are usually infected by wading or swimming in water (or mud) contaminated by the urine of infected animals.** Although the disease is more common in catchment water the bacteria may be present in clear streams. The spirochetes routinely enter through the victim's skin or mucus membranes. Abraded or cut skin increases the risk of transmission. Less common routes of transmission are ingestion or direct contact with an infected animal's urine, feces, or tissue.

The infection has two phases that begin after an incubation period that usually ranges from 7-12 days but may be as long as four weeks. During the initial phase, the infecting spirochetes may be cultured from the patient's blood or cerebrospinal fluid. The second phase begins after a short remission of one or two days. Fatalities are possible and usually due to liver or kidney failure. During the second phase the organisms are no longer present in the patient's blood or CSF but may be isolated from their urine.

Prevention

- Avoid wading or swimming in water that may be contaminated by urine from livestock or wildlife.
- Vaccines are limited to individual strains and are rarely practical.
- Prophylaxis is possible in epidemic areas with a weekly dose of doxycycline given orally at 200 mg per dose. [1,3]

Assessment

- *History of swimming or wading in potentially contaminated water within the last month.*
- The *initial phase* is characterized by a sudden fever, chills, headache, muscle pain (especially in the legs), and red watery eyes. Additional signs and symptoms may include nausea, vomiting, abdominal pain, and a nonproductive cough.
- The *second phase* begins after a 1-2 day remission and is characterized by a severe headache that is unresponsive to pain medications and may indicate developing meningitis. Nausea, vomiting, abdominal pain, and muscle pain may continue; some patients may develop a red skin rash. In severe cases jaundice is present.
- Definitive diagnosis is through blood or CSF culture during the first 7-10 days and from the patient's urine after the tenth day.

Treatment

- Oral antibiotic treatment is effective if begun during the first phase (week) of the disease.
- Doxycycline is the treatment of choice given orally at 100 mg twice a day for seven days. Doxycycline causes extreme sun hypersensitivity; sun block is usually ineffective in preventing sunburn. Alternate antibiotics include penicillins, cephalosporins, and erythromycin. [1,3]

Hantavirus Pulmonary Syndrome

Pathophysiology

Hantavirus Pulmonary Syndrome is a *viral disease transmitted by aerosolized rodent urine.* It is prevalent in the desert Southwest of the United States. Deer mice, pack rats, and chipmunks are the primary carriers. The incubation period varies from a few days to six weeks with a two week average. There is a 50% mortality rate.

Prevention

- Avoid disturbing rodent nests or burrows.
- Store food and water in rodent proof containers.
- Do not use caves, cabins, or enclosed areas that have been infested by rodents.
- Do not camp in or near areas with a large rodent population.
- Maintain high standards for camp hygiene.
- The virus is susceptible to most disinfectants (bleach, etc.). Spray contaminated areas thoroughly prior to cleaning.

Medical

Assessment

- *History of exposure to rodents within the last six weeks.*
- The disease usually begins with general muscle soreness, fever, nausea, vomiting, and abdominal pain. The initial signs and symptoms are *quickly* followed by severe respiratory distress.

Treatment

- Because the infection is viral, **treatment is supportive** in nature and focused on intensive respiratory care.

Plague
(Bubonic and Pneumatic forms)

Pathophysiology

The Plague is a **bacterial infection that is transmitted by the fleas of infected rodents or by the respiratory droplets of infected patients**. Risk is highest in rural mountain areas (including the United States). The bacteria cannot penetrate unbroken skin and transmission may be prevented by washing after exposure. A serious infection may lead to meningitis and/or secondary pneumonia.

Prevention

- Avoid flea bites.
- Avoid close contact (face to face or within an enclosed space) with plague patients. The disease is transmitted by respiratory droplets.
- Avoid areas with known outbreaks.
- The bacteria cannot penetrate unbroken skin and transmission may be prevented by washing after exposure.
- Vaccination: 2 doses one month apart with a final booster after six months. Plague vaccination is of questionable effectiveness and not currently available in the United States.
- Preventive antibiotic therapy should be taken if risk of exposure is high. Prophylaxis may be obtained through oral tetracycline dosed at 15-30 mg per kg per day in four divided doses for one week following exposure. [3]

Assessment

- *Recent history of travel and flea bites in Plague epidemic areas or areas infested with rodents within the last week.*
- Infection is characterized by a rapid onset of flu-like symptoms including fever, chills, headache, extreme exhaustion, and muscle soreness.
- Acute swelling of lymph nodes in the groin and occasionally the underarms is characteristic of the **Bubonic form**.
- Coughing and respiratory distress is present in the **Pneumonic form**.
- Definitive assessment is accomplished by culture and identification of the specific microorganism from the patient's blood, skin abscesses, cerebrospinal fluid (CSF), or sputum.

Treatment

- The drug of choice is Streptomycin IM given at 2-4 grams per day in 2-4 divided doses (adult dose) for 7-10 days. 4 Alternate treatment is doxycycline.[6]

Malaria

Pathophysiology

There are four different strains of Malaria, each a derivation of the same parasite: Plasmodium falciparum, P. vivax, P. ovale, and P. malariae. The infecting *parasite is carried and transmitted by infected Anopheles female mosquitos*. Anopheles mosquitos primarily feed during the night between dusk and dawn. Malaria is common in Africa, Southeast Asia, Central and South America, the Indian subcontinent, and the Middle East. All wilderness travelers in these areas are at high risk for contracting malaria. Once infected, the parasite matures first in the host's liver and then within red blood cells, eventually destroying them. Once mature, the parasite acts like a "web" that "catches" red blood cells, causing micro clots. The clots may then migrate to the joints, lungs, kidneys, heart, spinal cord, and brain where they become lodged in small arteries and cut off perfusion, causing death in severe cases. Signs and symptoms follow an incubation period of 6-12 days. Improperly treated, infections of P. vivax, P. ovale, P. malariae can cause the disease to reoccur for years after the initial episode. *Accurate diagnosis requires a blood test to identify the specific strain. Treatment varies depending upon the infecting strain. Some strains in some areas have become resistant to specific drugs.* Therefore effective treatment hinges upon an accurate diagnosis, identifying resistant strains, and administering appropriate drug therapy.

Prevention

- No vaccine is available.
- *Avoid mosquito bites.* The Anopheles mosquito tends to feed early evening, throughout the night, and early morning; sleeping under protective netting is strongly advised.
- Prophylaxis is possible using antimalarial drugs (chloroquine, mefloquine). In some cases, doxycycline may be an effective chemoprophylaxis. Strains *resistant* to these drugs are common and regional. Outbreaks are unpredictable. *The effectiveness of the prophylaxis depends on the correct drug choice and dose. An overdose of antimalarial drugs can be fatal. Self medication is not advised.* Contact the **Center for Disease Control Malaria Hotline at 404-332-4555** for current recommendations immediately prior to travel.
- *Travelers can still get malaria despite the use of preventive measures.*

Assessment

- *History of travel and mosquito bites within the past three weeks in countries where malaria is present.*
- Travelers can still get malaria despite the use of prophylaxis.
- Flu-like symptoms follow the incubation period: headache, chills, fatigue, loss of appetite, muscle soreness, nausea, and vomiting.

Medical

- Early symptoms are soon followed by episodes of severe headache and joint pain, high fever and sweating, followed by intense chills. Jaundice (yellow skin color) may be present due to the destruction of both liver and red blood cells.
- The episodes commonly last 1-8 hours but may be as long as 30 hours.
- Episodes are usually repeated every 2-3 days but may occur more frequently with a more severe infection.

Treatment

- *Because of resistant strains, treatment for malaria is best done in a hospital setting. Self treatment is not recommended.*
- Drugs used in the treatment of Malaria include chloroquine, quinine, primaquine, Fansidar, artemether, artesunate, or artemisinin. In some cases Fansidar may be used as a field treatment until definitive care is reached. Artemether, artesunate, and artemisinin are derivatives of Chinese herbal remedies known to be clinically effective against malaria and without apparent significant toxicity. The drugs are currently available only in Southeast Asia. [1,3,7]

Yellow Fever

Pathophysiology

Yellow Fever is a *viral disease transmitted by the infected Aedes aegypti mosquito.* Nicknamed "Jungle Fever," it is common in the tropical and forested areas of Africa, Central and South America, and some islands in the West Indies. After a 3-6 day incubation period flu-like symptoms appear. Jaundice (yellow skin) occurs in most cases. In severe cases, as the virus continues to destroy red blood cells, the jaundice increases. The virus may also limit the patient's ability to clot and the patient may bleed easily. Liver and kidney failure are possible; the disease is *fatal* in 50% of jaundiced patients.

Prevention

- *Vaccination:* one dose followed by a ten day waiting period; the vaccine is good for ten years.
- The vaccine is a live virus vaccine. Infants, pregnant women, people allergic to eggs (the vaccine is prepared in embryonated eggs), and people with a suppressed immune system (HIV infection, AIDS, leukemia, lymphoma, etc.) should carefully weigh the risk of exposure to the risks associated with the vaccine.
- *Cholera and Yellow Fever vaccines should be given three weeks apart.*
- A certificate is issued and remains valid for 10 years. It must be presented to meet entrance and exit requirements to some areas.
- Avoid mosquito bites.

Assessment

- *Unvaccinated persons with a recent history of travel and mosquito bites in countries where Yellow Fever is present during the past week.*
- Flu-like symptoms follow incubation period: sudden fever, headache, muscle soreness, nausea, and vomiting.

- Jaundice is possible and the patient may bleed easily.
- Skin rashes are possible but rare.

Treatment

- Because the infection is viral, *treatment is supportive* in nature and focused on relieving the patient's signs and symptoms.

Japanese Encephalitis

Pathophysiology

Japanese Encephalitis is a *mosquito borne viral disease common to rural rice growing and pig farming regions* in China, Korea, the Indian subcontinent, the Philippines, southeast Asia, eastern Russia, and the Japanese archipelago. The Culex mosquitos that carry Japanese Encephalitis represent a small portion of the entire mosquito population. The majority of persons infected do not develop any illness or show only mild signs and symptoms. Infants and older people are at increased risk of developing serious signs and symptoms. Of those who develop encephalitis (brain infection) only one third recover without further incident. A second third survive with severe brain damage or paralysis and one third of cases are fatal. AVPU and behavioral changes may occur as the disease progresses to infect the patient's brain.

Prevention

- **Vaccination:** a total of three doses; the second and third doses follow the initial dose on days 7 and 30. A waiting period of 10 days is necessary before exposure. A booster dose is required every two years. Medical supervision for anaphylaxis is recommended for 48 hours following each dose. The vaccine should not be given to people who are acutely ill, to those who have heart, kidney, or liver disorders, pregnant women, and people with a history of anaphylaxis.
- Avoid mosquito bites.

Assessment

- *History of travel and mosquito bites within the last 3 weeks in countries where Japanese Encephalitis is present.*
- Initial symptoms are flu-like with headache and fever.
- AVPU and behavioral changes may occur as the disease progresses to infect the patient's brain.

Treatment

- Because the infection is viral, *treatment is supportive* in nature and focused on relieving the patient's signs and symptoms.

Dengue Fever

Pathophysiology

Dengue Fever is a *viral disease transmitted by the infected Aedes aegypti and rarely the Aedes albopictus mosquitos.* The Aedes mosquitos feed during the day. Dengue Fever is endemic to the semi-tropical and tropical regions of the Caribbean, Central and South America, Africa, Mexico, the Indian subcontinent, the Philippines, New Guinea, Southeast Asia and northern Australia. Symptoms begin after a 3-14 day incubation period; the disease is self-limiting. Fatalities are rare with Dengue Fever. Dengue Hemorrhagic Fever, a different but related disease, has similar signs and symptoms but is much more serious. Left untreated Dengue Hemorrhagic Fever has a mortality rate of 50%. The risk of contracting both diseases is high in endemic areas and low elsewhere; it is rarely found at elevations above 4,000 feet.

Prevention

- The mosquitos that transmit Dengue Fever tend to feed during the daylight hours and bite below the waist; avoid mosquito bites.
- There is no vaccine available.
- Persons who have had previous bouts of Dengue Fever are more susceptible to Dengue Hemorrhagic Fever.

Assessment

- *History of travel and mosquito bites within the past two weeks in countries where a Dengue Fever is present.*
- Dengue Fever is commonly known as "bone-break" fever and is characterized by an acute fever and intense bone and joint pain. The febrile episodes usually last 3-5 days and no more than seven.
- Patients also complain of a severe headache, sore muscles, pain behind their eyes, and mild GI distress.
- A red, itchy rash usually appears on the patient's chest, abdomen, upper arms and legs as the fever dissipates. The rash may begin on the chest and expand outward; it is rarely visible on dark-skinned races.
- Microscopic hemorrhages occur in the vascular beds causing minor bleeding from the nose and gums, and pinpoint bruising throughout the body.
- Definitive assessment is by a blood test that detects the presence of the virus or antibodies.
- A simple field test using a blood pressure cuff can verify the presence of **Dengue Hemorrhagic Fever:** The cuff is inflated to a point halfway between the patient's systolic and diastolic pressures. The test is positive if pinpoint hemorrhages appear on the patient's skin distal to the cuff.
- Patients showing a clinical pattern for volume shock after the febrile episodes have subsided indicates **Dengue Hemorrhagic Fever.**

Treatment

- Because the infection is viral, **treatment is supportive** in nature and focused on relieving the patient's signs and symptoms; the disease is self-limiting.

- *Aggressive fluid replacement* and oxygen therapy significantly reduces fatalities in Dengue Hemorrhagic Fever.
- Do not give patients drugs containing aspirin or aspirin derivatives. Aspirin impedes the clotting process and exacerbates the bleeding.
- The disease may last up to 10 days; complete recovery often requires 2-4 weeks.
- Relapses are rare but possible.

Rocky Mountain Spotted Fever

Pathophysiology

Rocky Mountain Spotted Fever is caused by a **tick borne parasite active in the late spring and early summer.** Many ticks carry the parasite but dog and wood ticks are the most common. In order to transmit the disease the ticks must have been actively feeding for a minimum of four hours. The disease is more common with feeding times greater than six hours. Infections are prevalent in the southeast reaching as far north as Maryland and in the mid-west through Oklahoma and Kansas. Signs and symptoms follow an incubation period of 2-14 days. In severe cases the parasites multiply and progressively destroy the lining of the blood vessels. This destruction increases vascular permeability and leads to both organ dysfunction and volume shock. The mortality rate is 5%.

Prevention

- When in tick country wear light-colored protective long pants and long sleeved shirts with socks pulled over the pant cuffs; coat the clothing with DEET.
- Do a thorough check for ticks periodically during the day, before sleeping, and upon awakening. Remove and shake clothing before going inside a tent or shelter.
- Find and immediately remove any ticks. Attached ticks may be removed by grasping them close to the skin with a tweezers and applying a slow steady pulling pressure; the site should be thoroughly cleaned with povidone-iodine. Monitor patients with known tick bites for 14 days.

Assessment

- *History of tick bite within the past two weeks.*
- A sudden fever (103-104 degrees F) and chills immediately follow the incubation period and last for 2-3 weeks. They are accompanied by headache and muscle pain. Within 2-6 days of the onset of the fever, 50% of the patients develop a red spotted rash on their extremities that spreads towards their core. The rash emerges on the hands, wrists, and feet, and then spreads to include the chest, abdomen, and back. Other signs and symptoms include light sensitivity, joint pain, swollen hands and feet, coughing, and abdominal pain with nausea and vomiting.
- *Definitive assessment is difficult without the history of a tick bite.*

Treatment

- The infection is usually treated with 500 mg of tetracycline [6] 4 times a day OR 100 mg of doxycycline (adult dose) [4] twice a day for 4-7 days or until the patient is fever free for two days. Both drugs cause severe sun hypersensitivity; sun block is usually ineffective in preventing sunburn.

Medical

Lyme Disease

Pathophysiology

Lyme Disease is a *tick borne parasite* commonly carried by the adult and nymphal forms of the deer tick. Cases of Lyme Disease have been reported throughout the United States, Canada, Soviet Union, Australia, Europe, Scandinavia, Japan, and China. Signs and symptoms appear 3-32 days following an infected tick bite. Left untreated the disease progresses through three stages. If diagnosed and treated during the first stage, before antibodies are present (usually 3-6 weeks), a complete recovery is likely. During the second stage the disease begins to affect the heart, the central and peripheral nervous systems, the liver, the digestive system, and the musculoskeletal system. If still untreated the disease will progress to chronically infect the patient's nervous system, skin, eyes, and joints. Excessively late treatment may result in an incomplete recovery. Many patients complain of persistent fatigue, sleep disorders, depression, and cognitive difficulties.

Prevention

• A vaccine is available. It is given in two doses a month apart with a booster at 12 months. Efficacy is high after the booster dose but the vaccine is NOT 100% effective against preventing infection. Lyme Disease does NOT confer protective immunity and people who have had the disease should be vaccinated.
• When in tick country wear light-colored protective long pants and long sleeved shirts with socks pulled over the pant cuffs; coat the clothing with DEET.
• Do a thorough check for ticks periodically during the day, before sleeping, and upon awakening. Remove and shake clothing before going inside a tent or shelter.
• Find and immediately remove any ticks. Attached ticks may be removed by grasping them close to the skin with a tweezers and applying a slow steady pulling pressure; the site should be thoroughly cleaned with povidone iodine.
• *Monitor patients with known tick bites for five weeks.*
• In animal experiments ticks infected with Lyme Disease did not transmit the disease if attached less than 24 hours.

Assessment

• *History of tick bite.*
• Normal incubation period is 2-32 days.
• Most infections occur during the late spring and early summer when ticks are most active.
• The *first stage* is usually heralded by a distinctive rash. The rash begins as a small red spot and grows outward forming an irregular circle; the rash may also appear in the form of hives. The classic bulls-eye pattern occurs in a small percentage of the population. The rash may be accompanied by nonspecific flu-like signs and symptoms. Left untreated, the rash disappears after 1-4 weeks and the flu-like signs and symptoms appear or intensify.
• The *second stage* leaves the patient with a feeling of extreme lethargy, loss of appetite, general malaise, low grade fever, chills, swollen lymph glands, severe headaches, conjunctivitis, light sensitivity, and muscle and joint pain. Abdominal pain, nausea, and vomiting are possible. 60% of the patients in this stage develop arthritis.
• Definitive diagnosis is reached through the analysis of the patient's blood for the presence of Lyme specific antibodies.
• Because early treatment is highly successful, assessment often consists of a positive history of a tick bite together with the presence of a rash.

Treatment

- Early treatment consists of an oral course of 100 mg of doxycycline (adult dose) twice a day for 2-3 weeks. Doxycycline causes severe sun hypersensitivity; sun block is usually ineffective in preventing sunburn. Amoxicillin may be used in place of doxycycline. Amoxicillin is given orally at 500 mg four times a day for 2-3 weeks. Patients allergic to penicillin are also allergic to amoxicillin. [3]
- *Once the disease has become established internally it must be treated more aggressively* with an oral course of doxycycline at 200 mg twice a day for three days followed by 100 mg twice a day for 25 days. Doxycycline causes extreme sun hypersensitivity; sun block is usually ineffective in preventing sunburn. Alernatively, erythromycin or ceftriaxone may be used. [3]
- Intravenous antibiotics (usually high doses of ceftriaxone or penicillin) are required for difficult cases. [3,5]

Colorado Tick Fever

Pathophysiology

Colorado Tick Fever is a *viral infection transmitted by the wood tick* and common to all areas of the mountain west. Signs and symptoms follow an average incubation period of 3-5 days. The worst part of the infection is usually self-limiting within 5-7 days; however, the patient may continue to feel weak with general malaise for another 3-4 weeks.

Prevention

- When in tick country wear light-colored protective long pants and long sleeved shirts with socks pulled over the pant cuffs; coat the clothing with DEET.
- Do a thorough check for ticks periodically during the day, before sleeping, and upon awakening. Remove and shake clothing before going inside a tent or shelter.
- Find and immediately remove any ticks. Attached ticks may be removed by grasping them close to the skin with a tweezers and applying a slow steady pulling pressure; the site should be thoroughly cleaned with povidone iodine.
- Infection usually confers lifelong immunity.

Assessment

- *Recent history of a tick bite within the past week.*
- Signs and symptoms are flu-like. Fever (102-104 degrees F), severe headaches, muscle pain, and lethargy are common. In greater than 50% of the cases the fever disappears for a few days and then returns. Light sensitivity, eye pain, nausea, vomiting, and abdominal pain occur occasionally. In a small number of cases a mild skin rash may appear.
- Definitive diagnosis may be made by isolating the virus from the patient's blood.

Treatment

- Because the infection is viral, *treatment is supportive* in nature and focused on relieving the patient's signs and symptoms.

Medical

Cholera

Pathophysiology

Cholera is wildly prevalent throughout the world; 50% of the reported cases occur in the western hemisphere. Cholera is a **bacterial infection caused by fecal-oral transmission and the ingestion of contaminated food or water**; it may remain active for weeks in some foods. Cholera may also be transmitted in "hand to mouth" person-to-person contacts. The cholera bacteria may also live in coastal rivers and waters, contaminating shellfish. In most cases the bacteria are destroyed by normal stomach acids. Infection occurs when the bacteria are able to establish themselves in the small intestine and multiply. The incubation period is 1-5 days. The bacteria produce a toxin that prevents fluid absorption *and* causes an influx of fluids into the gut from the rest of the body; the result is profuse, watery diarrhea. Most infections occur without symptoms or are extremely mild. A severe cholera infection occurs in one fifth of the cases causing extreme and painless diarrhea. **Once diarrhea begins, death from dehydration can occur within hours.** There is a 50% fatality rate associated with untreated cases.

Prevention

- **Treat suspected food and water.**
- Active immunization with the current killed cell vaccine is only 50% effective and not recommended. [3]
- Two types of new oral vaccine provide a high level of protection lasting up to several months for 01 strains. One is a live virus vaccine (Orachol) and is given in a single dose. The other contains a inactivated virus and a synthetic derivative given in two doses. [3]
- Cholera and Yellow Fever vaccines should be given three weeks apart.

Assessment

- **History of ingestion of potentially contaminated food and water or contact with an infected person within the past 5 days.**
- The disease causes fluid accumulation, distention, and diarrhea. The diarrhea may initially be brown in color but quickly becomes a watery-gray. Severe fluid loss occurs within the first 24 hours.
- Vomiting may occur and is usually a result of dehydration.
- Fever is present in one quarter of the cases.
- Definitive diagnosis is made via a stool culture.

Treatment

- **Death from dehydration can occur within hours.**
- **Begin immediate and aggressive fluid and electrolyte replacement** until the patient's urine is clear. If the patient is not producing clear urine aggressively continue fluid replacement. Fluid replacement should continue as long as diarrhea is present. In 90% of the mild to moderate cases oral rehydration is successful. The World Health Organization (WHO) recommends the following oral fluid replacement formula: 20 g/L glucose (table sugar), 3.5 g NaCl (table salt), 1.5 g KCl, 2.5 g NaHCO3 (baking soda).

- IV therapy may be necessary in severe cases. Use WHO diarrhea solution and replace 30 ml/kg of fluid IV within the first 30 minutes then switch to oral replacement.
- With fluid treatment the disease is self-limiting.
- An oral course of antibiotics shortens the duration of the disease. Tetracycline is the antibiotic of choice. Adult dose is 500 mg 4 times a day for three days. Tetracycline causes severe sun hypersensitivity; sun block is usually ineffective in preventing sunburn. Trimethoprim-sulfamethoxazole (TMP/SMX) may be substituted for tetracycline at 320 mg TMP/1600 mg SMX 2 times a day for three days. Patients allergic to sulfa medications should not take TMP/SMX. [3]

Bacterial Dysentery

Pathophysiology

Shigella bacteria are extremely hardy (they can survive freezing) and easily *transmitted by the fecal-oral route through ingestion of contaminated food or water (including ice). Person-to-person spread ("hand to mouth") is common especially among groups with close physical contact. Expeditions with questionable sanitary conditions are at high risk of contracting the disease.* Shigella is responsible for many cases of traveler's diarrhea. The incubation period is 1-3 days. Shigella produces local toxins that affect the patient's intestinal tissue. Mild cases are common and indistinguishable from other illnesses that cause headache, fever, abdominal cramps, watery diarrhea, muscle soreness, and general exhaustion. If the bacteria become established in the large intestine they may invade local tissue causing a severe infection and ulcers. This classic form of infection is characterized by a fever, severe abdominal cramps, and bloody diarrhea. Mild infections tend to resolve within 7 days but severe cases may last up to a few weeks. One quarter of untreated cases result in death.

Prevention

- *Treat all suspect food and water.*
- *Maintain high sanitary procedures.*
- Avoid contact with the fecal matter of infected persons.
- No commercial vaccines are available.

Assessment

- *History of ingestion of potentially contaminated food and water or close contact with an infected person within the past week.*
- Initial signs and symptoms include headache, fever, abdominal cramps, watery diarrhea, muscle soreness, and general exhaustion.
- After 1-3 days dysentery may develop. The signs and symptoms of dysentery are fever and bloody diarrhea. The urgency and frequency of diarrhea increases as the volume decreases; 20-30 watery yellow, green, or brown movements with mucus and blood are possible per day. Most patients report that each bowel movement requires effort and strain. Vomiting is present in 50% of the cases.
- Definitive diagnosis is made via a stool culture. Since antibiotic resistance is common with Shigella, bacteria cultured from the patient's stool are subjected to laboratory trials to determine which antibiotics would be most effective.

Medical   **128**

Treatment

- In cases involving severe fluid loss, treatment is focused on fluid and electrolyte replacement. The disease is self-limiting and fluid replacement is highly effective in preventing fatalities.
- *Vomiting and diarrhea should not be controlled by medications.*
- An oral course of antibiotics decreases the severity and duration of the disease. Administer ciprofloxacin; adult dose is 500 mg two times a day for 3-5 days. [1,4]

Hepatitis A

Pathophysiology

Hepatitis A is a *viral infection transmitted through a fecal-oral route by contaminated food and water or "hand to mouth" contact with an infected person.* It is the most common serious viral infection among travelers and world wide. It is prevalent in countries with poor sanitation. The incubation period is 2-7 weeks. The virus replicates in the liver destroying liver cells in the process. In most cases the cells regenerate without complications after the disease has run its course. Signs and symptoms include loss of appetite, nausea, vomiting, abdominal pain, and fever. Jaundice usually follows within a few days or weeks. The disease is usually self-limiting within three weeks of the appearance of jaundice; however, it may take months for a full recovery.

Prevention

- *Treat suspect food and water.*
- A new vaccine is available and recommended for persons with repeated or long term exposure (greater than 6 months). The vaccine is given in a single dose with full protection complete within thirty days. With boosters it may confer livelong immunity.
- An *immune globulin shot* will help prevent infection and is recommended for persons with intermittent or short term exposure (3-6 months). The immune globulin interferes with normal antibody development and should be given 2-4 weeks after other vaccines and immediately prior to potential exposure since its protection disappears after 3-6 months. The shot may also be given within two weeks after exposure.
- Infection confers lifelong immunity.

Assessment

- *History of ingestion of potentially contaminated food and water or "hand to mouth" contact with an infected person within the past 7 weeks.*
- Sign and symptoms include loss of appetite, nausea, vomiting, abdominal pain, and fever.
- Enlargement of the spleen and liver usually accompanies the initial signs and symptoms.
- Jaundice follows within a few days or weeks.
- A few patients may initially present with a rash and joint pain.
- Definitive assessment is possible through a blood antibody count.

Treatment

- Because the infection is viral, *treatment is supportive* in nature and focused on relieving the

patient's signs and symptoms.
- Do not attempt to restrict vomiting and diarrhea unless they interfere with necessary fluid and electrolyte replacement.
- A liver-friendly diet consisting of bland low-fat foods is recommended.

Typhoid Fever

Pathophysiology

Typhoid Fever is a **bacterial disease transmitted through a fecal-oral route by contaminated food and water or direct "hand to mouth" contact with an infected person.** The disease is common in third world and developing countries with poor sanitation. In a majority of the cases, most of the bacteria are destroyed by stomach acids while the remaining pass through the gut without transmitting the disease. If the bacteria become established in the digestive tract they multiply, invade local tissues, and multiply again. Incubation period is typically 7-21 days but may extend to three months. From the digestive tract the disease moves into the blood causing a systemic infection that may last 2-3 weeks. Untreated, typhoid fever may resolve itself within 3-4 weeks; however, life-threatening complications cause a 12-32% fatality rate.

Prevention

- *Treat all suspected food and water.*
- An oral vaccine is available in four doses over eight days, one capsule every other day. A booster is required every five years. An older vaccine, given by injection, is less effective.

Assessment

- *History of ingestion of potentially contaminated food and water or "hand to mouth" contact with an infected person within the past three weeks.*
- The systemic signs of the disease are usually proceeded by gastrointestinal distress, abdominal pain, and constipation. Diarrhea may occur but is less common.
- A slowly increasing fever follows and indicates a systemic infection. Left untreated, fever will remain constant for 2-3 weeks.
- Symptoms include headache, not eating, muscle soreness, and general exhaustion. A skin rash develops in 25% of the patients on the trunk of their body.
- Enlargement of the spleen and liver is common.
- Definitive diagnosis is through a blood or bone marrow culture.

Treatment

- Administer by mouth 960 mg (one double strength tablet) trimethoprim sulfamethoxazole twice a day for two weeks. Do not use TMP/SMX with patients allergic to sulfa drugs. [6]
- Ciprofloxacin may be used as an alternative treatment for those patients allergic to TMP/SMX. Adult dose is 500 mg twice a day for 10 days. [4]
- The fever will usually subside after 3-4 days of antibiotic treatment.
- *Relapse* can occur after two weeks and requires retreatment; consider an alternative antibiotic.
- *Do not attempt to restrict diarrhea unless it interferes with necessary fluid and electrolyte replacement.*

Medical

Giardia

Pathophysiology

Giardia Lamblia is a *flagellate protozoan that is transmitted in cyst form in contaminated water*. The adult organism is a filter feeder and restricts itself to clear running brooks and streams. Except during runoff it is not usually found in large rivers or lakes; although, the mouths of streams where they join rivers or lakes should remain suspect throughout the year. The protozoan may remain dormant in its cyst form for long periods of time and it is the cysts that are transmitted in the feces of most animals, including humans. *Fecal-oral "hand to mouth" contamination is currently considered a major method of transmission.* The incubation period ranges from 7-20 days. Once the cysts are ingested they emerge in a form that damages the lining of the small intestine, restricting food absorption. Most patients present with mild signs and symptoms while a small percentage experience an acute infection. The disease is usually self-correcting and often requires weeks or months for a complete recovery.

Prevention

- *Treat all suspect water.*
- *Maintain high standards for personal and group hygiene.*

Assessment

- *History of ingestion of potentially contaminated water or poor expedition hygiene within the past three weeks.*
- Most patients present with mild signs and symptoms that include flatulence, loose and foul-smelling stools, nausea, and mild abdominal cramps.
- A small percentage of patients experience an acute infection with severe abdominal cramps, explosive, foul-smelling diarrhea, sulphurous burps, fever, nausea, and vomiting. An acute infection may result in severe dehydration. Fever and vomiting are usually limited to the first few days of the acute form while general malaise, loose stools, and mild GI distress may continue for weeks to months.

Treatment

- Giardia is eventually self-correcting (weeks to months) and treatment is usually symptomatic. Fast relief may be obtained by administering one of the following drugs.
- Within the United States, Metronidazole (Flagyl) is the drug of choice given at 250 mg 3 times a day for 7 days. Supplement patients taking metronidazole with acidophilus capsules and/or yogurt containing live cultures to prevent yeast infections. [4,6]
- Quinacrine hydrochloride (Atabrine) is a rarely used alternative to metronidazole and for adults only. Oral dose is 100 mg 3 times a day for five days. [4,6]
- Tinidazole (available in Nepal and other foreign countries) is the preferred treatment when overseas and is taken by mouth in a single 2 g dose. Supplement patients taking tinidazole with acidophilus capsules and/or yogurt containing live cultures to prevent yeast infections. [4,6]
- *Do not attempt to restrict vomiting and diarrhea unless they interfere with necessary fluid and electrolyte replacement.*

Common Diseases

Atherosclerosis

Pathophysiology

Arteries may become obstructed over time by a buildup of plaque due to a poor diet, low exercise, high blood pressure, genetics, etc. The normal elastic nature of the arterial walls is significantly reduced as the arterial plaque thickens. Nicotine and diabetes also effect the development of plaque by reducing the elasticity of the arterial walls. Over time the body accepts the existence of arterial plaque as a normal development. If a piece of plaque breaks free of the wall the body senses an "abnormal" disturbance in the wall and initiates the clotting process at the site of the disturbance. Once the clot is in place it cuts off perfusion to the tissue serviced by the artery. If the tissue is not adequately supplied by collateral circulation it will die. *If a clot develops in the brain causing the death of brain tissue, the patient will present with the signs and symptoms of a stroke. If a clot develops in the heart, a heart attack will ensue.*

Prevention

- Eliminate the associated risk factors by eating a healthy diet low in cholesterol and fats; engage in a daily aerobic exercise program, don't smoke, treat high blood pressure, and eliminate stress.
- Minerals that help strengthen the circulatory system include: copper, chromium, calcium, magnesium, and selenium.
- Additional supplements include: vitamins E and C, lecithin, and coenzyme Q. Avoid vitamin D.
- Helpful herbs include raw garlic and licorice.
- Medications are available to decrease serum cholesterol and control high blood pressure.

Stroke

Pathophysiology

The development of a *clot in a cerebral artery* (usually due to atherosclerosis) or the *rupture of a cerebral artery* (cerebral aneurism) are the common causes of stroke. The tissue serviced by the artery looses perfusion and dies within a few minutes. The signs and symptoms reflect the amount of brain damage. In extremely mild cases the patient has no noticeable loss of function and the stroke may go undetected. Serious cerebral blocks or aneurysms may be large enough to be instantly fatal. The loss of sensation and motor function in the patient is proportional to the severity and location of the stroke. Because the cerebrum is divided into two hemispheres by the corpus callosum (right and left brain) and each hemisphere is serviced by a separate arterial supply, tissue damage due to stroke is usually confined to a single side. Motor and sensory functions for the head and face are serviced by cranial nerves while the remainder of the body is serviced by spinal nerves. Because the spinal nerves cross in the brain stem, loss of sensation and motor function in the head and face reflect damage to the same side of the brain while a loss of function below the head reflects damage to the opposite side of the brain. While increased ICP is a potential anticipated problem for patients surviving a stroke, it is rare. Generally, if the stroke is severe enough to cause and increase in ICP it is severe enough to cause death from the stroke itself.

Prevention

- Eliminate the risk factors for atherosclerosis.
- Consider medications for controlling serum cholesterol levels and high blood pressure.

Assessment

- History may indicate amnesia.
- Patients present with a loss of sensation and motor function involving a single hemisphere (same side face, opposite side body).
- Most awake patients are lethargic and tired immediately following a stroke.
- Some patients may present with a depressed level of consciousness. These patients generally have a poorer prognosis.

Field Treatment

- Administer oxygen.
- Sleep is a necessary part of the recovery process. A stroke patient should be permitted to sleep, closely monitored while sleeping, and awakened every few hours during the 24 hour period following the event.
- *Evacuate all stroke patients to a major hospital.* Thrombolytic medications are indicated within three hours if the stroke is due to a blocked blood vessel. Surgery may be indicated if the stroke is due to a ruptured vessel. A CT scan is required to distinguish between the two.

Heart Attack

Pathophysiology

Developing atherosclerosis and subsequent clotting of a coronary artery is the most common cause of heart attacks. Signs and symptoms commonly appear immediately and are due to a lack of oxygen in the affected tissue. Cardiac arrest evolves along a continuum and is not predictable. Arrest is ultimately due to a change in the electrical impulses and conduction pattern (cardiac arrhythmia) in the specialized cardiac nerves that stimulate normal cardiac contractions. An injury to these nerves blocks the conduction pathway. The block prevents or delays the electrical impulses from reaching their destination and causes cardiac arrest. The potential for arrest from a heart attack is directly related to the type, location, and size of the compromised tissue. If the blocked artery services the specialized nerve cells that coordinate the pumping action of the heart, arrest occurs within seconds or minutes. If the blocked artery services the heart's muscle fibers rather than its specialized nerve cells, the pumping action of the heart may be compromised. A reduction in the heart's ability to pump blood efficiently may cause a back pressure in the pulmonary vessels and force fluid into the alveoli causing respiratory distress (congestive heart failure). Complete pump failure and arrest may develop if a significant amount of heart muscle has been injured and the heart cannot continue to meet the body's demands for nutrients (cardiogenic shock).

The longer arrest is delayed the more likely the patient will survive without immediate hospital treatment. Patients who survive heart attacks are usually tired and "feel sick" with slightly elevated pulse and respiration rates. Recovery often takes months or years. Subsequent heart attacks are possible.

Atherosclerosis reduces the amount of oxygen available to the heart by effectively shrinking the size of the arteries with plaque deposits. Exercise and stress can increase the heart's need for oxygen beyond the delivery capacity of the restricted arteries. The resulting hypoxia causes heart pain or *angina*. Once the exercise or stress is removed the oxygen requirements of the patient's heart will return to normal levels and the chest pain will subside; usually within 20 minutes.

Prevention

- Eliminate the risk factors for atherosclerosis.
- Herbs that help control blood cholesterol levels, triglyceride levels, and blood pressure include: hawthorn, globe artichoke, black cohosh, evening primrose, and lily of the valley.
- Persons with atherosclerosis should consider taking two tablets of chewable baby aspirin per day to prevent coronary clotting.
- Persons with atherosclerosis should consider medications for controlling serum cholesterol levels and high blood pressure.
- Persons with atherosclerosis should consider cardiac medications (e.g.: nitroglycerin) to relieve angina.

Assessment

- The classic signs and symptoms of a heart attack are non-traumatic, non-tender chest pain or pressure accompanied by shortness of breath and diaphoresis (pale sweating skin). *Initially it is difficult to tell the difference between angina and a heart attack.*

Angina

- Patient complains of non-traumatic chest pain when exercising or under stress.
- The chest pain is relieved by stopping the exercise or removing the stress; usually within 20 minutes.
- The chest pain is relieved within minutes after administering nitroglycerin.

Heart Attack

- Patient complains of non-traumatic non-tender chest pain. The pain may mimic indigestion (it is not relieved with antacids) and is typically described as pressure or squeezing. There is no change in the pain with patient movement. The pain may radiate to the patient's neck or arms (classically the left arm).
- Shortness of breath is common as are sweating and pale skin.
- Fatigue and weakness are present.
- Many patients deny the possibility of a heart attack.

Cardiac Arrest

- Cardiac arrest evolves along a continuum and is not predictable. From the onset of chest pain arrest may occur within seconds to minutes if cardiac nerve cells are affected or within hours if a "large" area of cardiac muscle is damaged and pump performance is decreased (cardiogenic shock). Arrest is unlikely if a very small area of cardiac muscle is affected and pump performance remains relatively unaffected.

Medical

Cardiogenic Shock

- Rising pulse and respiration rates, decreasing mental status, and a falling blood pressure indicate cardiogenic shock.

Congestive Heart Failure (CHF)

- Increased respiratory distress and developing edema (fluid) in the lungs indicates congestive heart failure.

Field Treatment

Angina & Heart Attack

- Because it is difficult to distinguish between angina and a heart attack in the initial stages, field treatment is identical.
- If respiratory distress is present allow patient to sit or support them in a sitting position. Provide rest, reassurance, and oxygen.
- *Immediately evacuate with ALS all patients who complain of non-traumatic non-tender chest pain.*
- Administer two tablets of chewable baby aspirin with the onset of chest pain. The aspirin acts as an anticoagulant and may help minimize cardiac damage.
- Administer nitroglycerin in awake patients. Adult dose is one tablet (.4 mg) dissolved under the patient's tongue OR .4 mg delivered as a metered spray. The dose may be repeated every 5 minutes for three doses. Nitroglycerin will cause a tingling or burning sensation if it is active. Headaches are common following the administration of nitroglycerin and rarely last longer than 20 minutes. [6]

Cardiac Arrest

- If your patient arrests, begin positive pressure ventilations and chest compressions. Recovery with CPR alone is not possible. If CPR is initiated immediately following the arrest and ALS is on scene within 4-8 minutes the patient has a 43% chance of recovery. The chance of recovery goes down significantly with longer ALS response times. There is no chance of recovery after 30 minutes. *Consider stopping CPR after 30 minutes of documented arrest.*

Cardiogenic Shock

- *Support critical systems and immediately evacuate with ALS to a major hospital.*

Congestive Heart Failure

- Allow the patient to sit or support them in a sitting position. Provide rest, reassurance, and high liter flow oxygen.
- If the patient has a history of CHF and their own diuretic medication allow them to continue taking it on schedule.
- *Immediately evacuate with ALS to a major hospital.*

Diabetic Emergencies

Pathophysiology

Diabetes is a disease that effects the entire body by compromising systemic circulation. It is a disease of the pancreas and results from insufficient insulin production.

Sugar is required for cellular metabolism; however, sugar molecules are too "big" to pass through the cell walls without assistance. Insulin increases the permeability of the cell walls enabling sugar to enter the cells. As blood sugar levels rise to meet cellular demands, the pancreas releases insulin into the blood. Insulin facilitates the entry of sugar into the cells. If the pancreas does not produce enough insulin, sugar (even if it is available in the blood) cannot enter the cells. Because of a constant cellular demand for more sugar the blood sugar level of the uncontrolled diabetic is extremely high. As blood sugar levels continue to rise the kidney's filter system is overwhelmed and some sugar is released into the urine. The presence of massive amounts of sugar in the microvascular beds indirectly damages the vascular walls and permanently reduces perfusion to the local tissue. If the diabetic remains uncontrolled, the damage to their circulatory system continues and may lead to general perfusion problems, kidney and liver failure, stroke, heart attack, blindness, delayed healing, higher risk of infection, etc. Because of circulatory system damage, all diabetics are at a higher risk for most environmental injuries including hypothermia, hyperthermia, and frostbite.

There are *two types of diabetes:* juvenile onset and adult onset diabetes. *Juvenile onset diabetes* may appear anytime during childhood through early adulthood (mid 30s). Signs and symptoms include increased thirst, increased urination, sugar in the urine, and rapid weight loss. Control of juvenile onset diabetes usually requires daily shots of insulin.

Adult onset diabetes generally emerges later in life with symptoms similar to the juvenile type but without weight loss. Because insulin is also required for fat storage, people whose diet contains a large amount of fats and/or processed sugar place a higher demand on their pancreas. As their pancreas works overtime, it may eventually tire leading to a lower level of insulin production. People with this type of diabetes often control it through weight loss and a low fat, low sugar diet. They may also require oral medications to stimulate their pancreas. Some adult onset diabetics need daily shots of insulin. A diabetic that controls their diabetes by diet alone is less likely to develop acute hypoglycemia.

Diabetics who control their diabetes with intramuscular injections of insulin are referred to as *insulin dependant diabetics*. Because the insulin dependant diabetic is more fragile, life-threatening problems can arise when they are exposed to unusually high energy demands (hypoglycemia), a limited supply of calories (hypoglycemia), and/or an abrupt change in their medications (hyperglycemia).

Because the *uncontrolled diabetic* tends to be extremely tired, irritable, and generally sick they are not usually found in a wilderness setting. However, it is common to find *controlled diabetics* in the backcountry. Patients under treatment for diabetes can slow the development of disease and lead normal lives. Since all patients who suffer from diabetes have a compromised circulatory system they are at a significantly higher risk for most environmental injuries and are more challenged by severe trauma and disease. In addition, insulin dependent diabetics must balance their sugar intake, energy output, and insulin requirements to avoid the associated problems of hypoglycemia or hyperglycemia.

Prevention

General

- A vegetarian diet low in processed sugars and fats.
- Chromium and vanadium may prevent and treat (replace insulin) adult onset diabetes.
- Prickly pear is helpful in controlling adult onset diabetes.[12]

Prevention of Diabetic Emergencies

- Contact the diabetic's personal physician before leaving on a trip or expedition for specific recommendations.
- Balance food intake (complex carbohydrates) with energy output; diabetics have limited energy stores. *Diabetics new to most outdoor pursuits severely underestimate the amount of energy required for the activity and commonly do not carry enough food with them to avoid hypoglycemia.* Avoid simple sugars, alcohol, and fats.
- Maintain the patient's water balance; monitor urine output and color. *Avoid dehydration.*
- The patient should closely monitor and balance their blood insulin levels with their energy (and sugar) requirements. Some diabetics are more sensitive than others and require multiple doses of insulin to maintain a balance. Any activity that requires additional energy will require more sugar and perhaps more insulin. *Unless you have been thoroughly trained, you should not attempt to balance a patient's blood insulin levels.*
- Over time, as the disease develops, all diabetics are at higher risk for hypothermia, hyperthermia, infection, heart attack, stroke, kidney and liver failure, blindness, etc. than non-diabetics. *Plan wilderness outings and expeditions with diabetics to minimize exposure to circulatory system problems.*

Assessment

General

- *All diabetics who travel in a wilderness environment will have a previous history,* be in a treatment program, and may be taking insulin to control the disease. Some will be wearing a Medical Awake Tag or tatoo on their chest, wrist, or ankle. Get a complete history including medications, dose, and schedule.
- *Most diabetic emergencies are due to hypoglycemia.* Hyperglycemia is extremely rare in a wilderness environment.

Hypoglycemia

- In most cases, the patient has been taking their insulin but has not eaten enough to maintain their blood sugar levels. Hypoglycemia means "low blood sugar." In rare cases the patient may have taken too much insulin (with the same results).
- Onset of acute hypoglycemia may occur within minutes once the patient has run out of sugar.
- Watch for a change in normal mental status to awake and lethargic or awake and irritable. Awake hypoglycemic patients often appear "drunk."
- Any voice responsive, pain responsive, or unresponsive diabetic patient is assumed to be suffering from hypoglycemia.
- Seizures are common; death is possible.

Hyperglycemia

- The patient has not taken their usual dose(s) of insulin.
- The onset of signs and symptoms is delayed 24 to 72 hours or more as the controlled diabetic reverts back to being uncontrolled. Hyperglycemia means "high blood sugar" and is due to a decrease in insulin.
- Severe signs may include coma and death.

Field Treatment

Hypoglycemia

- *Always feed a diabetic patient.* Begin with simple sugars (sublingual sugar paste, or honey if the patient is voice responsive, pain responsive, or unresponsive). Once the patient is awake follow with a complete meal consisting of complex carbohydrates.
- Administer 0.5-1 unit of glucagon IM for severe hypoglycemic reactions in an patient with a depressed mental status (V, P, or U). The dose may be repeated up to a total of three injections if the patient does not respond in 10-20 minutes. Glucagon is a hormone that releases glucose stores from the patient's liver. [6]
- IV glucose is the definitive treatment for patients with a depressed mental status.
- Maintain fluid balance; monitor the patient's urine.
- Restrict exercise for 24 hours.
- If patient is awake and cooperative, rescuers may assist them in administering their scheduled insulin dose. *Untrained rescuers should not give insulin as a treatment for any diabetic problem. An overdose may be fatal.*
- Protect the patient from all circulatory system insults. Aggressively prevent hypothermia, hyperthermia, and frostbite.
- *Immediately evacuate all diabetic patients who are not awake with ALS to a major hospital.*

Asthma

Pathophysiology

Asthma is a respiratory disease that with exposure to a causal agent produces an immediate bronchial spasm, increased mucus production, and subsequent bronchial constriction. Secondary swelling due to the inflammatory response is possible during the 24 hours following the attack. In persons suffering from chronic and severe asthma the smooth muscular walls of the bronchi thicken making subsequent attacks increasingly more dangerous. The primary agents for inducing an asthmatic episode are cold, exercise, allergens, and stress. Patients present with the signs and symptoms of respiratory distress immediately following exposure. *Severe asthma attacks may be fatal if not treated.*

Prevention

- Avoid exposing people with a prior history of asthma to the specific causal agents.
- If exposure is unavoidable prophylaxis may be obtained through the use of an inhaler. Patients who suffer from chronic asthma usually carry medication for both prevention and treatment of

Medical   **138**

an episode. The most common inhalers are Rx: albuterol (Ventolin), isoetharine (Bronkosol), or metaproterenol (Alupent). The adult dose is 2-4 initial puffs followed by 2 puffs every 6 hours.

Assessment

- *Most asthma patients have a prior history and are familiar with the disease and treatment procedures.*
- Most patients will present with mild respiratory distress accompanied by wheezing that may or may not progress depending on the severity of the attack.
- In severe cases a patient typically assumes an erect, eyes forward, sitting position and is focused on their breathing. Acute episodes may quickly develop into severe respiratory distress accompanied by a decrease in AVPU levels and cyanosis; respiratory arrest is possible. Severe asthma attacks may be fatal if left untreated.

Field Treatment

- Remove the patient from the causal agent (e.g.: stop exercise; warm and humidify the patient's air; remove the stress; remove the patient from the irritant or allergen).
- Reassure the patient to help slow their breathing rate and permit more complete lung expansion. Supplemental oxygen is helpful.
- Fast treatment with a Rx inhaler may completely control the attack by dilating the patient's bronchioles. The drug is most effective when the patient is able to inhale deeply and hold their breath for 10 seconds. Wait one minute between puffs to permit a deeper inhalation with the following puff. Spacers (a tube with a mouthpiece that attaches to the inhaler) increase the effectiveness of the delivery. Do not exceed the recommended dose.
- Administer .3-.5 cc of epinephrine subcutaneously or intramuscularly (usually in the upper thigh) *if the patient does not respond to their inhaler*. Repeat as necessary every 10-15 minutes until the respiratory distress is relieved. *Epinephrine may be fatal to patients with a history of cardiac problems.* [2,6]
- Patients who have required corticosteroids in the treatment of prior asthmatic episodes or patients who do not show a marked improvement after the administration of epinephrine should begin a course of oral prednisone. Adult dose is 50 mg the first day; each subsequent day the dose is lowered by 5 mg for eight days. Steroids act to decrease mucus production and inflammation. [2]
- *Evacuate all patients who suffer severe asthma attacks to a hospital. Avoid patient exertion during the evacuation.*

Seizures

Pathophysiology

Seizures indicate a disturbance in the normal electrical activity of the brain and can have many causes. *Epilepsy* is defined as a condition where a patient suffers from chronic seizures that are often controlled with anti-seizure medication. The type and dose of the medications vary with each patient. Common medications used in the control of epilepsy are diphenylhydantoin (Dilantin), phenobarbital, and diazepam (Valium). The most common cause of seizures in a person under treatment for epilepsy is a failure to take their medication. Often persons with epilepsy are able to distinguish a particular smell, metallic taste, or feeling immediately prior to a seizure. *Seizures unrelated to epilepsy* often accompany other injuries or illnesses that affect the brain. Increased ICP, drug overdose, heat stroke, severe hypoglycemia, and high fevers are some examples. Seizures may take various forms. With a grand mal seizure the patient has violent and repetitive muscular contractions and often loses control of their bladder and bowels. Patients are unable to breath effectively during sustained grand mal seizures greater than two minutes and usually require ALS intervention. Petit mal seizures often go unnoticed and are characterized by a generalized confusion; the patient may appear to be day dreaming. Most seizures are self-limiting and followed by an indeterminate recovery period dependent upon their cause. Initial field treatment is supportive while definitive care must address the cause.

Prevention

- Patients under treatment for epilepsy should closely follow their medication schedule.

Assessment

- A grande mal seizure is characterized by severe and repetitive muscular contractions, unresponsiveness, and a loss of bladder and bowel control.
- Causes may vary. Persons under treatment for epilepsy or diabetes will have a medical history and may wear a medic awake tag.

Field Treatment

- Initial treatment is to protect the patient from injury caused by their muscular contractions. Do not place anything in the patient's mouth.
- Positive pressure ventilations as necessary after the seizure has ended.
- Prolonged or multiple seizures may require immediate ALS intervention.
- Definitive care is based upon the MOI.
- *Consider evacuating all seizure patients to a major hospital for evaluation.*

Expedition Medicine

Lower Respiratory Tract, Throat & Sinus Infections

Pathophysiology

Most lower respiratory tract, throat, and sinus infections are transmitted through close contact with an infected patient usually through shared water bottles, coughing, sneezing, or poor sanitation. These infections commonly infect most members of small expeditions where close contact is unavoidable. Respiratory infections are also associated with near drowning episodes and rib fractures. Most respiratory tract infections are either bacterial or viral in origin. Viral infections destroy the integrity of the infected tissue and are often followed by secondary bacterial infections. A bacterial infection often produces colored phlegm (yellow or green) while in viral infections the mucus is usually clear. A culture may provide definitive diagnoses.

In *lower respiratory tract infections* the microorganism makes its way into the lower airway causing increased mucus secretion, a productive cough, and mild respiratory distress. This is usually accompanied by muscle soreness, a low grade fever, and general fatigue. If the infection becomes well established it may spread into the alveoli (pneumonia) and respiratory signs and symptoms will increase. Rales (wet lung sounds) are often heard and increased fever, chills, and chest pain may develop; death is possible.

In *throat infections* the infecting organism becomes established in the soft tissue of the throat causing inflammation, a sore throat, and dry cough. More serious infections may become systemic. A systemic infection exhibits fever, chills, muscle soreness, swollen lymph nodes, and increased fatigue. A serious bacterial infection (Strep) may lead to cardiac or kidney damage. Throat infections may spread to include the sinuses.

Sinus infections are often transmitted by sneezing and are characterized by a runny nose (increased mucus production), sneezing, congestion, headache, and (rarely) fever. Severe sinus infections may travel up the eustachian tubes and become established in the middle or inner ear.

Prevention

- Avoid close contact with infected persons and maintain good expedition hygiene.
- Nutrition and rest strengthen the immune system and are useful in preventing respiratory tract infections.

Assessment

General

- Recent history of close contact with an infected patient; usually through coughing, sneezing, shared water bottles, etc.
- A bacterial infection often produces colored phlegm (yellow or green) while in viral infections the mucus is usually clear. A culture may provide definitive diagnosis.

Lower Respiratory Tract Infections

- Patient may have a history of near drowning or fractured ribs.
- Signs and symptoms include a productive cough, fatigue, and mild respiratory distress. Severe cases may develop rales and fever.
- An anticipated problem is pneumonia.

Throat Infections

- Signs and symptoms include local inflammation, a sore throat, and dry cough. Fever is possible with more severe infections.
- *Heart and kidney complications related to bacterial strep throat are possible if improperly assessed and treated.*

Sinus Infections

- Patient may have a recent history of severe throat infection.
- Signs and symptoms include runny nose (increased mucus production), sneezing, congestion, headache, and (rarely) fever.
- An anticipated problem is a middle or inner ear infection.

Field Treatment

General

- Provide rest and assistance with thermoregulation.
- Replace fluids and electrolytes. Encourage patients to increase their normal fluid intake (force fluids). Monitor the patient's urine to access their hydration status.
- Fevers above 102 degrees F are best controlled with acetaminophen using the OTC dose. Herbs that help control fever include yarrow and bark from white and black willows (aspirin). Because of the potential for developing Reye's syndrome aspirin is contraindicated in children under 17.
- Do not use an antihistamine in the treatment of symptoms associated with cold, flu, or sinus infections. Antihistamines inhibit mucus production (and the associated runny nose) and restrict drainage permitting the infecting microorganism to multiply.
- Herbs that stimulate the immune system include: echinacea/golden seal combination, ginseng/astragalus combination, and hyssop. All have antibiotic and antiviral properties.
- Herbal teas specific to colds and flu include: catnip, bone set, osha, sage, thyme, and angelica.
- Because of the serious potential complications of leaving respiratory tract infections untreated in a backcountry setting a broad spectrum antibiotic may be indicated. Indications for antibiotic use include local infections that do not respond to supportive treatment, infections that appear to get worse, and all systemic infections. The extended range erythromycins (clarithromycin, azithromycin) are expensive but target all respiratory tract infections. Clarithromycin is given by mouth at 250-500 mg 2 times a day for 10-14 days.[6] Axithromycin is given by mouth at 500 mg 4 times a day on day 1 then 250 mg 4 times a day for four more days.[6]
- *Consider evacuation to a clinic or hospital.*

Lower Respiratory Tract Infections

- An OTC expectorant may be useful during the day. Herbal expectorants include skunk cabbage, pleurisy root, and lung wort.
- An OTC nonnarcotic cough suppressant may be administered before bed to permit rest. Black cherry bark or mullein taken as a tea are two effective herbal cough treatments.
- Steam inhalation therapy may ease daily episodes of respiratory distress. Sage or eucalyptus oil may be added for their antimicrobial properties.
- Alternative antibiotics include TMP/SMX, ceftriaxone, and ciprofloxacin.

Throat Infections

- An OTC cough suppressant or cough drops may be useful to suppress irritation due to a dry nonproductive cough. Mullein and black cherry bark are effective herbal cough suppressants. Give as syrup, tea, or lozenge.
- Gargling with warm salt water or thyme tea may help reduce inflammation.
- Penicillin VK is the drug of choice; however, the extended range erythromycins are also effective against strep.

Medical

Sinus Infections

- Steam inhalation therapy may ease congestion and pressure headaches.
- A systemic OTC decongestant is useful to relieve general congestion and promote drainage. Eyebright tea may also be used to relieve nasal congestion.
- A local OTC decongestant (nasal spray) is helpful before bed to promote rest. Have the patient inhale the spray deeply into their sinuses and hold for ten seconds.
- TMP/SMX or Amoxicillin are the drugs of choice but the extended range erythromycins are also effective.

Ear Infections & Problems

Pathophysiology

Internally each ear is a single tube divided by a thin membrane. The **external ear canal** is open to the general environment and ends with the ear drum. The **middle ear** begins (or ends) at the ear drum and contains the body's specialized hearing apparatus while the **inner ear** contains the balance center. Both are connected to the sinuses via the eustachian tubes. Invading bacteria or viruses are confined to the external ear canal unless the ear drum has ruptured. Infecting organisms may also travel from the sinuses, through the eustachian tubes, and into the middle or inner ear. External ear infections are usually caused by water trapped in the external ear canal. Middle ear infections are usually secondary to sinus infections. Dizziness and fever are characteristic of a middle ear infection. In rare instances the infection may spread to the brain and cause death.

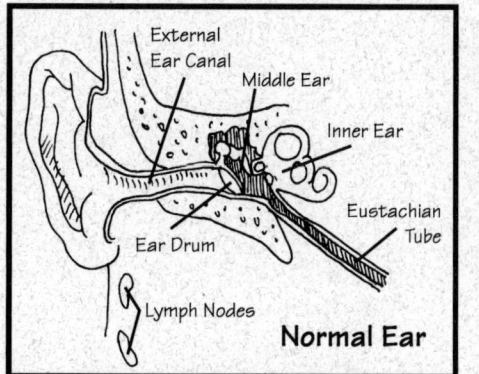

Normal Ear

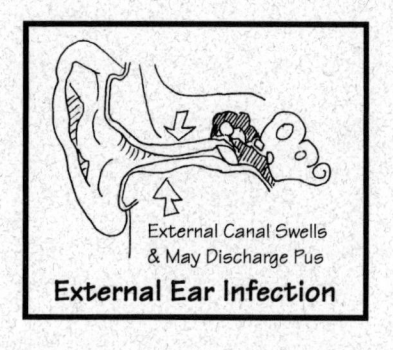

External Canal Swells
& May Discharge Pus

External Ear Infection

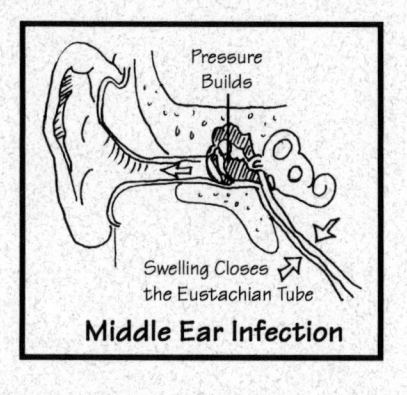

Pressure
Builds

Swelling Closes
the Eustachian Tube

Middle Ear Infection

Prevention

External Ear Infections

- Avoid swimming in contaminated water.
- Thoroughly remove all water from the external ear canal using a few drops of alcohol in each ear or flush with a 1:1 diluted vinegar solution.

Middle and Inner Ear Infections

- Aggressively treat all sinus infections.
- Do not flush or use ear drops with a ruptured ear drum.

Ruptured Ear Drum

- Avoid abrupt pressure changes.

Assessment

External Ear Infections

- History of swimming (usually in contaminated water).
- Ear pain with an inflamed and tender external ear canal.
- Rarely severe infections may cause a fever and swollen lymph glands.

Middle or Inner Ear Infections

- Patient may have a recent history of a severe sinus infection or (rarely) ruptured ear drum.
- Symptoms include ear pain, a full feeling in the ears, dizziness, and fever.
- An anticipated problem is a brain infection (meningitis or encephalitis).

Ruptured Ear Drum

- Possible MOIs are: a foreign object thrust into the ear, an abrupt ascent while SCUBA diving, a loud noise or pressure, a nearby lightning strike, or a severe middle or inner ear infection.
- Immediate and severe ear pain usually accompanied by a hearing loss.
- Dizziness, nausea, and occasionally vomiting may occur.

Field Treatment

External Ear Infections

- Mild infections (without fever or swollen lymph glands) may be treated with diluted vinegar.
- Antibiotic drops containing hydrocortisone should be administered when the patient has a severe infection with fever and swollen lymph glands. In addition, a systemic antibiotic should be considered. Consider penicillin VK or the extended range erythromycins (clarithromycin, azithromycin). Penicillin VK and clarithromycin are given by mouth at 250-500 mg 2 times a day for 10-14 days. [6] Axithromycin is given by mouth at 500 mg 4 times a day on day 1 then 250 mg 4 times a day for four more days. [6]

Middle or Inner Ear Infections

- A systemic OTC decongestant is useful to relieve general congestion and promote drainage.

Medical

Medical

- All middle ear infections should be treated aggressively with systemic antibiotics to prevent spreading to the brain.
- Provide rest and assistance with thermoregulation.
- Replace fluids and electrolytes. Encourage patients to increase their normal fluid intake (force fluids). Monitor the patient's urine to assess their hydration status.
- Fevers above 102 degrees F are best controlled with acetaminophen using the OTC dose.
- If the infection appears bacterial in nature a broad spectrum antibiotic may be administered. Consider the extended range erythromycins (clarithromycin, azithromycin) or TMP/SMX. Clarithromycin is given by mouth at 250-500 mg 2 times a day for 10-14 days. [6] Axithromycin is given by mouth at 500 mg 4 times a day on day 1, then 250 mg 4 times a day for four more days. [6] Adult dose for TMP/SMX is one double strength (960 mg) twice a day for 10 days. [6]
- Consider evacuation to a clinic or hospital.

Ruptured Ear Drum

- Cover to prevent contamination; do not flush.
- Administer OTC pain medications: aspirin, ibuprofen, naproxen sodium, acetaminophen. Because of the potential for developing Reye's syndrome aspirin is contraindicated in children under 17.
- Monitor for a middle or inner ear infection. Most ruptured ear drums heal without complications.

Eye Problems

Pathophysiology

The musculature surrounding the eyes and the eyeball itself are reasonably tough. **Penetrating injuries** are extremely rare and must be attended by a specialist. **Blunt trauma** is also rare and is usually treated as a stable musculoskeletal injury. The most **common injuries** associated with the eyes are general irritation, sunburn, small foreign bodies, corneal abrasions, and infection. All of these problems involve the conjunctiva and, if more severe, the cornea. Signs and symptoms often include itching, redness, a burning sensation or pain, tearing, headache, and light sensitivity. Normal movement of the injured eye is usually uncomfortable but possible. Eyes are highly vascular and minor injuries usually heal within 24-48 hours.

Prevention

- Sunglasses that filter 100% UVB and 80% blue light (UVA) are mandatory in mountain, river, ocean, and desert environments where sunlight and glare are unavoidable. Consider goggles, wraparound glasses or glasses with side protection.
- Protective goggles are helpful in brushy areas and while working with machinery.
- Contact lens wearers should consider wearing glasses instead of contact lenses.
- If contact lenses are worn, wearers should take care to maintain a clean environment when working with their lenses.

Assessment

General Irritation

- Smoke and other chemicals (sunscreen, insect repellent, etc.) often irritate the conjunctiva and occasionally the cornea.
- Signs and symptoms are usually nonspecific with redness, tearing, and general irritation.

Sunburn

- UVB radiation usually effects the conjunctiva causing pain, redness, swelling, headache, and light sensitivity.
- Severe burns may cloud the cornea.

Foreign Bodies

- Onset is abrupt and usually associated with small flying insects and blowing dirt or sand.
- Signs and symptoms include irritation or pain, tearing, and redness.

Corneal Abrasions

- Abrasions may occur on the conjunctiva through contact with branches, foreign bodies, etc.
- Only large scratches will be visible on examination; most corneal abrasions cannot be seen although the patient continues to report a foreign body or general irritation.
- The eye is red and tearing.

Infection

- Infections of the conjunctiva may follow the removal of foreign bodies or the treatment of corneal abrasions. They are also associated with poor contact lens hygiene and close contact with infected persons.
- With bacterial infections the general signs and symptoms are accompanied by a yellow or green pus that often "glues" the eyelids together with a crust during sleep.
- *Bacterial infections of the eye are usually contagious.*

Field Treatment

General Irritation

- Treatment consists of removing the person from the irritant and flushing with sterile saline. The saline solution in squeeze bottles common to contact lens wearers is an extremely effective way to flush an eye.
- *When flushing chemicals, flush towards the outside of the face to avoid contaminating the other eye.*

Sunburn

- The person should be protected from further exposure to sunlight until the signs and symptoms subside; usually within 24-48 hours.
- Severe cases may require bandaging.
- Headaches may be treated with OTC medications: aspirin, ibuprofen, naproxen sodium, acetaminophen.

Medical   146

Small Foreign Bodies

- Remove the object by flushing with sterile saline.
- Stubborn objects may require pulling back the eyelid and using the wet corner of a gauze pad to lift or push the object from the eye.

Corneal Abrasions

- Flush with sterile saline.
- Abrasions usually resolve themselves within 24-48 hours without additional treatment.

Infection

- Herbs used as an eye wash to treat infection include: chamomile, agrimony, and eyebright.
- Bacterial infections may be treated with antibiotic ointment or drops every two hours while the patient is awake. Consider Rx medications ophthalmic gentamicin or Neomycin-polymyxin B-gramicidin ophthalmic. Do not use antibiotics containing steroids. [2,4,6]

Tooth and Gum Problems

Pathophysiology

Problems associated with teeth and gums can be mildly irritating to unbearable. Teeth may be broken or knocked out. Broken teeth or gums can become infected. Fillings or caps can loosen and fall out. Once established a local infection may become severe, systemic, and difficult (if not impossible) to treat in the field.

Prevention

- *Have all dental work done prior to leaving on a expedition.*
- Floss and brush on a regular basis.

Assessment

Broken Teeth, Lost Fillings or Caps, & Knocked Out Teeth

- Tooth is broken but the *pulp is not exposed*. The tooth is sensitive and painful. There is a low risk of infection.
- Tooth is broken and the *pulp is exposed*. The tooth is extremely painful and there is a moderate or high risk of infection.
- The tooth has been knocked out and the socket is exposed and painful. There is a moderate or high risk of infection.
- A filling or cap has loosened or fallen out.

Infection

- The mouth is swollen and extremely painful. The patient may have swollen lymph glands and fever. An abscess may be noticeable in the gums.

Field Treatment

Broken Teeth and Lost Fillings or Caps

- Pain may be controlled with oil of clove (eugenol). OTC medications: aspirin, ibuprofen, naproxen sodium, or acetaminophen.
- The damaged area should be flushed well with salt water, a dilute vinegar solution, or an iodine solution and covered with a wax compound (Orabase) or temporary dental filling material. (DENTEMP).
- Monitor for infection and evacuate all patients who have exposed pulp.

Knocked Out Teeth

- Replace teeth that have been knocked out if they are clean and have been out less than 15 minutes.
- To replace a tooth, first rinse both the socket and the tooth with normal saline then place firmly in the socket. *Do not scrub the connective tissue from the tooth.*
- Do not replace teeth of patients who have not had a tetanus booster within the last five years.
- Secure the tooth to the adjacent teeth using DENTEMP or by "lashing" in place with dental floss or fishing line. Monitor for infection. The tooth should remain splinted for 7-10 days.
- To insure proper alignment and receive antibiotic prophylaxis, patients should be seen by a dentist within 48 hours.
- If evacuation is not possible begin antibiotic prophylaxis. Administer oral penicillin VK or erythromycin. Both are dosed at 250-500 mg 4 times a day for 10 days. [2,4]
- If an infection develops remove the tooth and treat for an infection.

Infection

- Apply hot, moist compresses to the infected area inside the patient's mouth. Do not apply heat to the outside of a patient's face when their tooth or gum is infected. Abscesses move towards heat.
- Consider lancing any obvious pustule heads.
- Thoroughly clean the infected area with a salt water, a dilute vinegar solution, or an iodine solution.
- Administer a systemic antibiotic. Consider penicillin VK or erythromycin. Adult dose for both drugs is 500 mg 4 times a day for 10 days. [4]
- *Evacuate to dental care.*
- If evacuation is not an option and the tooth becomes severely infected consider pulling the tooth with pliers, thoroughly flushing the socket, and continuing antibiotic therapy. To pull a tooth: Wrap the tooth in gauze and grasp firmly with a pair of pliers. Use a wiggling motion to gradually, over many, many hours (8+) loosen the tooth. The attachment of the tooth to the gum is often stronger than the root. If the tooth is loose but still attached at the gum line, you will need to cut the gum using a thin scalpel blade.

Gastrointestinal Problems

Pathophysiology

Problems with the digestive system are primarily those associated with the structure and function of its tubes. These tubes can become blocked, kinked, cut, ruptured, irritated by toxins, or infected.

Medical   **148**

Blocked tubes, especially the small and large intestine, commonly produce abdominal pain and cramps. The small intestine is often blocked by gas. Gas stretches the intestinal wall causing cramps and abdominal pain. Once it has passed, the pain subsides and the system returns to normal. A hernia, a kink in the small intestine, functions like a block. The most common form of hernia occurs in men, usually while lifting a heavy object. In this case the pressure associated with lifting forces a piece of the small intestine through the abdominal wall and into the scrotal sac. The accompanying pain is instantaneous and severe. If a piece of intestine remains inside the scrotal sac it may block the intestinal tract, lose perfusion, and die. The large intestine is commonly blocked by consolidated fecal matter causing constipation. And the bile duct is occasionally blocked by gall stones. All blocked tubes are accompanied by a loss of function, cramping, abdominal pain, and in more severe cases guarding and tenderness. The pain is usually nonspecific, mild or severe, and does not necessarily relate to the severity of the problem.

Invading bacteria, viruses, one cell organisms, and yeast commonly produce varying degrees of *infections* that may have local or systemic consequences. Some infecting organisms may travel from a tube into the bloodstream or connecting organs. Most intestinal infections usually produce diarrhea, vomiting, and abdominal cramps. More severe infections may cause fever, chills, severe pain, guarding, and tenderness. A local infection may cause the appendix to swell, become ischemic, and eventually rupture. If this occurs in the backcountry the patient may die.

Rupture and penetrating trauma may cause digestive fluids to leak into the abdominal cavity. The stuffsack lining the abdominal cavity, the peritoneum, is highly innervated and easily inflamed. Fluids from any of the digestive tubes can quickly activate the inflammatory response and cause massive amounts of fluid loss to edema; volume shock is possible. If the fluids contain invading bacteria the subsequent infection may be fatal if the fluid loss is not. Blunt trauma may also cause a rupture of the liver or spleen and lead to volume shock. Patients who have a mechanism for abdominal fluid loss (trauma, infection, ulcers, etc.) and present with severe abdominal pain and tenderness often require surgery.

It is extremely difficult to diagnose the cause of abdominal pain and its associated signs and symptoms without a specific mechanism. Fortunately most abdominal pain, signs, and symptoms are self-limiting within 12 hours and benign. Field treatment is usually limited to treating the signs and symptoms. Abdominal pain that is accompanied by blood, either in the vomitus or in the stool, fever, or extreme tenderness should be considered serious. Partially digested blood looks like coffee grounds when vomited and smells foul. Blood in the stool is black and tarry. An evacuation should be initiated if the abdominal problem is persistent, uncomfortable, and not relieved by supportive treatment.

Prevention

- Treat all suspect food and water.
- Maintain good expedition hygiene.
- Maintain hydration and monitor urine color and output.
- Eat a healthy diet with complete nutrition and fiber.

Assessment

- A thorough history focused on discovering the specific MOI is indicated. Gastrointestinal signs and symptoms may have numerous mechanisms (e.g.: flu, pregnancy, ulcers, etc.). Evaluate each tube separately. Carefully examine what has gone into, what has come out of, and the current function of each tube.

- General abdominal pain associated with nausea, vomiting, and/or diarrhea that resolves and doesn't compromise the patient's hydration status.

Serious

- Abdominal pain associated with a *fever*.
- Abdominal pain associated with **blood** in vomitus or stool.
- **Persistent** abdominal pain, tenderness, vomiting, and diarrhea greater than 12 hours.
- **Increasing** abdominal pain and tenderness associated with trauma.
- Abdominal pain and tenderness associated with the signs and symptoms of volume shock.
- Abdominal pain not relieved by supportive treatment.

Field Treatment

- Provide bed rest and assist thermoregulation.
- Replace and force fluids and electrolytes. Encourage patients to increase their normal fluid intake (force fluids). Monitor the patient's urine to access their hydration status.
- Herbal teas that help relieve general GI signs and symptoms include: hops, chamomile, peppermint, licorice, and bayberry.
- If the patient is hungry, their diet should consist of clear fluids and bland neutral foods. The diet should be enforced until all GI signs and symptoms have been absent for a minimum of 24-48 hours.
- In most cases **vomiting** is self-limiting and should be permitted to run its course. Consider controlling *persistent* vomiting (greater than 12 hours) OR vomiting that compromises the patient's hydration status with promethazine (adults only). Oral dose 25 mg every 6 hours. Suppository: 25 mg every 6 hours. Alternately, 50 mg of diphenhydramine (Benadryl) may be given every six hours for 4 doses. [6] Both drugs are contraindicated in pregnant women.
- In most cases **diarrhea** is self-limiting and should be permitted to run its course. Mild diarrhea may be controlled using tea made from five finger grass or the inner bark of slippery elm. Consider controlling *persistent* diarrhea (greater than 24 hours) OR diarrhea that compromises the patient's hydration status with loperamide (Imodium): adult dose is 4 mg initially followed by 2 mg after each loose bowel movement. Do not exceed 16 mg within a 24 hour period. [6] Constipation and abdominal cramps are possible.
- **Constipation** may initially be treated with increased fluids and intestinal bulking agents (Metamucil). Local lubricants (mineral oil by mouth or suppository) and oral OTC laxatives are next followed by bisocodyl suppositories (10 mg as needed inserted in the patient's rectum). Warm water enemas are a last resort.
- **Fevers** above 102 degrees F are best controlled with acetaminophen using the OTC dose.
- The herb agrimony (given as a tea) increases clotting and may be useful in the treatment of mild GI bleeds.
- **Evacuate all patients with serious signs and symptoms** (as outlined above under assessment).

Medical

Genitourinary Problems

Pathophysiology

Problems with the genitourinary system are primarily those associated with the structure and function of its tubes which commonly become blocked or infected.

Women are predisposed to urinary tract infections (UTI), vaginitis, and some sexually transmitted diseases because their urethras are short and close to their anus. Gonorrhea and Chlamydia are two common sexually transmitted diseases that may spread into a woman's uterus and cause pelvic inflammatory disease (PID). PID is an infection of the uterus. It is accompanied by nonspecific abdominal cramps, pressure, and pain. Because both gonorrhea and chlamydia are often asymptomatic the initial signs and symptoms may indicate a serious infection; left untreated PID may be fatal.

Within a woman's vagina, bacteria and yeast coexist in a balanced state. If the bacteria are destroyed, the balance is disturbed, and yeast is able to grow unchecked, often causing a vaginal yeast infection. All antibiotics are capable of upsetting the vaginal balance. Women taking antibiotics are at risk for yeast infections.

During the first trimester, tubal (ectopic) pregnancies and miscarriages may cause serious problems. An ectopic pregnancy may obstruct a fallopian tube causing extreme pain. If not treated promptly ectopic pregnancies may rupture and cause death. Pregnant women may undergo a spontaneous abortion or miscarriage during the first trimester that is usually not physically significant unless accompanied by severe bleeding. Secondary infection is possible if a portion of the fetus remains attached to the uterine wall. Miscarriage is unlikely, unless caused by trauma, during the second and third trimesters. All pregnant women should consult a physician before joining an expedition.

Men rarely suffer from urinary tract infections because their urethras are longer and at a greater distance from their anus; however, they are susceptible to sexually transmitted diseases.

Prevention

Urinary Tract Infections and Vaginitis

- Maintain hydration and urinate on a frequent basis to flush bacteria. Don't "hold it in."
- Women should wash and dry a minimum of twice a day.
- Keep genital area cool and dry. Wear clean cotton underwear or skirts without underwear whenever possible.
- Good hygiene is important. Women should consider using "pee rags" to pat dry after urination; avoid "drip drying." Wipe front to back after a bowel movement to prevent contamination of the vagina.
- Direct trauma to the urethra from bicycles, climbing harnesses, vigorous sexual activity, etc. contributes to the development of urinary tract infections. A significant number of UTIs occur from bacteria exchanged during oral sex. In addition to washing, women prone to UTIs should urinate before and after sex to help flush unfriendly bacteria.
- Women taking antibiotics should take oral acidophilus or eat yogurt with live cultures to help maintain or reestablish normal vaginal bacteria and prevent yeast infections.

Sexually Transmitted Diseases

- Use condoms.
- Get tested and, if necessary, treated prior to any lengthy expedition.
- Know your partner's sexual history.
- Abstain.

Assessment

Urinary Tract Infections

- Burning pain or urethral spasms upon and shortly following urination.
- Increased urgency and frequency of urination with increasingly smaller amounts of urine.
- The urine may be cloudy or tinged with blood.
- Fever and/or back pain and tenderness (lower thoracic or upper lumbar region) usually indicate a UTI that has spread to the kidneys.

Vaginitis

- *Definitive assessment for all forms of vaginitis require a vaginal smear.* In the absence of definitive care, signs and symptoms may guide field treatment. If the patient does not respond to the prescribed drug therapy or the condition worsens, discontinue therapy and evacuate to definitive care.
- Vaginal itching and a thick white cheesy discharge characterize a *yeast infection*. Recent history often reveals antibiotic therapy. Women who have previously been treated for yeast infections easily recognize the signs and symptoms.
- With *bacterial vaginitis* the discharge is usually thin, white, and foul smelling. The odor is often stronger following menstruation. Bacterial infections may be accompanied by low pelvic pain.
- In rare instances vaginitis may be caused by a *protozoan*. Signs and symptoms are similar to a bacterial infection but with an abundant foamy discharge. The infection may spread to include abdominal pain and fever.
- Urination may irritate already inflamed tissues causing a burning vaginal pain. Although the pain is different from the pain associated with urinary tract infections, confusion is common.

Miscarriage

- History of pregnancy or sexual intercourse within the past three months.
- Signs and symptoms may include unusually heavy vaginal bleeding outside the woman's normal menstrual period accompanied by abdominal pain or cramping.

Ectopic Pregnancy

- Signs and symptoms are general or localized abdominal cramps, pressure, and pain that progressively increases.
- Spotting or minor vaginal bleeding is common.

Sexually Transmitted Diseases

- *Definitive assessment is only possible through culture and examination by trained medical professionals.*
- Varieties of the *Herpes* virus cause outbreaks of open sores. Herpes is extremely contagious during an outbreak and predisposes people to other sexually transmitted diseases.

Medical

- Many people, both males and females, are asymptomatic carriers of **gonorrhea** and **Chlamydia**. In women, gonorrhea and Chlamydia may be accompanied by a burning pain with urination and a rotten fishy smell. Burning pain with urination and/or a white milky discharge in a male usually indicates either gonorrhea or Chlamydia.
- **Syphilis** has an incubation period of 10 days to 3 months and initially presents with localized sores that begin to subside after 4-6 weeks. The disease then enters a latent stage with occasional episodes of oozing sores. Eventually the disease damages the brain or heart causing death.
- **PID** is characterized by abdominal cramps, pressure, and pain. PID may be accompanied by a fever. It is difficult to distinguish from other causes of abdominal pain.

Field Treatment

Urinary Tract Infections

- Force fluids.
- High concentrations of vitamin C or cranberry juice may help in the early stages or with mild infections.
- Herbs useful in treating UTIs include gravel root, couch grass, boldo, and parsley. These herbs act as a diuretic and have antimicrobial properties. Prickly pear juice may be used to alleviate the pain but has no antimicrobial action.
- Urinary tract infections should be treated aggressively with antibiotics to prevent spreading to the kidneys and blood. Consider administering trimethoprim with sulfamethoxazole or ciprofloxacin. Adult dose for TMP/SMX is one double strength tablet (960 mg) twice a day for 7-10 days. Do not give TMP/SMX to patients allergic to sulfa drugs. Adult dose for ciprofloxacin is 250 mg twice a day for 7-10 days. [4,6]
- *Evacuate the patient if antibiotic therapy is not available .*

Vaginitis

- **Mild infections** may be treated with regular douching using a diluted solution of povidone-iodine (1 teaspoon per quart of water) or vinegar (1 tablespoon per quart of water).
- OTC medications are highly effective for **yeast infections** as are vaginal suppositories, tablets, or creams. Clotrimazole (Gyne-Lotrimin): insert one applicator full of cream or one 100 mg vaginal tablet at bedtime for 7 days. Miconazole nitrate (Monistat): insert one applicator full of cream or one 100 mg suppository at bedtime for 7 days.
- For **bacterial vaginitis** (Gardnerella) treat with Rx intravaginal metronidazole (MetroGel) given as a vaginal insert twice daily for 5 days. [4,6]
- For **protozoal vaginitis** (Trichomoniasis) a systemic antibiotic metronidazole (Flagyl) should be used. Adult dose is 500 mg twice a day for 7 days. Therapy has also been successful using a single 2 g dose of metronidazole. [4]
- *If the patient does not respond to the prescribed drug therapy or the condition worsens, discontinue therapy and evacuate to definitive care.*

Miscarriage

- Monitor for the signs and symptoms of infection for 3-4 days.
- The herb agrimony (given as a tea) increases clotting and may be useful in the treatment of heavy menstrual bleeding or bleeding due to miscarriage.
- *Evacuate to a major hospital if persistent bleeding occurs.*

General Drug Theory

Drugs are chemical toxins designed to kill specific microorganisms. Many have potentially dangerous side-effects and their benefits and complications must be carefully weighed prior to use. Unfortunately side-effects can vary greatly from patient to patient and some risk is unavoidable. Drugs based in sulfa or penicillin preparations may cause a life-threatening allergic reaction (anaphylaxis) in some people. Toxic overdose is possible in others. Infants, children, and pregnant women often have a significant increase in risk.

The **dose and schedule** may also vary greatly depending upon the severity of the disease and the drug used. Drugs may be delivered via intravenous drip, subcutaneous or intramuscular injection, by oral tablet or capsule, inhalation, or via topical preparations. The human body metabolizes and treats drugs in the same way it handles other chemical compounds that require neutralization and/or elimination. Neutralization is usually accomplished in the liver while elimination is the primary responsibility of the kidneys. If the drug is given by mouth it must first survive stomach acids and then be absorbed by the small intestine. Different drugs have different "clearance" times and pathways within the body depending upon the specific drug and delivery method. Therefore drugs are specific to both the infecting organism and its location within the body. Indiscriminate substitution is highly discouraged and can be dangerous.

Ideally the perfect drug will have minimal or no side-effects and quickly destroy the invading organism. Drugs are usually taken in courses that are commonly 7-14 days in length. This amount of time permits the level of toxicity to remain consistent for a period of time long enough to destroy all invading organisms and prevent mutation. If the choice of drug is correct, symptoms often subside within 3-4 days. If the drug is discontinued before the end of the prescribed course, resistant organisms may develop, multiply, and cause a relapse that is no longer treatable with the original drug. **Once started, it is important to complete a course of drugs.**

Because of the potential dangers associated with the use of drugs it is best to have a patient diagnosed and treated by a trained physician. Unfortunately trained physicians are often unavailable during long remote expeditions where drug therapy may make the difference between the life and death of a patient. Any expedition that carries drugs in the absence of a physician should receive specific training for that drug prior to the expedition. The specific drug therapies discussed within this field manual are offered in order to promote understanding and stimulate additional learning.

Drug Table Index

The following tables indicate the route of administration, some contraindications, some potential side effects, and general information relative to drugs discussed in this manual. Additional information may be found by referring to the numbered reference(s).

Antibiotics[6]	Rt	Contraindications	Side Effects	Notes
Amoxicillin	PO	Hypersensitivity to penicillins. Pregnancy.	GI: diarrhea, nausea, vomiting. GU: vaginal yeast infections.	
Ceftriaxone	IM	Hypersensitivity to cephalosporins. Pregnancy.	GI: diarrhea, abdominal cramps. GU: vaginitis.	
Ciprofloxacin	PO	Hypersensitivity to quinolones. Pregnancy, nursing mothers, children.	CNS: headaches, vertigo, malaise, seizures. GI: nausea, vomiting, diarrhea, cramps.	Increase fluid intake. Avoid caffine.
Clindamycin	PO	Hx of hypersensitivity. Pregnancy. Caution with Hx of GI Px.	GI: diarrhea, nausea, vomiting, abdominal pain. Skin: rashes.	Stop drug if severe diarrhea develops. Do not take concurrently with diarrhea drugs.
Doxycycline	PO	Sensitivity to tetracyclines. Pregnancy, nursing mothers, children.	GI: nausea, vomiting, abdominal cramps, diarrhea. Skin: increased sun sensitivity.	Avoid sun during therapy and for a period of 5 days after the course is completed. Sunblocks are ineffective.
Erythromycin	PO	Hypersensitivity. Pregnancy. Pts with impaired liver function.	CNS: vertigo, tinnitus. GI: nausea, vomiting, diarrhea, abdominal cramps. GU: vaginal yeast infections.	Not for prolongued use due to the potential for developing resistant organisms and superinfections.
Penicillin G	PO IV	Hypersensitivity or allergies to penicillins or cephalosporins. Pregnancy.	Anaphylaxis. CNS: fever, malaise. Skin: rash.	Take oral medication on an empty stomach 1 hour before or 2 hours after a meal.
Penicillin VK	PO	Hypersensitivity or allergies to penicillins or cephalosporins. Pregnancy.	Anaphylaxis. GI: nausea, vomiting, diarrhea.	
Streptomycin	IM	Hypersensitivity or allergies to aminoglycosides. Pregnancy, children.	Anaphylaxis. CNS: headache, weakness, vertigo, tinnitus.	
Tetracycline	PO	Hypersensitivity to tetracyclines. Pregnancy, children.	GI: nausea vomiting, diarrhea. Skin: phototoxicity. General: yeast infections, superinfections.	Avoid sun during therapy and for a period of 5 days after the course is completed. Sunblocks are ineffective.
Trimethoprim sulfamethoxazole (TMP–SMR)	PO	Hypersensitivity or allergies to sulfa drugs. Pregnancy.	GI: nausea, vomiting, diarrhea. Skin: rashes, photosensitivity, jaundice.	Discontinue if skin rash or jaundice appear.

Drug Tables

Antimalarial	Rt	Contraindications	Side Effects	Notes
Artemether$_{1,3}$	IM		CNS: potential neurotoxicity.	For severe cases with quinine resistant strains and in combination with other antimalarials.
Artemisinin$_{1,3}$				For severe cases with quinine resistant strains and in combination with other antimalarials.
Artesunate$_{1,3}$	IM IU		CNS: potential neurotoxicity.	For severe cases with quinine resistant strains and in combination with other antimalarials.
Chloroquine$_{3,4}$	PO		GI: nausea, vomiting, abdominal pain. CNS: dizziness, headache.	Avoid prolonged use.
Fansidar$_{3,4}$	PO	Hx of sulfonamide intolerance.		Taken with chloroquine. Tx is temporary; seek medical evaluation ASAP.
Mefloquine$_{3,4}$	PO	Pregnancy, children, pts on cardiac drugs, pts with psychiatric disorders, epilepsy.	GI: nausea, abdominal pain, diarrhea. CNS: dizziness, insomnia, strange dreams.	
Primaquine$_{3,4}$	PO	Pregnancy.	Circ: hypertension, arrhythmias. GI: abdominal cramps	
Quinine$_{3,4}$	PO IU	Avoid tetracyclines. Do not use if pt. has taken mefloquine during the past 2 weeks.	CNS: tinnitus, vertigo, confusion. GI: nausea, vomiting, diarrhea.	

Antiviral Drugs$_6$	Rt	Contraindications	Side Effects	Notes
Acylovir	PO	Pregnancy, children.	CNS: headache, lightheadedness, fatigue. GI: nausea, vomiting diarrhea. GU: acute renal failure. Skin: rash.	Most effective when started with the onset of S/Sx. Avoid contact with eyes.

Antimicrobials	Rt	Contraindications	Side Effects	Notes
Metronidazole[1,3,6]	PO	Pregnancy, nursing mothers, and pts. with preexisting yeast infections.	CNS: vertigo, headache, depression, fatigue. GI: nausea, diarrhea, abdominal cramps, constipation. GU: UTI, pelvic pressure, dryness of vagina and vulva, yeast infection.	Avoid alcohol. Pts urine may be dark or reddish brown. Discontinue if seizures or peripheral numbness develop. Supplement with acidophillus capsules and/or yogurt containing live cultures.
Quinacrine Hydrochloride[3,6]	PO	Pregnancy.	CNS: headache, vertigo, irritability, insomnia. GI: nausea, vomiting, diarrhea, abdominal pain. Skin: yellow color.	Skin discolorations disappear about 2 weeks after Tx.
Tinidazole[1,3]	PO	Pregnancy, nursing mothers, and pts. with preexisting yeast infections.	GI: nausea, vomiting, abdominal cramps, diarrhea, constipation. GU: UTI, pelvic pressure, dryness of vagina and vulva, yeast infection.	Supplement with acidophillus capsules and/or yogurt containing live cultures.

AMS Drugs	Route	Contraindications	Side Effects	Notes
Acetosolamide[6] (Diamox)	PO	Hx of hypersensativity to sulfa drugs. Pregnancy. Caution with diabetic pts.	CNS: malaise, depression, fatigue, muscle weakness. GI: nausea, vomiting, diarrhea, thirst, dry mouth.	Take with food to minimize GI problems. Increase fluid and electrolyte (esp. potassium) intake.
Dexamethasone[6]	PO, IM	Systemic fungal infections, acute infections, concurrent with live virus vaccine.	CNS: euphoria, insomnia, increased ICP, vertigo. Cardiovascular: CHF, hypertension, edema. Endocrine: menstrual irregularities, hyperglycemia. GI: hiccups, nausea, abdominal distension, ulcers, oral yeast infections. Musc: weakness, tendon rupture, pathogenic fractures. Skin: impaired wound healing.	Increase potassium intake.
Nifedipine[1]	Sublingual		Cardiovascular: hypotension.	

Asthma Medications[6]	Rt	Contraindications	Side Effects	Notes
albuterol (Proventil, Ventolin)	Inhaled	Pregnancy, nursing mothers. Caution in pts with cardiovascular disease and diabetes.	CNS: anxiety, hallucinations, headache. Cardiovascular: hypotension, hypertension. Eye: blurred vision. GI: nausea, vomiting. General: muscle cramps.	Avoid OTC cold medicines or drugs that mimic sympathetic nervous system actions.
Epinephrine	IM	Hypersensitivity to drugs that mimic sympathetic nervous system actions. Uolume or cardiogenic shock. Pts. with hx of cardiac problems. Pregnancy.	Cardiac: MI, tachyarrhythmias. CNS: anxiety, dizziness, severe headache, stroke. GI: nausea, vomiting. Skin: sweating, pale color.	May increase blood glucose levels; pts with diabetes may experience control problems.
Isoetharine (Bronkosol, Bronkometer)	Inhaled	Hx of hypersensitivity to drugs that mimic sympathetic nervous system actions and bisulfites. *Do not use with epinephrine.*	Cardiac: tachycardia, palpitations, MI. CNS: headache, dizziness, anxiety, insomnia. GI: nausea, vomiting.	Keep spray away from eyes during use. Increase fluid intake. Excessive use may cause an increase in symptoms.
Metaproterenol (Alupent, Metaprel)	Inhaled	Hx of hypersensitivity to drugs that mimic sympathetic nervous system actions. Pregnancy.	Cardiac: palpitations, MI. CNS: anxiety, headache, fatigue. GI: nausea, vomiting.	
Prednisone	PO	Systemic fungal infections, hx of hypersensitivity. Pregnancy. Caution with pts suffering from infections and hypertension.	CNS: euphoria, headache, insomnia, psychosis. Cardiac: CHF. GI: nausea, vomiting, ulcers. Musc: weakness, delayed wound healing. Osteoporosis. Endocrine: hyperglycemia, carbohydrate intolerance.	Avoid aspirin during Tx. Discontinue use gradually if course is greater than a week.

Hypoglycemia[6]	Rt	Contraindications	Side Effects	Notes
Glucagon	IM	Hypersensitivity. Pregnancy.	GI: nausea, vomiting.	After pt. becomes alert (5-20 minutes) follow with complete carbohydrate meal. Headache, nausea, and weakness may persist hours after recovery.

Ointments, Creams & Suppositories[6]

	Route	Contraindications	Side Effects	Notes
Clotrimazole (Gyne–Lotrimin)	Vaginal	Pregnancy, nursing mothers, children.	Local: mild burning sensation. GI: lower abdominal cramps, bloating. GU: UTI.	Refrain from intercourse during Tx. Supplement with acidophilus capsules and/or yogurt containing live cultures.
Metronidazole (MetroGel)	Vaginal	Pregnancy, nursing mothers, and pts. with preexisting yeast infections.	CNS: vertigo, headache, depression, fatigue. GI: nausea, vomiting, abdominal cramps, diarrhea, constipation. GU: UTI, pelvic pressure, dryness of vagina and vulva, yeast infection.	Avoid alcohol. Pts urine may be dark or reddish brown. Discontinue if seizures or peripheral numbness develop. Supplement with acidophilus capsules and/or yogurt containing live cultures.
Miconazole (Monistat)	Vaginal	Pregnancy, nursing mothers, children. Hx of allergic reactions.	Anaphylaxis. Cardiac: tachycardia, arrhythmias. GU: vulvovaginal burning, itching, pelvic cramps. GI: nausea, vomiting, diarrhea:	The organism should be identified prior to Tx. Improvement should occur within 1–2 weeks. Avoid intercourse during Tx.
Gentamicin	Eye	Hx of hypersensitivity to any aminoglycoside antibiotic	Photosensitivity, burning, stinging, redness.	
Neomycin Sulfate	Ear Eye Skin	Do not use over large skin areas or with ruptured ear drum.	Redness, scaling. High incidence of allergic dermatitis.	Short term use only.
Promethazine	PO PR	Hypersensitivity to phenothiazines.	CNS: Sleep, drowsiness. Respiratory depression. N/V, constipation. Skin: photosensitivity. GI:	Avoid prolonged sun exposure.
Silver sulfadiazine	Skin	Hypersensitivity to sulfer drugs.	Pain, burning , itching, rash.	Normal color of cream is white; do not use if cream is dark.

Heart Medications[6]

	Route	Contraindications	Side Effects	Notes
Nitroglycerin	Sublingual	Hypersensativity to nitrates. Head trauma, increased ICP. Hypotension. Pregnancy, nursing mothers, children.	CNS: headache, vertigo Cardiovascular: postural hypotension, palpitations. circulatory collapse. Skin: flushing, cold sweat.	Tingling or burning sensation under tongue is normal. Once pain is relieved with sublingual tablet, the remaining portion may be expelled.

Allergy Medications₆	Rt	Contraindications	Side Effects	Notes
Diphenhydramine (Benadryl)	PO	Hypersensitivity to antihistamines. Asthma. GI obstruction. Pregnancy, nursing mothers, children under 12. Caution in pts with cardiovascular disease and diabetes.	CNS: drowsiness, dizziness, headache, impaired coordination, insomnia, tinnitus, vertigo. Cardiovascular: palpitation, tachycardia, cardiovascular collapse. GI: vomiting, diarrhea, constipation. Resp: wheezing, thickened secretions.	May by used to prevent motion sickness. Take with food. Avoid alcohol and other CNS depresssaants. Avoid activities that require alertness. Increase fluid intake.
Epinephrine	SQ IM	Hypersensitivity to drugs that mimic sympathetic nervous system actions. Volume or cardiogenic shock. Pts. with hx of cardiac problems. Pregnancy.	Cardiac: MI, tachyarrhythmias. CNS: anxiety, dizziness, severe headache, stroke. GI: nausea, vomiting. Skin: sweating, pale color.	May increase blood glucose levels; pts with diabetes may experience control problems.

Pain₆	Rt	Contraindications	Side Effects	Notes
Aspirin	PO	Hypersensitivity to salicylates and other NSAIDs. Hx GI bleeding or bleeding disorders. CHF. Children suffering from Chicken Pox or influenza-like illnesses (Reye's syndrome).	*Anaphalaxis.* ENT: tinnitus, hearing loss. GI: nausea, vomiting, heartburn, GI bleeding.	GI irritation can be reduced by taking with H₂O or food. Do not crush or dissolve tablets.
Acetaminophen	PO	Hypersensitivity to acetaminophen or phenacetin. Alcoholism. With recurrent fever or fever above 103˚F.	Negligible with recommended dosage.	May be crushed and taken with fluids. Do not take with food. Limit use to 10 days for adults, 5 for children.
Ibuprofen	PO	Hypersensitivity to other NSAIDs. Hx GI ulcers.	*Anaphalaxis.* GI: heartburn, nausea. GI bleeding.	Taking with food slows absorption rate. Do not exceed 2400 mg in 24 hours.
Naproxen Sodium	PO	Hypersensitivity to other NSAIDs. Hx GI ulcers.	*Anaphalaxis.* CNS: headache, drowsiness, dizziness. GI: heartburn, nausea, GI bleeding.	May be taken with food to reduce GI irritation.
Ketorolac Tromethamine	PO IM	Hypersensitivity to ketroloac and other NSAIDs.	CNS: drowsiness,dizziness. GI: nausea, pain, *hemorrhage.*	Limit use to 5 days. Do not take concurrent with other NSAIDs. Avoid alcohol.

Medicinal Herbal Theory & Use

Medicinal herbs have been successfully used to treat ailments for thousands of years. Their gathering, preparation, and use have been documented in the writings and folklore of numerous cultures worldwide. Their use has been refined by generations and provides a built-in safety factor unavailable in modern drugs. Although herbs may be evaluated according to their pharmacological actions and chemical compounds, herbalists believe (and recent studies have proven) that the constituents of the entire plant are greater than the sum of its parts. Some plant components are synergistic and enhance the herb's action far beyond the synthesized "active" compound, while other constituents buffer chemicals that would, without their presence, cause harmful side-effects. In addition to their direct therapeutic affect herbs provide necessary trace elements and vitamins required for effective healing. Because the line between therapeutic and toxic doses is much broader with herbs than with modern drugs, *most medicinal herbs may be safely used by lay persons.* Herbs may be gathered and stored for use as the dried herb, dried powders, essential oils, tinctures, ointments, liniments, capsules, lozenges, and syrups. Teas may be made from fresh or dried herbs, tinctures, and tonics.

- *Essential oils* extracted from the plant are used as inhalants and, when diluted, for massage; they should not be taken internally.
- Fresh herbs steeped in alcohol or cider vinegar produce concentrated *tinctures.* Tinctures are taken internally or used to make teas, compresses, or ointments. A single tincture made from multiple herbs is referred to as a *tonic.*
- *Infusions* are teas made from the flowers and leaves of fresh or dried herbs. To make an infusion pour boiling water over the herb, cover, and allow it to steep for 10-15 minutes before straining. Infusions preserve the volatile oils present in the herb.
- *Decoctions* are teas made by boiling the hard, woody parts of an herb. The roots, woody stems, bark, or nuts are first chopped (or ground) and then boiled for 10-15 minutes before straining.
- *Compresses* are made by soaking a clean cloth in an infusion or decoction. *Poultices* are similar to compresses but are made by wrapping the herb in gauze before applying to the skin. Both compresses and poultices are applied hot to the injured area and changed when they become cool. The active components are absorbed through the skin.
- *Ointments* are made by combining the fresh herb or tincture with a base of wax, fat, or oil that is then applied to the skin.
- *Liniments* are an oil based herbal extract and used externally.
- *Capsules* are gelatine containers filled with powdered herbs or oils.
- *Lozenges* are powdered herbs or oil combined with gum or dried sugar.
- *Syrups* are tinctures added to sugar.

Herbs may be carried and stored in a chopped or powdered form for later use in infusions, decoctions, compresses, or poultices. Since they do not keep well, *water-based infusions and decoctions should be used immediately.* Essential oils, ointments, liniments, and tinctures are prepared prior to use and for specific purposes; they are easily carried and last for years.

The following tables indicate the common and Latin names, parts used, route of administration, and action of the medicinal herbs discussed in this manual. Additional information may be found by referring to the numbered reference(s).

Common Name	Latin Name	Parts Used	Route	Action
Agrimony[18]	Agrimonia eupatoria	aerial parts	tea	Increase clotting up to 50%. Tones mucus membranes. Slows profuse menstration. Mouthwash, gargle, eye wash, wound irrigation.
Aloe[1,18]	Aloe vera	fresh juice and gel	poltice	Burns, cuts, wounds. Encourages skin regeneration.
Angelica[18,13]	Angelica archangelica	roots, stems, seeds	tea	Colds, UTIs. Sweat inducing expectorant. Antimicrobial. Antiseptic. Antispasmodic. Relieves abdominal cramps. Diuretic.
Arnica[1,18,11]	Arnica montana	dried flowers or extract	poltice compress ointment	Bruises & sprains. Increases resistance to bacterial infection. Stimulates local circulation. *Do not take internally.*
Astragalus[18]	Astragalus membranaceus	root	tea	Strengthens the immune system. Use with ginseng.
Bayberry[18]	Myrica cerifera	dried root bark	tea	Colds & fevers. Inflamation and infection of digestive tract. Antibacterial. Stimulating astringent.
Black Cherry[18]	Prunus serotina	bark collected in the fall	tea	Cough suppressent.
Black Cohosh[18]	Cimicifuga racemosa	dried root, rhizome	tea	Dilates blood vessels and lowers BP. Antispasmodic. Anti-inflammatory. Reduces menstral cramps. Relieves asthma.
Boldo[18]	Peumus boldo	leaves	tea	UTI. Diuretic and urinary antiseptic.
Boneset[18,13]	Eupatorium perfoliatum	aerial parts	tea	Colds & flu. Stimulates circulation & promotes sweating. Weak anti-inflammatory.
Catnip[18,11,13]	Nepeta cataria	dried aerial parts	tea	Colds, flu, infectious diseases. Promotes sweating. GI sedative that counters flatulence and diarrhea. Relieves menstrual cramps.
Chamomile[1,18,11]	Chamomilla	dried flowers	tea wash	Sedative. Induces sleep. Relaxes smooth muscle of the intestine and uterus. Wound irrigation (relieves pain & promotes healing). Eye wash. Antimicrobial. Antifungal. Antispasmodic. Antihistamine.

Herb Tables

Common Name	Latin Name	Parts Used	Route	Action
Clove[18]	Eugenia aromatica	dried buds	oil	Relieves pain of toothache.
Comfrey[1,10,13]	Symphytum officinale	fresh or dried roots or leaves	poltice compress salve	Fractures, bruises, burns.
Couch Grass[18]	Agropyron repens	rhizome	tea	UTI. Soothing diuretic and antibacterial.
Echinacea[18,12]	Echinacea	dried root, rhizome	tea wash	Strengthens immune system. Wound irrigation. Antibacterial & antiviral. Increases general tissue repair.
Eucalyptus[18,11,12]	Eucalyptus	oil of leaves	oil	Strong antiseptic. Inhalation therapy for colds & flu. Chest rub. *Do not use internally.*
Eyebright[18]	Euphrasia officinalis	aerial parts	tea compress	Nasal congestion. Eye infections. Mouthwash.
Evening Primrose[18,11,13]	Oenothera lamarkiana, O, biennis	extracted oil	oil	PMS. Heart Disease. Reduces blood clotting & BP. Relieves menstrual cramps. GI sedative. Antiarthritis.
Five Finger Grass[18]	Potentilla erecta	root	tea ointment	GI infections & diarrhea. Cuts & wounds. Eye wash.
Garlic[1,18]	Allium sativum	cloves	crushed raw poltice	Lowers blood cholesterol and fats. Reduces BP and blood clotting. Antifungal. Antibacterial. Lowers blood sugar levels.
Ginger[1,18]	Zingiber officinale	rhizome	tea raw	Nausea, poor circulation, colds. Stimulates heart and circulation. Lowers cholesteral. Anti-inflammatory. Expectorant.
Ginseng (oriental)[18]	Panax ginseng	dried root	tea	Strengthens immune system. Especially useful for people weakened by disease.
Globe Artichoke[18]	Cynara scolymus	flower heads, leaves, root	tea	Lowers blood cholesterol and triglyceride levels. Diuretic.
Goldenseal[1,18]	Hydrastis canadensis	rhizome, roots	tea	Antibacterial & antiviral. Heals inflamed mucus membranes. Skin wash for infections. Gargle for sore throat and gums. Eye wash.

Common Name	Latin Name	Parts Used	Route	Action
Gravel Root[18]	Eupatorium purpureum	rhizome, roots	tea	UTIs, PID, menstrual cramping. Diuretic.
Hawthorn[18]	Crategus oxyacantha, C. monogyna	flowers, leaves, berries	tea	Dilates coronary & peripheral arteries. Slows pulse and reduces high BP. Relieves Reynauds disease.
Hops[10,11]	Humulus lupulus, H. americana	dried female strobiles	tea	Relaxes the smooth muscle of the digestive tract. Antibacterial. Anti-inflammatory.
Horse Chestnut[18]	Aesculus hippocastanum	fruit, bark	tea ointment	Strengthens veins. Externally for hemorrhoids. *The nuts are poisonous.*
Hyssop[18]	Hyssopus officinalis	flowering herb	tea compress	Use internally in small doses. Expectorant. Externally for bruises, burns, and cold sores.
Jewelweed[13]	Impatiens pallida	stems, leaves	raw juice ointment	Juice from crushed stems and leaves prevents or relieves poison ivy.
Licorice[18]	Glycyrrhiza glabra	roots, runners	tea	Anti-bacterial. Anti-inflammatory. Antiarthritis. Antiallergenic. Gentle laxative. Expectorant. Soothes sore throats. Lowers blood cholesterol.
Lily of the Valley[18]	Convallaria majalis	leaves	tea	Increases strength of heart contractions. Lowers high BP. Encourages arterial vasodilation. Diuretic.
Lung Wort[18]	Pulmonaria officinalis	dried flowering plant	tea	Soothing expectorant.
Mullein[10,11,13]	Verbascum thapsus	leaves, flowers	tea	Soothing expectorant. GI sedative. Diuretic.
Osha[11]	Ligusticum porteri	root	tea	Colds & lung infections. Wound irrigation.
Parsley[18]	Petroselinum crispum	leaves, root, seeds	tea raw	UTIs. Strong diuretic.
Peppermint[18]	Mentha peperita	flowering herb	tea	Antispasmotic effect on smooth muscle of the digestive tract. Anti-inflammatory. Antibacterial & antiparasitic.
Pleurisy Root[18]	Asclepias tuberosa	root	tea	Sweat inducing expectorant. Respiratory sedative.

Herb Tables

Common Name	Latin Name	Parts Used	Route	Action
Prickly Ash (northern & southern)[18]	Zanthoxylum	bark, berries	tea	Stimulates circulatory system. Promotes peripheral circulation, sweating, and reduces fevers. Chew the bark for toothache.
Prickley Pear[12]	Opuntia	inner flesh, flowers	raw juice poltice tea	Externally for bruises & burns. Take juice internally for: Anti-inflammatory diuretic. Reduces pain associated with UTI. Adult Onset Diabetes. Tea from the flowers strengthens capilary beds and submucosa.
Rue[18,11]	Ruta graveolens	aerial parts	ointment	Strains & sprains. Chilblains. Strengthens blood vessels.
Sage[18,12]	Salvia officinalis, S. lyrata, S. urticifolia	leaves	tea	Antibacterial & antiseptic. Stops sweating. Strengthens the nervous system. Relieves congested sinuses and eustachian tubes. Steam can be inhaled. Mix with appple cider vinegar and gargle for sore throats.
Slippery Elm[18]	Ulmus fulva	inner bark	tea poltice	Diarrhea. Lubricates and relieves GI irritation. Wounds.
Skunk Cabbage[18]	Symplocarpus foetidus	root	tea	Antispasmodic & expectorant with sedative properties.
Thyme[18]	Thymus vulgaris, T. serpyllum, T. pulegioides	flowerinig aerial parts	tea	Sore throats, colds, cough. Antibacterial & antifungal. Antispasmodtic. Sweat inducing expectorant. Gargle. Relieves flatulence.
Witch Hazel[18]	Hamamelis virginiana	leaves, bark	tea compress	Bruises. Stops mild bleeding. Eye wash.
Willow (White & Black)[18,11]	Salix	bark	tea	Fevers, arthritis. *Aspirin.* Antipyretic. Antirheumatic. Analgesic. *Do not give to persons allergic to aspirin.*
Yarrow[18,11,13]	Achellea millefolium, A. lanulosa	Aerial parts, especially flowering heads	tea	Sweat inducing. Reduces fever. Expels toxins. Anti-inflammatory. Lowers BP.

First Aid Kits

Introduction

Whether you are traveling alone, part of an expedition, or a member of a rescue team, you will need a first aid kit. An effective first aid kit is designed for you and your use. What you should take and how you should package it depends on many things.

Here are a few basic concepts that you will need to know in order to assemble your first aid kit.

Size & Weight

There is no generic first aid kit. The type activity or expedition defines the amount of weight and space available for your kit (eg: a sailboat can usually carry more than a raft and a raft can carry more than a climber etc.). The longer you are from "help" generally the bigger your first aid kit will be; consider resupply(s). The level of training of the medical "officer" will limit how much invasive equipment or Rx drugs you can carry. Examine the medical history of each expedition or team member; you may need to add special equipment or drugs to your kit. Pay attention to any allergies. Consider carrying a first aid manual (preferably this one).

Expedition vs Rescue Kits

First aid kits used by expeditions are conceptually very different from those used by rescue teams. Expeditions hope that they will NOT use their first aid kits; therefore, they usually adhere to the principles of improvisation and limit specialized items, focus on multipurpose equipment, and adapt expedition gear for medical uses (splints or litters). As your ability to improvise essential equipment increases the size of your expedition first aid kit decreases.

Rescue teams know they WILL use their equipment and often carry specialized gear with them rather than scavenge their personal gear for improvisation.

Packaging

Packaging is extremely important. Well thought out organized packaging protects valuable and irreplaceable equipment. It permits fast and easy access to emergency gear without "vomiting" kit contents everywhere. Critical concepts to organization and packaging are:

- Use different colored compartments or mini-packs. *DO NOT* use plastic bags as pack or compartment substitutes.
- Clearly label each compartment or pack: Major Trauma or Emergency, Drugs or Meds, Minor Trauma, and Personal Care. In many expeditions each expedition member carries their own personal care kit (blisters, sun, OTC meds, personal Rx meds, minor cuts & scrapes) leaving the expedition first aid kit for emergencies and minor trauma (more serious wounds and unstable injuries). This helps ensure that the expedition first aid kit is complete when it is needed.
- Laminate a contents list for each pack and indicate the intended use for each item.
- Consider sealing soft goods in plastic to protect them from moisture. Use mini zip-locks or "Seal-a-Meal" freezer type packages.
- Use a drug log for ALL medications so that you know who is using them and why.

First Aid Kits   166

Training

Train your expedition or team members to use your kit. Until they are trained only you know why you assembled the kit as you did. Without specific training most people will not know how to use the equipment you have so thoughtfully assembled. *Restrict access* to compartments or packs that members are not trained to use.

Possible Problems and Contents

An effective first aid kit is built from a comprehensive possible problem list. Divide your list into Trauma, Environmental, and Medical problems. Choose the problems that you will likely encounter (rule out zebras) and prioritize them. Once you are satisfied with your possible problem list, compile a list of items needed to treat them; carry more of the stuff that you WILL need. Consider a resupply for long expeditions. Use the possible problem lists in this field manual as a guide. Remember to consider how you can improvise from the equipment you are already carrying.

the Wilderness Medicine Training Center has developed packs and assembled quality first aid materials to assist you in designing your first aid kit. For detailed description of each item and cost go to our website (www.WildMedCenter.com) and click on "First Aid Kits".

References

1. Auerbach, Paul S.: **Wilderness Medicine,** fourth edition, St. Louis, Mosby-Year Book, Inc, c2001.

2. Auerbach, Paul S.: **Medicine for the Outdoors,** second edition, Toronto, Little, Brown & Company, c1991.

3. Benenson, Abram S.: **Control of Communicable Diseases Manual,** sixteenth edition, Washington, D.C., American Public Health Association, c1995.

4. Brown, Tom: **Tom Brown's Guide to Wild Edible and Medicinal Plants,** New York, The Berkley Press Publishing Group, c1985.9.

5. Centers for Disease Control: **Health Information for International Travel,** Washington D.C., U.S. Government Printing Office, c1995.

6. Forgey, William W: **Wilderness Medical Society Practice Guidelines,** ICS Books, Old Saybrook, Connecticut, c2001

7. Goth, Peter: **Spine Injury: Clinical Criteria for Assessment and Management,** Augusta, Medical Care Development, Inc., c1994.

8. Hien, T.T., White N.J.: Qinghaosu, **Lancet** 341:603, c1993

9. Mabey, Richard: **The New Age Herbalist,** Londen, Gaia Books. Ltd., c1988.

10. Moore, Michael: **Los Remedios: Traditional Herbal Remedies of the Southwest,** Santa Fe, Red Crane Books, c1992.

11. Moore, Michael: **Medicinal Plants of the Desert and Canyon West,** Santa Fe, Museum of New Mexico Press, c1989.

12. Sanford, Jay P., Gilbert, David N., Sande, Merle A.: **Sanford Guide to Antimicrobial Therapy,** 25th Edition, Dallas, Merck & Company, c1995.

13. Stewart, Charles E.: **Environmental Emergencies,** first edition, Baltimore, Williams & Wilkins, c1990

14. Wilson, Billie Ann, Shannon, Margaret T., Stang, Carolyn L.: **Nurses Drug Guide,** Stamford, Appleton & Lange, c2000.

Medical Abbreviations

A

ALS	Advanced Life Support
ASR	Autonomic Stress Response
AVPU	Alert, Voice-responsive, Pain-responsive, Unresponsive

B

BLS	Basic Life Support
BP	Blood Pressure

C

c̄	with
c/o	complaining of
C̄C	Chief Complaint
CHF	Congestive Heart Failure
CNS	Central Nervous System
CO_2	Carbon Dioxide
CPR	Cardiopulmonary Resuscitation
CSF	Cerebrospinal Fluid
CSM	Circulation, Sensation, Motor

E

ET	Endotrachial Tube

F

Fx	Fracture

G

GI	Gastrointestinal
gtts	Drops
GU	Genitourinary

H

Hx	History

I

IM	Intramuscular
ICP	Intra Crainial Pressure
IV	Intravenous

K

K	Potassium

L

LOC	Loss of Consciousness

M

MDR	Mammalian Diving Reflex
MI	Myocardial Infarction (heart attack)
MOI	Mechanism of Injury

N

Na	Sodium
N/V	Nausea/Vomiting

O

O_2	Oxygen
OTC	Over the Counter

P

PAS	Patient Assessment System
PFA	Pain Free Activity
PO	by mouth
PPV	Positive Pressure Ventilations
Pt	Patient
Px	Problem

Q

q	every
q.d.	every day
q.i.d.	four times daily
q.o.d.	every other day

R

RICE	Rest, Ice, Compression, Elevation
ROM	Range of Motion
Rt	Route
Rx	Perscription or Medical Treatment

S

s̄	without
S/Sx	Signs/Symptoms
SOB	Shortness of Breath
SPF	Sun Protection Factor

T

TIP	Traction into Position
Tx	Treatment or Evacuation

Y

y/o	year old

Symbols

+	positive or good
–	negative or bad
↑	increasing
↓	decreasing
♀	female
♂	male
1°	primary
2°	secondary to (due to)
△	change

Abbreviations & Symbols   170

ASSESSMENT

Possible Problem List	Time	Problem List	Anticipated Problem List
Trauma			
↑ ICP/ Concussion			
Respiratory Distress			
Volume Shock			
Unstable Spine			
Musculoskeletal Injuries			
Wounds			
Environmental			
Dehydration/Low Na$^+$			
Hypothermia/Cold			
Heat Stroke/Exhaustion			
Frostbite/Burns			
Local/Systemic Toxin			
Local/Systemic Allergy			
Near Drowning			
Altitude			
Diving/SCUBA			
Other:			
Medical			
Infectious Disease			
Other:			

PLAN

Field Treatment

PHYSICAL EXAM: Look for: discoloration, swelling, abnormal fluid loss, and defor mity. Feel for: tenderness, crepitus, and instability. Check range of motion and distal CSM. Consider assessing breath sounds.

TIME

UITAL SIGNS: Continually monitor both the patient's pulse and mental status. If the pulse varies in either direction by ten or more points *OR* the patient's level of consciousness changes, record a complete set of vitals. Once a clinical pattern has been identified, treatment and evacuation should not be hindered to take fur- ther sets of vital signs *UNLESS* a change in the patient's vital signs would indicate a change in treatment.

TIME	PULSE	RESP	BP	SKIN	TEMP	AVPU

SOAP Notes   3

SOAP Notes

A LLERGIES: Consider: Cause, Severity (local or systemic), & Treatment.

M EDICATIONS: Consider: Rx, OTC, Herbal, Homeopathic, & Recreational.

DRUG	REASON	DOSE	CURRENT
			Y/N
			Y/N
			Y/N
			Y/N

P AST RELEVANT MEDICAL HISTORY: Relate to potential MOI

L AST FOOD & FLUIDS: Assess available calories, electrolytes, and hydration status.

URINE COLOR: ☐ Clear ☐ Dark   URINE OUTPUT: ☐ Increased ☐ Normal ☐ Low

E VENTS: Have the patient describe in detail the events leading up to the injury or illness. Patient: ☐ Remembers event   ☐ Does not remember event

PATIENT SOAP NOTE

PATIENT INFORMATION: Name:_____ M / F

Age:_____ Weight: _____ # / Kg Address: _____

_____ Phone:_____

Contact Person: _____ Phone:_____

Time: _____ Date:_____ Briefly Describe MOI:_____

_____

_____

_____

_____

ENVIRONMENTAL CONDITIONS: Consider: Temperature, sun, wind, rain, snow, etc.

_____

_____

_____

_____

PATIENT FOUND: _____

INITIAL PROBLEM LIST: ☐ Unstable Spine   AVPU on arrival: _____

☐No Pulse ☐No Respirations ☐Severe Bleeding ☐Blocked Airway ☐Vomiting

INITIAL TREATMENT: _____

_____

_____

_____

_____

_____

SUBJECTIVE

SYMPTOMS: Detailed Description including Onset, Cause, & Severity (1-10).

TIME

SOAP Notes   1

Possible Problem List	Time	Problem List	Anticipated Problem List	Field Treatment
Trauma				
↑ ICP/ Concussion				
Respiratory Distress				
Volume Shock				
Unstable Spine				
Musculoskeletal Injuries				
Wounds				
Environmental				
Dehydration/Low Na$^+$				
Hypothermia/Cold				
Heat Stroke/Exhaustion				
Frostbite/Burns				
Local/Systemic Toxin				
Local/Systemic Allergy				
Near Drowning				
Altitude				
Diving/SCUBA				
Other:				
Medical				
Infectious Disease				
Other:				

OBJECTIVE

PHYSICAL EXAM: Look for: discoloration, swelling, abnormal fluid loss, and defor mity. Feel for: tenderness, crepitus, and instability. Check range of motion and distal CSM. Consider assessing breath sounds.

TIME

VITAL SIGNS: Continually monitor both the patient's pulse and mental status. If the pulse varies in either direction by ten or more points *OR* the patient's level of consciousness changes, record a complete set of vitals. Once a clinical pattern has been identified, treatment and evacuation should not be hindered to take fur- ther sets of vital signs *UNLESS* a change in the patient's vital signs would indicate a change in treatment.

TIME	PULSE	RESP	BP	SKIN	TEMP	AVPU

SOAP Notes   3

SOAP Notes

ALLERGIES: Consider: Cause, Severity (local or systemic), & Treatment.

MEDICATIONS: Consider: Rx, OTC, Herbal, Homeopathic, & Recreational.

DRUG	REASON	DOSE	CURRENT
			Y/N
			Y/N
			Y/N
			Y/N

PAST RELEVANT MEDICAL HISTORY: Relate to potential MOI

LAST FOOD & FLUIDS: Assess available calories, electrolytes, and hydration status.

URINE COLOR: ☐ Clear ☐ Dark   URINE OUTPUT: ☐ Increased ☐ Normal ☐ Low

EVENTS: Have the patient describe in detail the events leading up to the injury or illness. Patient: ☐ Remembers event   ☐ Does not remember event

PATIENT SOAP NOTE

PATIENT INFORMATION: Name:_____M / F

Age:_____ Weight: _____ # / Kg Address: _____
_____ Phone:_____

Contact Person: _____ Phone:_____

Time: _____ Date:_____ Briefly Describe MOI:_____
_____
_____
_____
_____

ENVIRONMENTAL CONDITIONS: Consider: Temperature, sun, wind, rain, snow, etc.
_____
_____
_____
_____

PATIENT FOUND: _____

INITIAL PROBLEM LIST: ☐ Unstable Spine   AVPU on arrival: _____
☐No Pulse ☐No Respirations ☐Severe Bleeding ☐Blocked Airway ☐Vomiting

INITIAL TREATMENT: _____
_____
_____
_____
_____
_____

SUBJECTIVE

S YMPTOMS: Detailed Description including Onset, Cause, & Severity (1-10).

TIME

SOAP Notes   1